MANAGEMENT, WORK AND ORGANISATIONS

Series editors:

Gibson Burrell, The Management Centre, University of Leicester
Mick Marchington, Manchester Business School
Paul Thompson, Department of Human Resource Management, University of Strathclyde

This series of new textbooks covers the areas of human resource management, employee relations, organisational behaviour and related business and management fields. Each text has been specially commissioned to be written by leading experts in a clear and accessible way. The books contain serious and challenging material, take an analytical rather than prescriptive approach and are particularly suitable for use by students with no prior specialist knowledge.

The series is relevant for many business and management courses, including MBA and post-experience courses, specialist masters and postgraduate diplomas, professional courses and final-year undergraduate courses. These texts have become essential reading at business and management schools worldwide.

Published

Paul Blyton and Peter Turnbull **The Dynamics of Employee Relations** (3rd edn)
Sharon C. Bolton **Emotion Management in the Workplace**
Sharon Bolton and Maeve Houlihan **Searching for the Human in Human Resource Management**
Peter Boxall and John Purcell **Strategy and Human Resource Management**
J. Martin Corbett **Critical Cases in Organisational Behaviour**
Keith Grint **Leadership**
Irena Grugulis **Skills, Training and Human Resource Development**
Damian Hodgson and Svetlana Cicmil **Making Projects Critical**
Marek Korczynski **Human Resource Management in Service Work**
Karen Legge **Human Resource Management:** anniversary edition
Patricia Lewis and Ruth Simpson (eds) **Gendering Emotions in Organizations**
Stephen Procter and Frank Mueller (eds) **Teamworking**
Helen Rainbird (ed.) **Training in the Workplace**
Jill Rubery and Damian Grimshaw **The Organisation of Employment**
Harry Scarbrough (ed.) **The Management of Expertise**
Hugh Scullion and Margaret Linehan **International Human Resource Management**
Adrian Wilkinson, Mick Marchington, Tom Redman and Ed Snape **Managing with Total Quality Management**
Colin C. Williams **Rethinking the Future of Work**
Diana Winstanley and Jean Woodall (eds) **Ethical Issues in Contemporary Human Resource Management**
Ruth Simpson and Patricia Lewis **Voice, Visibility and the Gendering of Organizations**

For more information on titles in the Series please go to www.palgrave.com/busines/mwo

Invitation to authors

The Series Editors welcome proposals for new books within the Management, Work and Organisations series. These should be sent to Paul Thompson (p.thompson@strath.ac.uk) at the Dept of HRM, Strathclyde Business School, University of Strathclyde, 50 Richmond St Glasgow G1 1XT

Series Standing Order
If you would like to receive future titles in this series as they are published, you can make use of our standing order facility. To place a standing order please contact your bookseller or, in case of difficulty, write to us at the address below with your name and address and the name of the series. Please state with which title you wish to begin your standing order.
Customer Services Department, Macmillan Distribution Ltd
Houndmills, Basingstoke, Hampshire RG21 6XS, England

Reading Management and Organization in Film

Emma Bell

palgrave
macmillan

First published in 2008 by
PALGRAVE MACMILLAN
Houndmills, Basingstoke, Hampshire RG21 6XS and
175 Fifth Avenue, New York, N.Y. 10010
Companies and representatives throughout the world.

PALGRAVE MACMILLAN is the global academic imprint of the Palgrave
Macmillan division of St. Martin's Press, LLC and of Palgrave Macmillan Ltd.
Macmillan® is a registered trademark in the United States, United Kingdom
and other countries. Palgrave is a registered trademark in the European
Union and other countries.

ISBN-13: 978–0–230–52092–9
ISBN-10: 0–230–52092–8

This book is printed on paper suitable for recycling and made from fully
managed and sustained forest sources. Logging, pulping and manufacturing
processes are expected to conform to the environmental regulations of
the country of origin.

A catalogue record for this book is available from the British Library.

A catalog record for this book is available from the Library of Congress.

10 9 8 7 6 5 4 3 2 1
17 16 15 14 13 12 11 10 09 08

Printed and bound in China

In memory of Janet Newton,
who made things happen

Contents

List of film plates

Acknowledgements

I would like to thank Nick Llewellyn, John Downey and Mark Jancovich for prompting the initial ideas for this book, Dave Buchanan, Stefano Harney, Peter Clark, Tony Watson, Martin Parker, Scott Lawley and Brendan George for their comments and suggestions, Martin Corbett for generously letting me use the term, 'the mad organization', Ursula Gavin and Mark Cooper at Palgrave Macmillan for their support of the project, and everyone else who suggested their favourite films. I would like to acknowledge the Queen Mary Drapers' Award for Innovations in Teaching and Learning and the staff of the British Film Institute, especially Dave McCall, for his support in accessing the film stills. Every effort has been made to contact all copyright holders, but if any have been inadvertently overlooked, the publisher will be pleased to make the necessary arrangements at the first opportunity. Thanks also go to the students at Queen Mary who took my course and introduced me to a wide variety of reader perspectives. And finally thank you to Scott – for everything.

Introduction

Why do I resort so often to examples from popular culture? The simple answer is in order to avoid a kind of jargon, and to achieve the greatest possible clarity, not only for my readers but also for myself. (Žižek, 2005, p. 56)

This book explores how the subjects of management and organization are represented in film. One reason for doing this relates to the general role that visual media play in contemporary society and their importance in determining the information we receive and the impressions and opinions we form. Film is also an important indicator of individual self-identity. For example, when you first meet and are getting to know someone, one of the first things you might try to find out is what their favourite films are, this giving you a potential insight into how they see themselves in relation to their social context. The sheer scale and potential impact of this powerful medium in shaping our understandings of the world and who we are within it thus provides a reasonably good argument for studying how it represents management and organization.

A further reason stems from the ability of film to represent management and organization at an emotional as well as an intellectual level, providing individuals with a way of making their own experiences of organization meaningful. While business school curricula, traditional case studies and textbooks tend to emphasize the rationality and order associated with organization, film draws attention to the embodied, personal and emotional nature of organizational life, showing such things as sex, romance, violence, power struggles and the consequences of success and failure, alerting students to the irrational, overlooked, hidden and disorderly aspects of organizational life (Cohen et al., 2006). Moreover, by offering a rich source of documentary and dramatic material (Hassard and Holliday, 1998), film enables a vicarious experience for the viewer which acts as a substitute for personal experience (Phillips, 1995) and so provides a 'safe' way of learning what it feels like to work in an organization at different historical moments and in different cultural contexts (Czarniawska-Joerges and de Monthoux, 1994).

Film also has the added advantage of being a form of entertainment, one that can seem more natural than, for example, a series of abstract letters and words written on

1

a page. Yet although we are able to understand and enjoy film relatively easily, we tend to accept the information it conveys without necessarily questioning how it tells us what it does. Several authors have argued that 'videocy', the ability to read visual images, is as important a skill as literacy in a society where our understandings are shaped increasingly by moving images as much as by written words (Denzin, 1991; Kress and van Leeuwen, 1996). Film provides a valuable source of material for developing this ability. But perhaps the most important reason for this book stems from the role of film in producing systems of discourse which have helped to shape our collective perceptions of management and continue to inform our experience of organized work. There are therefore significant advantages to be gained, for those of us who are interested in this subject, by developing a greater facility to interpret these representations with a view to understanding the effects of their consumption on our everyday experience.

Film as an aspect of popular culture

Film can be understood as a mechanism for the expression of mass popular culture, the cultural practices that characterize a particular society at a particular time and reflect everyday experiences. Czarniawska and Rhodes (2006, p. 198) argue that popular culture 'can express the ideals and describe the practices of its era' to large numbers of people. They additionally suggest that popular culture '*teaches practices* and provides a means through which *practices might be understood*', going on to note, 'abstract models do not teach you what to say or how to act during your first management meeting, a movie might' (Czarniawska and Rhodes, 2006, p. 199; emphasis in original). Popular culture also plays a role in the generation of 'transformational metaphors' which confer and confirm the identity of certain occupational groups in society (Hollows, 2002). Of course, film is only one aspect of mass-mediated popular culture and, as other writers have noted, there is great potential in studying how organizations are represented in other forms, whether it be television, radio, popular music or the printed media (Hassard and Holliday, 1998; Rhodes and Westwood, 2007). However, this book will focus exclusively on film as the motion picture products shown in cinemas, on television, video or DVD and the cinema industry that produces them, a focus that brings with it certain advantages.

Why film?

First, in the period since the 1960s, film studies has become established as an academic subject in its own right in the humanities and social sciences through the development of a range of theoretical approaches that have been informed by semiotics, psychoanalysis, Marxism, feminism, post-structuralism, cultural studies and postmodernism. These developments are relevant because they challenge and provide alternatives to the more traditional formal aesthetic approaches which have concentrated on identifying and evaluating the artistic merits of a film, thereby enabling greater focus on film's social-ideological potential.

Second, film is arguably a more globalized medium than many other forms of popular culture. Films, unlike television shows or newspapers, are produced with a view to being consumed on a worldwide scale rather than for specific national audiences. As a result, it is likely that students from a variety of cultural backgrounds and nationalities will have already watched some of the films mentioned in this book, and if they haven't they can rent or buy them on video or DVD relatively easily and watch them using subtitles in various languages. However, it must be acknowledged that, although this book attempts to incorporate a range of cultural perspectives, the majority of films analysed originate from the United States, reflecting cultural understandings of work and management that are specific to this society. Consequently, film tends to be somewhat ethnocentric, encouraging a view of management and organization based on a predominantly Western, Anglo-Saxon perspective. Yet this focus can be justified on the grounds that film has provided the medium through which American culture and mythology has been communicated and reinforced in a way that extends far beyond its geographical boundaries (Sadar and Wyn Davies, 2004). Film can provide insight into the moral basis of this economic system through which we can develop understanding of its cultural influence on a global scale.

Third, film provides a means of communication which is relatively accessible, unlike academic writing which follows a series of conventions which make it hard to produce an account that is theoretically informed but not pretentious (Grey and Sinclair, 2006). It is this issue that prompted Nichols and Beynon (1977) thirty years ago to suggest that 'so much of what passes for "theory" fails to connect with the lives that people lead', going on to observe that 'it is almost as if another way of writing has to be developed; something which "tells it like it is" even though in any simple sense this is not possible' (Nichols and Beynon, 1977, p. viii). Film provides a potential means of connecting theory with lived experience in a way that seeks to 'tell it as it is' even if, as will be discussed in Chapter 1, the status of these representations is complex and ambiguous.

Fourth, film provides a potential means of exploring the validity of theories about management and organization (Phillips, 1995). This book will show that many of the theories that can be applied to film are qualitative, often based on ethnography or participant observation, or even journalistic analyses, focusing on the lived experience of being part of an organization from an insider's perspective. This may be because of the similarities that exist between qualitative research and film, both of which rely on narrative processes of construction (see Chapter 1). Qualitative studies may also be more likely than quantitative research to engage readers' attention or challenge commonly held assumptions about a subject (Barley, 2006). Since it is the purpose of film to create something that people want to watch, it is perhaps unsurprising that there is a similarity to qualitative research in this respect. Finally, film is similar to qualitative research in that it seeks to provide a descriptive account of organizations based on the language and actions of social actors in the setting.

A fifth reason for focusing on film relates to the potential for historical analysis enabled through the exploration of archival artefacts which give the observer the possibility of immersion in other times and spaces (Doane, 2002). Indeed, one of the first films ever made and shown to an audience was about work, a documentary film by Louis Lumière entitled *Workers Leaving the Lumière Factory* (1895) comprising a minute-long record of female workers going home at the end of the day. The potential for historical analysis is realised through the coincidence between the 'birth of the cinematic society' in the period 1900–1930, a process whereby America became a cinematic culture that 'came to know itself, collectively and individually, through the images and stories that Hollywood produced' (Denzin, 1995, p. 24) and the rise of managerialism which is also suggested to be strongly located in American history and culture (Jacques, 1996). Hence, as Boozer (2002, p. 9) suggests, 'the history of this film form offers useful insights into important changes in the individual workplace experience, and its association with subtle changes in the larger success ideology'. Through its ability to represent the collective memories associated with these times, film represents various institutionalized facts about management at an earlier point of their social formation, thereby helping us to develop a better understanding of how they became dominant or to assume the cultural status of self evident truths (Jacques, 1996). Film thereby provides a resource through which to explore the enduring nature of many issues concerning management and organization, in addition helping to illustrate how understandings of these subjects have changed over time, as can be seen from representations of management fashions (Abrahamson, 1991) in film, like time and motion study in *Spotswood* (1991) (see Film Focus 3.5), culture building in *The Navigators* (2001) (Film Focus 2.11) and business process re-engineering in *Office Space* (1998).

A final reason for focusing on film stems from the potential for critical analysis that it affords through providing a basis for exploring the social relations through which management is accomplished and the exercise of power that underpins this (Alvesson and Willmott, 1996). As Fournier and Grey argue, one of the things that distinguishes critical from non-critical management studies is the latter's emphasis on knowledge that is geared towards enhancing the effectiveness of managerial practice. In contrast, film rarely represents management as a desirable given and tends only to be concerned with performativity in representing 'what is done in its name' (Fournier and Grey, 2000, p. 17). In addition, film often focuses on themes of power, control and inequality which lie at the heart of a critical approach to analysing organizations. Film represents the viewpoints and experiences of those who have relatively less power in organizations in addition to those who are more powerful, in so doing it provides insights that often contrast sharply with managerial rhetoric. Finally, film is critical of managerial discourses, often presenting them as the subject of humour or parody.

Defining film as popular

Because our focus is on representations of management and organization in popular film, we need to consider what is meant by the term 'popular' in this context. The commonsense understanding of popular suggests it to be something that is enjoyed by 'the people', in comparison to something enjoyed by an elite group (Hollows and Jancovich, 1995). Consequently, things are described as popular 'because masses of people listen to them, buy them, read them, consume them, and seem to enjoy them to the full' (Hall, 1981, p. 231). In addition, it is sometimes implied that people are manipulated into consuming such products on a mass scale. However, Hall (1981) suggests this neglects the importance of power relations in determining which films become popular and the importance of audiences in determining this.

> There is a continuous and necessarily uneven and unequal struggle, by the dominant culture, constantly to disorganise and reorganise popular culture; to enclose and confine its definitions and forms within a more inclusive range of dominant forms. There are points of resistance there are also moments of supersession. This is the dialectic of cultural struggle. In our times it goes on continuously, in the complex lines of resistance and acceptance, refusal and capitulation, which make the field of culture a sort of constant battlefield. A battlefield where no once-and-for-all victories are obtained but where there are always strategic positions to be won and lost. (Hall, 1981, p. 233)

Film does not become popular because it possesses a set of inherent characteristics which achieve certain effects, instead being labelled as popular is part of the process by which films are classified, this being affected by socio-cultural conditions and historical context. Hence what is at one point in time defined as elite and therefore as having appeal only to specialist audiences may over time lose its cultural status and be incorporated into popular culture of subordinate groups. For Hall (1981) the most important thing is that we are aware of the historical processes of incorporation, distortion, resistance, negotiation and recuperation through which notions of the popular are continually being redefined.

Narrative fiction and the linguistic turn

Several writers have put forward arguments for the analysis of a variety of forms of narrative fiction, including novels, short stories, plays, songs, poems and film, as a legitimate basis for the study of management and organization (Czarniawska-Joerges and de Monthoux, 1994; Phillips, 1995; Cohen, 1998; Czarniawska 1999; Linstead, 2003; O'Sullivan and Sheridan, 2005; Rhodes and Brown, 2005; De Cock and Land, 2006). Their arguments stem in part from the influence of postmodernism and the impact of the linguistic turn on the social sciences. The linguistic turn is based on the idea that language shapes our understanding of the world. Because, postmodernists argue, knowledge is constructed through language and language can never create an objective representation of external reality, meaning is uncontrollable and undiscoverable. This leads to a rejection of positivist scientists' claims to be able to produce reliable knowledge through a neutral process of exploration. Postmodernists argue that knowledge is never neutral and is constantly open to revision. They reject what they see as scientific 'grand' or 'meta' narratives which seek to explain the world from an objective viewpoint, suggesting that scientific investigation is nothing more than a type of 'language game' (Rorty, 1979) used by this particular community to produce localized understandings. These assertions have important implications for management researchers since it could be argued that *all* research is a form of fiction because it involves the telling of a story rather than the unproblematic articulation of certain privileged truth claims (Watson, 2000; Rhodes and Brown, 2005). Indeed, to argue otherwise or suggest that the writing up of empirical material about management is 'true' or 'factual' denies the responsibility of the researcher-as-author engaged in the creative process of producing the text.

Postmodernists therefore claim that there is a need to find alternative ways of representing the reality of management and organization that will blur the boundaries between science versus art, or 'fact' and 'fiction' (Linstead, 1993). Czarniawska (1999) advocates the development of narrative knowledge alongside scientific knowledge within organization theory, the value of the former being measured by the convincingness of the interpretation rather than whether it is based on fact or fiction. Locating these claims in the context of the study of organization implies that many of the social scientific conventions of study which have historically defined business school education are too narrowly defined. Calls for new ways of understanding management that do not rely so heavily upon rational analysis have come from a surprisingly wide variety of sources (e.g. Mintzberg, 2004). However, running parallel to the need to find alternative versions of reality is the need to deconstruct claims to represent 'objective' reality that business schools have traditionally relied upon to support their truth claims. A good example of this relates to the tradition of case study analysis, which Czarniawska-Joerges and de Monthoux (1994) suggest is a creative, narrative device. They argue that writing case studies involves a similar process of interpretation in dealing with multiple sources of information and constructing a narrative to that involved in writing narrative fiction. Furthermore, the objectives of the case study, to simulate real life situations and give students a taste of practice through adopting a professional personae and re-enacting a situation, can also be achieved through literary fiction.

> A good case should create 'the willing suspension of belief. In other words the willingness to take at face value the situation which the case presents, forgetting that this is artificial, so to speak, forgetting that this is a case, forgetting that this is a classroom, being willing to take the situation at face value and become the person concerned with it – that is the ideal that a case discussion ought to achieve.' (McNair, 1971, p. 4 cited in Czarniawska-Joerges and de Monthoux, 1994, pp. 2–3)

Czarniawska-Joerges and de Monthoux (1994) suggest that literary fiction exercises the reader's skills of criticism – judgement, interpretation and evaluation (which are also important managerial skills) and that this helps students to understand the complexity of organizations and to become more imaginative and creative. They also point out that narrative knowledge is older than scientific knowledge, suggesting that knowledge in classic literary fiction may be more enduring than the knowledge that is generated through management research, proposing that novels enable a focus that is simultaneously individual and organizational, enabling the portrayal of micro-events alongside macro-systems, something that is notoriously difficult to do within conventional social scientific analyses. Phillips (1995) puts the question of why we should use narrative fiction to understand organization somewhat differently, arguing that if a particular fictional narrative is popular with people who are members of organizations, we need to find out *why* it is popular, by asking what it reveals about people's experiences of work. He suggests that narrative fiction is therefore a way of testing the validity of a theory.

> If we can write a convincing dramatization that sensibly operationalizes a theory, then this provides one more bit of confirmatory evidence. On the other hand, if a sensible dramatization is not possible, then either the theory, or the domain in which it is applied, lacks validity. (Phillips, 1995, p. 641)

These viewpoints suggest a potential shift is taking place within managerial education whereby the social scientific knowledge base drawn primarily from the disciplines of economics, psychology and sociology that has traditionally defined the study of management may be giving way to a more pluralistic conception of potential theoretical sources from which insights into management and organization can be gained. For example, Gagliardi (2006) argues that the humanities, including philosophy, history, literary criticism, linguistics, the study of art and aesthetic experience, has the potential to bring ideas and fresh perspectives to management education, not least because these disciplines encourage the development of moral thought, rather than encouraging narrowly defined rational instrumentalism. Similarly, Kline Harrison and Akinc (2000) argue that there is a need for managers to be educated according to a broader liberal arts tradition through the study of artistic and literary works which enable a more flexible approach to learning that extends beyond the corporate environment.

Summary and structure of the book

This book is primarily intended for advanced undergraduate and postgraduate students of business and management, although it will also be of potential interest to students in sociology, film, communication, media and cultural studies. The reader may therefore have some knowledge of management and organization studies literature. A thematic approach is taken whereby themes related to management and organization that occur frequently in film are analysed in depth, on the grounds that if a film enables a particular theory to be operationalized it helps us to explore the validity of the theory (Phillips, 1995), both in terms of people's experience of work and their understanding of film. In this way it is argued that the analysis of film can enhance our understanding of subjects such as organizational behaviour, the sociology of work, organization theory and human resource management.

The analysis presented here is based on a sample of over one hundred films that in some way represent management and organization. Many of them contain scenes set in conventional work organizations such as offices, factories and shops, their stories involving management and organization, although these themes are often subsidiary to non-work related stories such as those relating to family or love. However, because management and organization often only provide the context within which these other stories are located, this should not be interpreted as an indication of their lesser significance. As Newitz (2006) notes, themes related to capitalism tend to operate as a subtext within film narratives where these ideas can be more safely contained through lurking 'in the background, shaping events and infecting the plot line' (Newitz, 2006, p. 3). A further point to be made in relation to the selection of films relates to the fact that work is an extremely broad category which encompasses social activity of various kinds, including criminal work (e.g. *The Godfather Trilogy*, 1992) and war work (e.g. *Full Metal Jacket*, 1987). Although these non-traditional forms of work are indeed interesting and potentially more exciting than many forms of more conventional paid work (which is probably why they have been the focus of a number of films), they do not constitute the norm of industrial, service and knowledge work that most of the readers of this book are likely to be engaged in for a large proportion of their lives. For this reason, this book focuses on more mundane experiences of management and organization as they are understood by the majority of people, most of the time, with a view to understanding how this relates to experience in our everyday lives.

The process of analysis that I adopted made use of my qualitative research training for dealing with other forms of rich, messy data (Coffey and Atkinson, 1996). This involved watching each film closely at least once, making notes on its salient features using the techniques explained in Chapter 1, identifying recurring themes and working with these themes in a way which enabled them to be related to theory. A technique not dissimilar to 'snowball sampling' (Bryman and Bell, 2007) was used to identify potential films for analysis. For example, I asked everyone I knew, including students taking my courses, what were the films that told them something about management and organization. Other sources included searching for films on websites like Amazon www.amazon.com which gave me recommendations based on what other people who watched one of the films on my list had also bought. A degree of saturation was achieved through this process, both in terms of the films selected as the same titles appeared over and over again, and at a theoretical level as new films added to my list confirmed the concepts and categories I had already identified in a way which did not reveal very much that was new. This process of analysis is of course not entirely objective since the inclusion of certain films and exclusion of others is inevitably affected by my subjective preferences. Readers may therefore wish to focus on films other than those included here. In so doing they may wish to consult comprehensive anthologies of films about management and work for inspiration, such as those written by Tom Zaniello, *Working Stiffs, Union Maids, Reds, and Riffraff: An Expanded Guide to Films About Labor* (1996) and *The Cinema of Globalization* (2007), which provide short descriptive summaries of a wide variety of well known and more obscure films including those made for television and online viewing.

The structure of the book is as follows. Chapter 1 sets the scene by setting out the arguments that justify the book's thematic structure. This involves explaining the approach to reading film as a 'text' and includes discussion of semiotics and deconstruction as well as ideological and audience analysis. Chapter 2 explores the processes of production and distribution of film, as an economic product and an industry, arguing that these organizational processes are vital to understanding why film represents organizations in various ways. Chapter 3 reflects on the predominance of negative portrayals of organizations in film, considering why such representations exist and their effects on the way that we think about management and organization. Chapter 4 considers representations of managerial work in large, bureaucratic, male-dominated American corporations, focusing on how the themes of motivation, hierarchy, power, reward and success, which were used to construct the discursive category of 'organization man' in the mid-twentieth century and continue to influence how we see managerial work today. Chapter 5 looks at the discursive construction of the worker within film in the context of the transition from modern industrial capitalism to post-industrial work and postmodernity. Chapter 6 focuses on what is left outside or excluded from representations of management and work in organization, predominantly through exploring representations of the working woman. Chapter 7 considers the preoccupation with the meaning of work that runs through representations of organization in film and explores the anxieties, including boredom, lack of motivation, deskilling, alienation, job insecurity and even fear of death that such a preoccupation reflects. Finally, Chapter 8 draws together the themes discussed so far in the book, concluding with an analysis of the role of film in challenging dominant views of management and organization by giving voice to groups who tend to be silenced by contemporary organizational practices.

Each chapter also contains a series of 'Film Focus' boxes that contain detailed description of scenes from particular films and approximate running times based on the playing time of a commercially purchased DVD copy. (☉ indicated by this symbol) The films analysed in this book have release dates anywhere from 1927 to 2006, the restoration and release of a growing number of Hollywood Classics on DVD and video ensuring that representations of management and organization in films of the 1930s to the 1960s can be analysed in addition to those found in more recent films.

This boxed material relates to issues discussed in the main text, drawing out themes and theoretical points and illustrating how they relate to particular films, this preventing the main text from becoming overly descriptive and helping to give the reader a sense of the wide range of films which can be incorporated into this analytical framework. Rather than being treated as definitive, these scene descriptions should be used as a starting point from which readers can form their own opinions and analyses of these and other films, which may or may not correspond to the ones provided here. Finally, there are a number of practical and legal issues relating to the use of film for educational purposes. First, the practical issues; while virtually all of the films included in this book are currently available on DVD, it is important if you intend to purchase or rent a DVD copy to note which format or regional code you require, this being dependant on the country in which you are based and your DVD player or computer. More information on DVD formats can be found on Amazon www.amazon.co.uk In relation to legal issues, as Huczynski and Buchanan (2004) note, in the UK, licenses granted to educational institutions under the Educational Recording Agency and Open University schemes enable the use of commercially available feature films for educational purposes. However, they also recommend that you check with your institution before using such material in teaching because copyright breaches incur expensive fines.

Plate 1 Norville Barnes becomes President of Hudsucker Industries in *The Hudsucker Proxy* (1994)

1

Reading film: studying management

Introduction

The approach taken in this book treats film as a series of texts which can be read for meaning in a similar way to written texts like books and other phenomena including objects. This approach entails two assumptions, first, that embedded within texts are the interpretations of their creators, and second, that the meaning of a text is acquired through its relationship to other texts. This chapter explores these parallel assumptions. It is based upon the notion that, through the provision of a system of conventions which represent the visible, film represents a specific 'way of seeing' (Berger, 1972) that reflects the obsessions of a particular culture. As Berger (1972, p. 8) notes, 'the way we see things is affected by what we know and what we believe'. Furthermore, the process of seeing does not occur in isolation, instead we are constantly looking at the relationship between the things that we see and ourselves. Thus, each of the films in this book constructs a particular image of management and organization in which we situate ourselves using our own cultural experience of these phenomena.

For example, when I show extracts from recent films such as *Erin Brockovich* (2000) and *Fight Club* (1999) to students in my classes it becomes evident from the discussion that they identify quite readily with these films. In so doing they are situating themselves *in* the image, based on their own cultural experiences of management and organization. That these are relatively contemporaneous films is also no coincidence since, broadly speaking, they express the view that it is easier to relate to films that represent a culture which is familiar to them. They thus have the cultural experience to be able to situate themselves in these images more easily than if they were watching a film released in the 1950s or produced in a country whose culture they are unfamiliar with. However, the process of seeing does not stop there. The popularity of Berger's book derives from the way that it challenges us to rethink the way we view images. By developing sensitivity towards these highly influential texts we become more able to read films from other time periods and other cultures, thereby potentially gaining insight into how other audiences situate themselves in relation to films that represent management and organization. Having the ability to read films and interpret their cultural and social significance relative to our own organizational experience and the experience of others is an important skill which this chapter seeks to develop.

Film aesthetics

The aesthetic dimension of film is important because, in addition to potentially enhancing the viewing experience of a film, it contributes to the meaning of the text and thus to its message. Moreover, if a film is deemed to be a 'classic' as a result of its aesthetic qualities, for example through winning awards or appearing in lists of the best movies of all time, this contributes to the historical and cultural significance of the text over the longer term, making it more likely that audiences will continue to refer to it. Therefore, a basic understanding of some of the principles that underpin 'film form', the internal structure of the text, is useful in enabling analysis. However, the focus of aesthetic analysis has traditionally been on establishing film as an art form, similar to music, art or literature (Monaco, 2000). Since our interest in this book is not primarily with the aesthetic value of film as an art form, these aspects of formal analysis merely provide a resource through which to explore what film says about management and organization.

Formal aesthetic analysis is concerned with the meanings which can be attributed to a film, which may be more or less explicit. Bordwell and Thompson (2004) distinguish between *referential meaning*, constituted through the basic plot and main events of the film; *explicit meaning*, as the openly asserted sentiment of the film; *implicit meaning*, the more abstract implications that derive from interpretation of the film; and *symptomatic meaning*, through which the film is situated in relation to societal trends and social ideology (see Film Focus 1.1).

FILM FOCUS 1.1: Four levels of meaning in *Wall Street* (1987)

Wall Street (1987) is the story of an ambitious young stockbroker from a working class background, Budd Fox, who gets a job working for corporate raider, Gordon Gekko. If we apply Bordwell and Thompson's (2004) four types of meaning to this film we might come up with the following analysis.

1. *Referential meaning*. A young man from a working class background struggling to build a career gets a job which brings financial success and status. He is asked by his boss to obtain information about companies illegally, betraying his own father by using information about the firm where he has been employed for many years. Only when he realizes his

---

boss plans to liquidate his father's company does he realize the error of his ways and seek to bring his corrupt mentor to justice.

Meaning depends on the spectator's ability to identify with the hopes and fears of the central character and his struggle for success in a context where the values of hard work and family are undermined by the pursuit of money.

2. *Explicit meaning.* A young man is corrupted by an older, highly successful man whom he admires into believing that 'greed is good' and hard work is 'not enough' in the intensely competitive world of finance. In the process he realizes how important the values instilled in him by his father are to his identity.

These assertions are made quite explicit in the film often through the words and actions of the central characters. For example, in a scene in the back of his limousine Gekko tells Fox that hard work alone is not enough to become successful and offers him a job on the condition that he provides him with inside information. In a later scene in which Gekko presents his philosophy to stockholders (see Film Focus 3.1) he makes the statement that 'greed is good'. In contrast, the internal conflict experienced by Fox is expressed through statements such as 'you've got to get to the big time first then you can be a pillar' and later, surrounded by the material evidence of his success, when he asks 'who am I?' Taken individually, each of these statements might not be taken to be a reflection of the meaning of the film as a whole. However, through their insertion at regular points throughout the narrative it becomes clear that they are important in defining the overall meaning of the text.

3. *Implicit meaning.* A young man's need for social recognition and esteem is not fulfilled through material wealth and status symbols but instead through the values of family, hard work and honesty communicated to him by his father.

This goes beyond what is explicitly stated in the film by relating the words and actions of the central characters to identify a set of underlying assumptions about morality and human nature. By tracing Fox's passage from seduction, to corruption and redemption the film ultimately represents him as a moral character.

4. *Symptomatic meaning.* In a society which explicitly promotes the idea that hard work and determination inevitably leads to career and economic success, those who are unable to attain this ideal can take comfort from the love and support they receive from their family.

This abstract meaning situates the film in the context of American society in the late 1980s, the American Dream (see Chapter 4) and Wall Street as a symbolic site

Continued

of capitalism. The narrative of the film seeks to expose the significant costs associated with realising this dream through the young man's struggle and eventual rise above it (Denzin, 1991). Symptomatic meaning relates to the values conveyed by a film by analysing the way that concepts like 'career' and 'work' are represented and by acknowledging that these portrayals are historically and culturally specific. However, formal analyses tend to shy away from detailed consideration of symptomatic meaning because of a concern that 'the more abstract and general our attributions of meaning, the more we risk loosening our grasp on the film's specific formal system' (Bordwell and Thompson, 2004, p. 58) instead urging a balance of concern between the formal system and its wider significance.

A second aspect of the formal structure of a film is the story that is told. Most films are structured according to some kind of narrative form or story which provides a way of organizing film according to a sequence of events that are often suggested to be causally related and involve goal-governed protagonists. Events are organized in a way that enables development of the narrative over time, whether over 50 years or one day, and there is a beginning, middle and an end, the ending often being established through resolution of conflicts and contradictions. The story also has a plot that contains 'conflicts, predicaments, trials, consequences, and crises that call for choices, decisions, actions, and interactions, whose actual outcomes are often at odds with the characters' intentions and purposes' (Gabriel, 2000, p. 239).

Film Focus 1.2 illustrates how the narrative structure of film can be explored using the technique of segmentation. Fictional film has tended to be dominated by a single mode of narrative form which Bordwell and Thompson (2004) refer to as the 'classical Hollywood cinema' – ' "classical" because of its lengthy, stable, and influential history, "Hollywood" because the mode assumed its most elaborate shape in American film studios' (Bordwell and Thompson, 2004, p. 89). Bordwell (2006) argues that despite numerous changes in the filmmaking industry, narrative conventions established between 1910 and 1920 continue to dominate the cinematic tradition of visual storytelling in a way which extends beyond Hollywood or the United States. The main structural principles of plot construction and characterization are as follows.

A film's main characters, all agree, should pursue important goals and face forbidding obstacles. Conflict should be constant, across the whole film and within each scene. Actions should be bound into a tight chain of cause and effect. Major events should be foreshadowed ('planted'), but not so obviously that the viewer can predict them. Tension should rise in the course of the film until a climax resolves all the issues. (Bordwell, 2006, p. 28)

Bordwell (2006) argues that the process of training contemporary screenwriters has embedded and formalized these rules to such an extent that they have developed into a template for designing a mass-market film made up of three distinct parts, like the acts in a play. The first, lasting around 25–30 minutes of a typical two-hour film, is known as the 'set up' and involves introducing the hero and their world, defining their purposes and culminating in a turning point or crisis. The second lasts approximately 40–60 minutes and comprises two stages, the first focusing on the main character's central problem which may be recast, the protagonist changing his or her tactics or facing an entirely new situation which causes them to recast their goals. The second stage also involves extending the hero's struggle towards their goals and often involves incidents which cause action, suspense or delay (Thompson, 1999). In the third and final part the protagonist solves the problem through a climax which is usually followed by an epilogue confirming the stability of the situation. The apparent rigidity of this structure might cause us to reflect on the extent to which film-making constitutes a creative act (a point that will be developed further in Chapter 2).

FILM FOCUS 1.2: A segmentation of the film *Human Resources* (1999)

One technique that can be used to trace the progression of a film and to gain a sense of the narrative is segmentation. This is simply a written breakdown of the parts of a film. The parts or scenes may be numbered and divided up into major and minor parts. Segmentation is a useful precursor to theoretical analysis because it encourages you to read the text closely. It is also useful in enabling recognition of patterns of repetition and narrative development. Film writers vary in their views about the best way to break a film up into segments and how long segments should be (Bellour, 1976) but a basic segmentation entails providing a descriptive account of time, place and action. Segmentation can also be used to record verbatim dialogue, such as a statement that strikes you as particularly meaningful or a particular phrase that is used, the names of characters, or your own responses to a film as you watch it (used in this way it also becomes a diary of your film viewing experience). It can be presented in diagrammatic or table format. The example provided here is of a segmentation from the film *Human Resources* (1999). This format includes approximate running times for each of the parts which has the advantage of enabling you to quickly return to a particular segment for closer analysis.

Time (mins)	Scene	Content
0	1	Credits
1.05	2	Frank returns home from University in Paris to start his industrial placement at his father's place of work – a factory in a small provincial town.

Continued

Time (mins)	Scene	Content
4.57	3	The next morning, Frank is ready for his first day at work. His mother admires her son's smart appearance. Frank walks with his father, Jean-Claude (JC) to the factory with some of his father's workmates. JC plays the role of introducer, explaining his son's presence to his workmates and proudly stating that his son will be working in the office.
8.22	4	Frank leaves his father to start his shift and takes a first tour of the factory, which is new and strange to him. He comes across his father who is working 'his machine' and sees his father being reprimanded by the supervisor for working too slowly.
12.23	5	Frank meets the human resources manager who explains the likely impact of the introduction of the 35 hour working week. Things are hard and he goes on to explain that 22 employees were 'let go' last year. The chief executive, Rouet, comes in. He asks Frank his views about the 35 hour week. Frank engages in some fence-sitting diplomacy in his response.

However, Bordwell (2006) argues that there is still considerable scope for innovation within this structure as long as it results in the production of a saleable commodity.

Huczynski and Buchanan (2004) argue that film narratives are inherently theory-laden, by encoding 'pattern and explanation, suggesting hypotheses and establishing causality' (Huczynski and Buchanan, 2004, p. 709). They suggest that film narratives typically encode process theories of organizational behaviour which are concerned with understanding flows of action rather than seeking to establish universal causal claims. However, others are more critical of film narratives, arguing that because they are 'subject-centred', they tend to deny contradiction in the social world by privileging the concerns of a central character. 'Conflict and struggle are therefore necessary to narrative, but they are not presented as the product of inherent contradictions within the social structure. Rather they are individualized and presented as the result of individual error or morality' (Jancovich, 1995, p. 130).

A final aspect of aesthetic approaches relates to the specific techniques – cinematography, *mise-en-scène*, editing and sound involved in making film. These stylistic elements combine with narrative to create overall film form (Film Focus 1.3).

FILM FOCUS 1.3: Using cinematography to convey organizational size and power in *The Crowd* (1928)

The Crowd (1928) is a silent film which tells the story of John Sims, a young and ambitious but undisciplined office clerk as he and his new wife, Mary, struggle to cope with financial pressures, being married and having a family in the midst of crowded New York City. The introductory sequence makes use of cinematography to convey a specific impression of the relationship between the individual and the organization in a way that has been repeatedly used in film, so much so that these innovations are suggested to have become clichés (Lopate, 2001) [http://qcpages.qc.cuny.edu/newlaborforum/old/html/9_article79.html – consulted 01.11.07]. At the start of the film the camera pans the skyline of New York City from overhead before the shot descends into the crowded streets below with their bustling people and various forms of transport passing across the view. The camera then alights on the frontage of a single tall building, before panning upward to the top of the building in a shot that is held for several moments. The focal length of this shot makes the skyscraper appear ominous through the way that it towers above the ground from the point of view of the individual standing below looking up at it. The shot is repeated several times with other skyscrapers and so the individual experiences a sensation of being surrounded by them. Then the camera moves to the inside of the building in another overhead shot, looking down at a vast open-plan or 'bullpen' office in which desks are organized in uniform rows and workers are seated at them. Gradually the camera focuses in on one figure, working at his desk. However, rather than moving towards the face of the character, the camera focuses down on the plaque fixed to the front of the desk, which reads 'number 137'. These stylistic techniques have the effect of emphasising the size and power of large-scale bureaucratic corporations that dominated US economic life in the 1920s. The effect is to emphasize the structure of organization, both in terms of its material (i.e. buildings) and immaterial (e.g. rules and resources) aspects. The individual is portrayed as relatively powerless in relation to this structure and anonymous, as a result of the increasing standardisation of workplace routines under the influence of Taylorism and scientific management. Referring to the office worker by desk number rather than by name makes explicit the extent to which the individual is treated as a means of achieving the rational goals of organization, in a similar way to a machine (see Chapter 3). [**currently unavailable on DVD**]

Reflectional readings

Several management writers have recommended the use of film as a teaching resource that can be used to bring management and organization theory 'to life' by helping students to understand concepts such as leadership (Comer, 2001), entrepreneurship (van Gelderen and Verduyn, 2003), gender relations (Comer and Cooper, 1998) and business ethics (Berger and Pratt, 1998). For example, Comer (2001, p. 430) suggests that undergraduates 'reared on video games and MTV' prefer watching a film to reading a book. Holmes (2005) argues that it is up to business school educators to respond to the millennial generation by creating 'new and inspiring teaching interventions that illustrate business principles in action' (Holmes, 2005, p. 70) while Cohen (1998) observes that more and more management educators are turning to fiction as a substitute for direct experience. Marx and Frost (1998) acknowledge the appeal of video technology to management educators while simultaneously cautioning for a more empirically grounded investigation as to the educational benefits, in particular the depth of learning associated with its usage. They suggest the need for film material to be used in conjunction with books and articles, the former to capture attention enabling greater comprehension of the content that follows (Marx, Jick and Frost, 1991). As Buchanan and Huczynski (2004) point out, 'film can illustrate topics in a manner more graphic than conventional instruction methods and is novel and entertaining and thus motivational for students' (Buchanan and Huczynski, 2004, p. 313). Even management consultants are keen to exploit the advantages of film as a learning resource for executives, arguing that film can teach lessons about human behaviour that are directly related to management and leadership (see Film Focus 1.7). However, interest in film has not only been confined to teaching, these texts having also been used in research as the basis for analysis with the aim of contributing towards our knowledge and understanding of how organizations work (e.g. Foreman and Thatchenkery, 1996; 2003).

Many of those who have advocated the use of film as a teaching resource have not confined themselves to focusing on films that deal with management and organization in any obvious way at all. Instead they have been concerned with developing metaphorical connections between film and management theory through analysis of the implications that arise from its central thesis or the experiences of characters. One of the most prolific advocates of the use of film as a teaching resource in management education is Champoux (2001b; 2004; 2005) who argues that animated film enables visual exaggeration of behaviours or characteristics which helps to illustrate and reinforce organizational behaviour concepts in the context of student learning (Champoux, 2001a). Similarly, Holmes (2005) shows how Disney's *Finding Nemo* can be used to illustrate organizational behaviour and management concepts. Even *Aliens* (1986) has been suggested to be useful in teaching students about leadership and power (Harrington and Griffin, 1990). However, it is not enough simply to invoke the 'popular-with-students argument' (Dyer, 2000) without being clear as to the point of analysing film to understand management and organization. As Cohen (1998) suggests, we risk diminishing and simplifying such texts by treating them as a direct substitute for 'real' life experience without due consideration for issues of context and the relationship between the author and the text. Although the use of film as an instructional tool to illustrate theory is a useful way of keeping students' interest in the subject, especially when they may have limited direct experience of managing or working themselves, it is not the purpose of this book to recommend film for this purpose.

These uses of film are problematic because they imply that film is able to reflect the social reality to which it refers. Students who analyse films in this way tend to spend a great deal of time considering whether or not the representations of management and organization that they see in film are an accurate reflection of reality. Their concerns relate to the validity of the text and the extent of its correspondence with the world (Czarniawska, 1999). While of course the production of texts does not take place in a vacuum, it is problematic to 'read off' meanings from film in a way which assumes them to be a resource that gives direct insight into the way things work in the 'real' world. As De Cock and Land (2006) argue, there are in-built problems with using literary resources such as film to improve our understanding of management and organization because this encourages a focus on their ability to reflect and tell us about reality. They propose that rather than being a means of reflecting the reality of management and organization, the influence of fictional forms is derived from its ability to represent unreality, thereby potentially disrupting audiences' views of these phenomena in everyday life.

Film tends to 'exaggerate, sensationalize and glamorize characters and events' (Buchanan and Huczynski, 2004, p. 314). Consequently, certain subjects, such as corporate corruption and entrepreneurship, are the focus of a great deal of filmmakers' and audiences' attention and some types of organization, such as financial institutions, are more commonly represented. Large commercial organizations tend to feature more often than small, not-for-profit ones, while white, male employees are likely to be more frequently represented than employees of other ethnic origin or women workers. A reflectional reading invites the assumption that films about management and organization reasonably accurately reflect how these subjects are regarded by society. A parallel can be drawn with reflectional theories of women in film which assume that that depictions of women in film mirror the values and beliefs of the society in which they are produced. While such theories grasp 'the ideological implications of cinema, images are seen as too easily detached from the texts and psychic structures through which they function, as well as the institutional and historical contexts that determine their form and their reception' (White, 2000, p. 116). Hence, as Hassard and Holliday argue in relation to the representation of organization in popular culture,

> The representation of reality depends on shared recognition by producers and audiences of dominant images and ideas, codes and conventions, rather than any deeper understanding of universal truths. But, despite shared recognition, there may still be little consensus on how to interpret those representations, and there will always be possibilities for alternative

readings. Texts that one person may judge realistic another may not, depending largely on life experiences or situated cultures. What is realistic is thus a controversial and subjective concept. (Hassard and Holliday, 1998, p. 2)

FILM FOCUS 1.4: Cinematic and everyday reality in *Erin Brockovich* (2000)

Many films are based on a story that is claimed to be true, drawing on non-fictional sources, such as biographical or autobiographical books and newspaper articles as the basis for the narrative and sometimes making this explicit at the start or end of the film, by telling the audience that the film is based on a true story or telling them how the 'real' story ended.

Comparisons between representation and reality provide the basis for the content on the film website *Chasing the Frog* [http://www.chasingthefrog.com/reelfaces – consulted 08.08.07] which claims to 'chase after the truth behind movies based on true stories'. The 'Reel Faces' feature compares the film actors and characters with people and events to which they are related. Such practices are founded on the principle of cinematic realism which presumes facts can be represented cinematically through a process of careful, journalistic investigation. Denzin (1995) suggests that the emergence of heightened cinematic realism can be traced to the 1930s when attempts were made to position filmmakers as seekers of truth, on a parallel with investigative journalists, by telling stories about reporters who bring down the powerful on behalf of the little people. Through articulating this powerful cultural myth of American democracy filmmakers 'cracked the barrier that had traditionally separated storytelling from everyday life' (Denzin, 1995, p. 23).

However, as Denzin (1995, p. 36) notes, the 'technologies for producing the real distort the real that is produced' to the extent that there can be 'two versions of reality; the cinematic and the everyday'. For example, the cinematic reality presented in *Erin Brockovich* (2000) has been questioned by several commentators who suggest many of Brockovich's and Masry's toxic-contamination lawsuits have been supported by questionable scientific evidence (Umansky, 2003). 'The real story of Erin Brockovich is simply this. A woman with no medical background goes to a small town and convinces residents that virtually every illness they've ever had, from cancer to rashes, are all related and all caused by a nearby corporation work almost $30 billion. Join our suit, she says, and I'll get you megabucks. They do, they get a settlement, and Brockovich's colleagues snatch away a cut of over $133 million. Brockovich gets more than 2 million. Only in Hollywood could such a person be made a heroine'. [http://www.fumento.com/brocklett.html; http://www.fumento.com/erinwsj.html – consulted 08.08.07] In this case it can be argued that the cinematic reality is the version which has become dominant, since it is this story which is known and understood by the greatest number of people, thereby confirming Denzin's assertion that 'the everyday is now defined by the cinematic' (Denzin, 1995, p. 36).

As Film Focus 1.4 illustrates, these issues are concerned with the truth-value which we accord to film and the extent to which we believe that there is an objective reality based on a set of externally verifiable facts that film represents. Most of us would readily agree that the making of films, even those which claim to be based on true stories, involves a process of creative construction whereby characters and events are subjectively interpreted. However, what is more problematic to ascertain is the extent to which we think there is an objective reality concerning social phenomena such as management and organization, which film more-or-less accurately reflects. The importance of true stories can also be related to the need for authenticity, which Peterson (1997) argues is important in ensuring audiences acceptance of a cultural product such as film (see Chapter 2). One of the techniques used to enhance authenticity involves the use of non-fictional film footage. For example, in *The Navigators* (2001) a factual corporate training video is watched by the railway track workers (see Film Focus 3.10). Peterson (1997) argues that even if the story is reinvented or revised in such a way that it bears little relation to the people or events on which it is based, this does not matter to the success of the product as long as the fabrication of authenticity is convincing.

The approach taken here assumes that social activities like management and organization are socially constructed and revised through the perceptions and actions of social actors as they go about their everyday lives, rather than objectively knowable entities that have a fixed reality which exists independently of the people who are involved with them. This implies that film is *part* of the process of social construction, by providing a certain view of social reality it contributes to the construction of knowledge in relation to the phenomena with which it is concerned. Hence if film is a medium of mass communication through which the social phenomena of management and organization are constructed and revised, we should surely be interested in understanding how it contributes towards the constitution of that emergent reality.

Genre and ideology

This book is concerned with identifying and classifying the features of these texts by analyzing the common conventions and characteristics which reappear in film after film about management and organization. These features define the boundaries of the genre, giving this group of films a common identity (Alloway, 1963; Hutchings, 1995). This approach encourages a focus on popular stereotypes, such as the drone-worker or corporate executive, commonly used settings, such as the open-plan office or elevator encounter, generic iconography, or visual conventions, such as the clock face or the towering skyscraper, and recurring subjects, such as the 1950s boardroom film (Lopate, 2001) or career movie (Boozer, 2002).

Here a slightly different approach to the analysis of genre is taken, one that emphasizes the interplay between audience, films and filmmakers in seeing genres as systems of conventions and expectations which are socially constructed. This presupposes that a particular text may engage with several genres at the same time but also that it rarely conforms to the conventions of any one genre completely (Derrida, 1980). By understanding texts as multiply generic, we allow ourselves not to be confined exclusively to films that embody all the characteristics of a genre instead being more flexible in exploring how these conventions seep into other texts. Genres also rely on the construction of what Neale (2000) describes as 'regimes of verisimilitude' which determine what audiences consider to be plausible, both in relation to the conventions of the genre and in relation to their social and cultural beliefs. Hence 'films are able to rely on the norms, rules and laws – the system of "everyday knowledge" – embodied in regimes of socio-cultural verisimilitude in accounting at a fundamental level for the actions, events and behaviour they represent' (Neal, 2000, p. 38). Since audiences can be relied upon to recognise and understand these conventions, they do not have to be explained every time they arise.

Each film text responds to and is organized in accordance with genres, both their formal, structural aspects which determine the shape of the material medium and how audiences encounter it, as well as their rhetorical and thematic dimensions (Frow, 2006). It is the thematic aspect of genre which we are most interested in here, this being understood as 'the shaped human experience that a genre invests with significance and interest' (Frow, 2006, p. 75). Thematic content is expressed through recurrence of certain topics, such as the meaning of work, the desire for career success, the fear of technology or the evil of bureaucracy. It is by focusing on the thematic aspect of the genre that we are able to identify the ideologies of management and organization that are communicated by it. Genre thus works to generate and shape our knowledge of management and organization in ways that involve the exercise of power, for as Frow (2006) states: 'Genres create effects of reality and truth, authority and plausibility, which are central to the different ways the world is understood' (Frow, 2006, p. 2).

This book argues that genre both shapes and constrains the production and interpretation of meaning in relation to management and organization in a way that 'is central to human meaning-making and to the social struggle over meanings' (Frow, 2006, p. 10). As Wright (1975) has argued in relation to Westerns, genre also provides the basis for constructing certain myths, timeless stories which conform to certain rules and are related to the dominant social order of the period. Film audiences are encouraged to identify with these myths and this binds them closer to the social order. Moreover, because films tend to reflect the economic and social conditions within which they are produced and disseminated, historical changes in the structure of these myths are likely to be reflective of changes in the dominant social institutions of the time. This takes us towards an understanding of film genres as having a socio-cultural significance, acting as a vehicle for collective expression in relation to societal ideals, values and dilemmas. Film can therefore be seen as a device though which these aspects of cultural identity are expressed and shared.

While it is relatively uncontentious to suggest that film has the potential to influence the cultural tastes and preferences of a worldwide audience based on the clothes worn, cars driven, houses lived in and jobs done by the people we see on the screen, ideological analyses go further than this in suggesting that film, alongside other aspects of mass media and popular culture has the ability to shape individual subjectivities including desires, hopes and fears in ways that serve the interests of a particular economic system. The implications of this assertion for reading and understanding management in popular film are significant. Althusser's theory of 'ideology-in-general' provides a basis for claiming that popular film creates illusions which perpetuate false consciousness in the general population in order to protect capitalist interests (Jancovich, 1995). This builds on the work of earlier Marxists, Horkheimer and Adorno who, having fled from Germany to New York in the 1930s, were struck by the extent of mass consumerism in US society which they saw as related to the controlling effects of the culture industry. In *The Dialectic of Enlightenment* (1944) they argued that the Hollywood film industry was an aspect of American mass culture that produced highly standardized products for consumption by passive audiences who were being fed propaganda 'from the time they leave the factory in the evening to the time they clock on in the morning' (Horkheimer and Adorno, 1944 [2002], p. 104). These authors saw the culture industry as a device of moral correction, its purpose to ensure individuals' continuing conformity and compliance by creating artificial desires for, and unrealizable promises of, the things and lifestyles they saw on the screen. Like Althusser, they saw cinema as an instrument of capitalist interests that distorts and impedes individuality by manipulating people's tastes and preferences and shaping them to fit the demands of the capitalist system.

Let us consider the implications of these assertions for understanding the role of film in informing how we understand management and organization. Through seeing what people in films desire, such as a demanding, high-status career where they wear expensive suits, get promoted, exercise power over others and earn lots of money, we learn to desire these things from our own everyday experiences of working, managing and being managed. Conversely, when we see things in films that apparently make people unhappy in their working lives, such as working in a routine, clerical job where there is no excitement or possibility of promotion, we learn not to desire this kind of work for ourselves. In other words, because ideological analysis implies that we imitate what we see in film, the fictionalized representations we watch on screen are significant in determining our behaviour in an everyday sense. One could even go so far as to speculate that the growing popularity of management as a degree subject and a career choice is in part influenced by the experiences of individuals who are socialized into seeing a managerial career as desirable through repeated exposure to these images. Critical ideological analyses further suggest that popular culture constitutes a means through which resistance to managerial ideology is diffused. For example, Rhodes (2001) questions whether TV shows like *The Simpsons* are really an effective method of resisting managerial ideology since by presenting a non-threatening form of entertainment they potentially discourage more meaningful political action. As he puts it, 'by encouraging viewers to laugh at their own employment situations' television shows like *The Simpsons* act as a 'safety valve that actually buttresses organizations from a more thoroughgoing critique' (Rhodes 2001, p. 382). Similarly, Gabriel (2000) sees film as a medium of mass entertainment that has undermined people's ability to tell stories based on their organizational experience, through a process of 'narrative deskilling' whereby the traditional craft of storytelling is lost.

However, the difficulty with ideological analysis is that it tends to overlook the variety of representations contained within film not all of which so neatly and consistently support the ideologies of management and organization that one might expect. A further problem arises from the tendency to portray audiences as passive, or as Garfinkel (1967) put it, as exhibiting the characteristics of a 'cultural dope', a caricature of a figure who absorbs the messages that a society puts out and unthinkingly acts in accordance with them, as the following quote from Horkheimer and Adorno illustrates:

> The familiar experience of the moviegoer, who perceives the street outside as a continuation of the film he just left, because the film seeks strictly to reproduce the world of everyday perception, has become the guideline of production. The more densely and completely its techniques duplicate empirical objects, the more easily it creates the illusion that the world outside is a seamless extension of the one which has been revealed in the cinema. (Horkheimer and Adorno, 1944 [2002], p. 99)

They see the culture industry as having successfully convinced readers that the text corresponds directly with the outside world, this tending to preclude the possibility that audiences read a film in a way that is different from that which is intended. In so doing, they portray film as inevitably reproducing systems of hierarchy and authority associated with the dominant culture. While ideological analysis has much to offer us in terms of understanding the potential for film to affect our values and actions, there needs to be a degree of caution in its application. The approach taken in this book characterizes film as a site of struggle over meaning, these processes being linked to social and historical changes in the way that the subjects of management and organization are perceived and understood. Hence different sometimes contradictory meanings of work and management may be present within the same text. As Gamman and Marshment (1988, p. 2) state: 'Between the market and the ideologues, the financiers and the producers, the directors and the actors, the publishers and the writers, capitalists and workers, women and men, heterosexual and homosexual, black and white, old and young – between what things mean and how they mean, is a perpetual struggle for control.' We must also be cautious in assuming that film popularity as measured by box-office success is an indictor of socio-cultural dilemmas and values, for as Neale (2000, p. 225) observes, 'there are all kinds of reasons why people pay to see films. And there are all kinds of reactions to them' which may have little to do with socio-cultural significance.

Intertextuality

The approach taken in this book entails analysis of film texts in relation to one another, focusing on their *intertextuality* or the way that 'texts are constituted as such by their relationship with other texts' (Frow 2006, p. 48). Rather than being self-contained, film texts contain references to and repetitions from other films. Moreover, texts are also defined by the *absence* of reference to other texts – by what they leave out as well as by what they include. To take an example, the film *The Hudsucker Proxy* (1994) picks up on many elements found in precursor films of the 1930s, 1940s and 1950s, self-consciously integrating them into its own construction to such an extent that one Internet Movie Database (IMDb) user is prompted to comment that it is as if the filmmakers 'wanted to charge every scene with symbolic meaning' (http://imdb.com/title/tt0110074/usercomments – consulted 27.10.07). These include the characters and plot of *Mr Deeds Goes to Town* (1936), the iconography of the clock as developed in films like *Metropolis* (1927) and *Modern Times* (1936), the cartoon-like character of Buzz the elevator boy who can be read as an exaggeration of the more restrained elevator girl Fran in *The Apartment* (1960), and the opulent film sets of senior executives' offices and boardrooms drawing on films such as *Executive Suite* (1954) and *Patterns* (1956). The film also draws on more recent film texts such as *Brazil* (1985) (see Film Focus 1.5). Through its elaborate reworking of these generic conventions *The Hudsucker Proxy* is a parody of the genre, appealing to the audience's ability to recognize these devices and thereby confirming their knowledge of film (Neale, 2000). However, even though these references are important and knowing about them might add to your understanding of the film, the meaning of *The Hudsucker Proxy* can still be followed even if you have not seen any of these precursor film texts. This is because the meanings belong to the genre rather than to any particular precursor text alone.

A further point about intertextuality relates to the social and historical context in which texts are located and the way that the genre is continually being remade, changes in the world being related to changes in the genre (Frow, 2006). The process whereby a particular text refers to other texts is inherently historical, drawing on what has been said before as well as anticipating what will be said in the future. For example, while *The Hudsucker Proxy* is set in 1959 it represents this era from the point of view of someone who lives in the 1990s, using exaggerated iconography such as the gigantic clock face or huge cigar to indicate that these things are not to be taken too literally or seriously. Traditional patterns of the genre are thus reinterpreted in a way that implies a playful knowingness in which the audience is invited to share (Bordwell, 2006). From this we conclude that genres have no essence, only historically changing use values that emerge, become popular and endure because they meet a demand.

FILM FOCUS 1.5: Intertextuality in *The Hudsucker Proxy* (1994) and *Boiler Room* (2000)

In the opening scene of *The Hudsucker Proxy* (1994) we meet Norville Barnes, a bright but naïve business school graduate from the small town of Muncie as he arrives by bus in New York looking for work. This instantly refers us to the opening scenes of precursor texts such as *The Crowd* (1928) or *Patterns* (1956). At the same time as Norville finds an advertisement for a job which is described as 'low pay – long hours' at Hudsucker Industries, the elderly executives of Hudsucker Industries are sitting in a dull meeting discussing profits. As the clock strikes noon the company president, Mr Hudsucker, rises from his seat and steps up onto the highly polished boardroom table, running along its full length and crashing through the plate glass window to plunge to his death just as Norville enters the building. The executives immediately proceed to analyse the impact of the president's suicide on the value of the company.

We return to Norville in the mailroom in the basement of the vast empire that is Hudsucker Industries, where he is being inducted into the 'The Hud' (the employee's nickname for their company) by a mailroom worker who shouts at great speed in a speech that lasts exactly a minute: 'You punch in at 8:30 every morning, except you punch in at 7:30 following a business holiday, unless it's a Monday, then you punch in at 8 o'clock. Punch in late and they dock you. Incoming articles get a voucher, outgoing articles provide a voucher. Move any article without a voucher and they dock you. Letter size a green voucher, oversize a yellow voucher, parcel size a maroon voucher. Wrong color voucher and they dock you! 6787049A/6. That is your employee number. It will not be repeated! Without your employee number you cannot get your paycheck.

Inter-office mail is code 37, intra-office mail 37–3, outside mail is 3–37. Code it wrong and they dock you! This has been your orientation. Is there anything you do not understand? Is there anything you understand only partially? If you have not been fully oriented, you must file a complaint with personnel. File a faulty complaint and they dock you!'

The rapid pace of work and furious movement of paper among the apron-clad postal workers in the mailroom, with its overhead ducts exposing the underbelly of the organization, can be read as a reference to the futuristic film *Brazil* (1985), where government workers toil in the basement of the building to the jaunty Latin-American tune 'Aquarela do Brasil' for only as long as their boss, Mr Kurtzmann's gaze is upon them, before returning to watch Western films on their computer screens.

In *The Hudsucker Proxy* the frenzied activity in the mailroom is interrupted by the arrival of a dreaded 'blue letter' which new-boy Norville is told to take up to the 44th floor of the Hudsucker Industries skyscraper. His progression up the organizational hierarchy to its highest level is indicated spatially by his ride up the elevator to the top of the building where the Art Deco-styled opulence of the high-ceiling rooms provide sharp contrast to the claustrophobic mailroom. Here the iconography associated with the genre is exaggerated almost to the point of parody, as in the scene where Norville first enters the office of the evil director Sidney Mussberger to see him sitting behind a huge desk at the far end of an echoing chamber of an office the size of a football pitch. 'This better be good' he tells Norville, 'I'm in a bad mood'. 💿 [**approximate running time: 3.45–21.10 mins.**]

In *Boiler Room* (2000) intertextuality is made explicit through the representation of other film texts within the film. When Seth is being socialized into the rules of his new job selling stock at brokerage firm JT Marlin he is asked if he has seen the film *Glen Garry Glenross* (1992). He replies that he has and is reminded of the message in the film to 'always be closing'. In another scene, the brokers relax at one of their homes drinking beer whilst watching the movie *Wall Street* (1987) on television. They are so familiar with the film that they can recite the dialogue as it is spoken by the characters on screen. Through its references to other texts, *Boiler Room* does two things. First, it represents the brokers as a film audience whose members share a common cultural frame of reference through which they make sense of their work context and reinforce their shared values about money and masculinity. Second, it indicates to the audience that the film seeks to confirm, adapt and extend other film texts with which the audience is likely to be familiar. 💿 [**approximate running time: 32.35–35 mins.**]

Film semiotics

If we take a film to be a text that can be analysed in the same way as written texts that use language then our task is to identify appropriate methodologies for analysing them. The approach developed in this book draws on semiotics, or the 'science of signs', which is concerned with how meaning is generated and conveyed through texts. Ferdinand de Saussure's (1916) ideas provide the starting point for semiotic analysis. Saussure suggests that language is comprised of signs which together constitute an entire system of meaning. For Saussure, a sign is something that stands for something else, being made up of a *signifier* or *sign vehicle* – the recognizable word, sound, or picture that attracts our attention and communicates a particular message, and the *signified* – the message or concept to which it refers. He further suggests that the relationship between the signifier and the signified is arbitrary, there is no logical connection between them. Therefore, its meaning depends on the conventions that are held by groups of sign users. 'From this perspective, language can no longer be regarded as a mirror of social reality. On the contrary, it provides the actual schemas and conceptual frames then used to organize one's experience of reality' (Prasad, 2005, p. 96).

Within these communicative systems, signs are defined by their relations with other signs in the overall system that ties them together. Sign systems thus work as a totality. Moreover, the most 'precise characteristic' of these concepts 'is in being what the others are not' (Saussure, 1966, p. 117, cited in Berger, 1991, p. 7). Signs are thus oppositional, being constituted by differences (Barthes, 1988) and the meaning of any particular sign is relational, determined through their difference from, or opposition to, other signs within the overall system. The work of Roland Barthes is useful to us here because it highlights the cultural ideologies that are embedded within any communicative system. Barthes (1972) asserts that, in addition to being used to analyse language, semiology can be applied to a whole variety of other sign systems in a wide variety of areas of communicative contexts that are concerned with conveying meaning, such as advertisements, TV soap operas and horror movies. In an influential collection of essays, he argues for the semiotic study of things that are produced and consumed by society including advertising, cookery, film and wrestling (see Film Focus 1.6).

FILM FOCUS 1.6: Signifying the manager in film

One of Barthes' (1972) essays involves a semiotic analysis of the Romans in film. Barthes begins by describing the Romans' hairstyles and draws attention to the signifier of the fringe that signifies their nobility. He also observes the signifier of profuse sweating (apparently achieved with the aid of Vaseline). In this case, the signified is the Romans' moral feeling. We can apply the same analytical

---

approach in relation to the physical appearance of other groups of characters in film such as office workers and managers where changes in signifier are often indicative of a shift in organizational status. For example, the bowler hat which is worn by the main character, Bud in *The Apartment* (1960) is important in signifying his promotion within the managerial hierarchy, replacing the trilby hat, which signifies his former status as an office clerk. Similarly, in *Working Girl* (1988) signifiers of heavy gold jewellery, back-combed hair and revealing tops relate to the general signified of Tess's status as a secretary. Later in the film it is the very absence of these things that signifies her status as an investment manager. In this example the meaning of being a manager is very clearly defined in relation to what it is not. Once we have learnt the meaning of particular signifiers of management such as the briefcase, bowler hat or cigar we can quickly recognize them when we come to watch a new film, even if we do so unconsciously and are unable to explain what rules or codes we are applying. Having an understanding of semiotics makes us more conscious of these rules and therefore better able to interpret them.

A further concept that is useful to us here is the notion of denotative and connotative meaning. Denotative meaning is the more obvious meaning of a signifier and as such it indicates its function, whereas connotative meaning is associated with the context in which it is applied. Within film connotative meaning is generated through the use of particular camera shots and editing techniques. For example, the decision to take an overhead shot of a male office worker sitting at his desk in a room full of other office workers conveys a sense of his insignificance relative to his social situation. Other examples of the way that camera work can be used to generate connotative meaning are given in Tables 1.1 and 1.2.

Connotative meaning is also derived from the use of metaphors and metonymy. Metonymy suggests a relationship based on association and it operates as a kind of cinematic shorthand (Monaco, 2000). It relies on the existence of codes that enable

Table 1.1   Camera shots as a sign system

Signifier (shot)	Definition	Signified (meaning)
Close-up	Face only	Intimacy
Medium shot	Most of body	Personal relationship
Long shot	Setting and characters	Context, scope, public distance
Full shot	Full body of person	Social relationship

Source: Berger, 1991, p. 26

Table 1.2 Camera work and editing techniques as a sign system

Signifier	Definition	Signified (meaning)
Pan down	Camera looks down	Power, authority
Pan up	Camera looks up	Smallness, weakness
Dolly in	Camera moves in	Observation, focus
Fade in	Image appears on blank screen	Beginning
Fade out	Image screen goes blank	Ending
Cut	Switch from one image to another	Simultaneity, excitement
Wipe	Image wiped off screen	Imposed conclusion

Source: Berger, 1991, p. 27

the reader to make the connection between an object (such as the clock), and the idea or thing that it represents (disciplined work). Metaphors have also been argued to be important in how we understand organization. As Morgan (1997, p. 4) argues, 'all theories of organization and management are based on implicit images or metaphors that lead us to see, understand, and manage organizations in distinctive yet partial ways'. However, metaphors do not simply reflect organizational reality. Instead each one highlights particular organizational features while drawing attention away from others. Hence the choice of one particular metaphor over another provides insight into the organizational theory that informs the message communicated by the text.

How it is that we are able to make these connections between say a clock and the idea of disciplined work that it symbolizes? In other words, what prior learning brings us to the point whereupon seeing a clock in a film we can immediately make this association? This question brings us to the concept of codes. Codes are structured patterns of association that help us to interpret signs. We learn codes as part of our socialisation into a culture and when we watch a film we apply the codes we have acquired in order to understand the film's meaning. As Berger (1991) explains, 'people carry *codes* around in their heads, highly complex patterns of associations that enable them to interpret metonymic communication correctly' (Berger, 1991, pp. 21–22, emphasis in original). However, codes are not necessarily universally shared, some of them depend on factors such as social class, education, political views, ethnicity and gender, while others are more general. In short, signs are polysemic and can be interpreted in different ways.

The role of the audience

Having established that there are a sufficient number of films which pursue themes related to management and organization to make their analysis worthwhile and outlined the approach that will be taken in analysing them, we can also speculate as to why it is that people watch films or, in other words, what 'gratifications' (Berger, 1991) they offer. Most obviously, people watch film to be entertained and amused. Film can also give people a common cultural frame of reference, providing a topic of conversation and helping people to relate to one other. It can also enable people to experience empathy. By relating to the characters on screen they are able to share their emotional experiences and prepare themselves emotionally for having to face similar situations in real life. For example, encountering a male film character in late middle-age who has worked in the same organization for twenty years can help us to antici-pate feelings about work that a younger viewer might not experience at first-hand for several decades. Film characters can also provide us with models of behaviour which can be imitated as a source of self-identity. This is one of the reasons why films such as *The Insider* (2000), *Glengarry Glen Ross* (1992), *Wall Street* (1987) and *Erin Brockovich* (2000) have been recommended as a way of helping students to under-stand subjects like business ethics (Van Es, 2003; Harrison, 2004; Shaw, 2004; Berger and Pratt, 1998). Film also enables us to see authority figures, such as senior managers or Chief Executive Officers, either exalted or deflated, thereby conveying a sense of how they should be dealt with. Finally, film can provide a vehicle for expression of some of our deepest fears, whether of the unconstrained power of big business, the threat of technology replacing human workers, or that we will reach the end of our working lives and wonder whether it was all worth it.

This raises some important questions alluded to earlier; namely, are film audiences the passive recipients of meaning imbued by filmmakers into the text or, are they active interpreters who can come up with alternative readings to those intended by producers of the text? This question relates to Barthes (1975) distinction between *readerly* texts, which envisage a passive, receptive reader who accepts the ideological claims of the text, and *writerly* texts, which call upon the reader to be active in creat-ing meaning. Readerly texts, or texts of pleasure, do not challenge audience percep-tions and are easily consumed, thus confirming the status quo and the reader's subject position within the culture. Writerly texts, on the other hand, challenge the reader's perceptions, forcing them to engage with the text in the production of mean-ing and thus provoking individual and social instability.

FILM FOCUS 1.7: The dangers of underestimating the audience

When four Italian management consultants (Bogliari et al., 2007) announced they had published a book which argued that managers could learn more from popular film than textbooks, the story was picked up by newspapers and web-sites in the US and Europe. The authors recommend 50 films including *The Terminal* (2004) for an insight into 'groundbreaking strategy' and creative

Continued

Consideration of audiences is further complicated by the fact that they are not a unified or homogenous group. Their interpretations will depend on their background and prior experiences and will be affected by cultural and social factors as well as individual psychology. It is therefore important to consider how different film audiences respond. In *The Role of the Reader* (1976) Umberto Eco draws attention to the misunderstandings or differences that can arise between the transmitters and receivers of messages. He suggests that the author of a text must assume that the codes s/he uses are shared by the reader of the text. The author must foresee a 'model reader' who is able to read the text in the same way as the author. However, Eco contends that the process of using linguistic codes is more fluid and open than structuralist semiotics suggests. Instead texts are subject to 'rule-governed creativity' that makes their meaning indeterminate. Similarly to Barthes (1975), Eco suggests that some texts are more 'open' to readerly interpretation than others. What is more, the potential for differences of understanding to arise between author and reader is greater in the mass media, including television, because of the wide gap, in terms of social class, politics and education that exists between those who create the text and those who receive it. Readers are therefore more likely to interpret these texts from their own perspective. However, more recently, Eco (1992) have cautioned against attributing too great a significance to the role of the reader, distinguishing between the *intention of the work*, the purpose of the text itself, and the *intention of the reader* and the purpose that the reader brings to their reading. Eco is resistant to the idea that texts are open to unlimited interpretation, instead seeing them as the subject of a dialectical interplay between the purpose of the text and the purpose of the reader.

Although the content of film is influenced by the industries that disseminate cultural material i.e. the media, it is not simply the result of these industries, instead it is the result of ongoing interaction between them and the people who consume their products and communicate with each other about them (Hall, 1980; Ang, 1991). This is what Hall (1980) refers to as the nonlinear 'circuit of communication' whereby he distinguishes between the discursive construction of products of mass communication like film and their translation into social practices or consumption. This circuit is nonlinear in the sense that it is comprised of a series of 'moments' – production, circulation, distribution/consumption and reproduction – each one shaping the overall message but none fully determining the others (Pillai, 1992). In contrast to earlier models of communication, Hall's (1980) analysis focuses on the significance of the role of the decoder (reader of the text) as well as the encoder (author of the text), suggesting that the decoder need not necessarily accept the encoder's intended meaning. He suggests that the experiences of watching, decoding, consuming, and receiving are contradictory and multiple. From this he develops three positions of the reader; first is the *dominant* (or *'hegemonic'*) *reading*, when the reader fully shares the text's code and accepts and reproduces the *preferred reading*, as intended by the author of the text. The code thus seems 'natural' and 'transparent'. The second possibility is the *negotiated reading* when the reader partly shares the text's code and broadly accepts the preferred reading, but sometimes resists and modifies it in a way which reflects their social position, experiences and interests. This position thus involves a degree of tension or contradiction. The third possibility is an *oppositional* (*'counter-hegemonic'*) *reading*, when the reader, whose social situation places them in a directly oppositional relation to the dominant code, understands the preferred reading but rejects this in favour of an alternative frame of reference, such as a radical or feminist reading (see Film Focus 1.8). Text and audience can therefore no longer be seen as independent and studied separately (Livingstone, 1993); instead we need to look at text *and* audience together.

> Texts attempt to position readers as particular kinds of subjects through particular modes of address, inviting readers to insert specific knowledge or perspectives into the interpretive flow. Readers may accept or neglect such textual invitations and constructions of subject positions, reading against the grain while avoiding aberrance, exploiting the inevitable degree of openness in the text, playing with textual conventions, and thereby jointly constructing different meanings on different occasions. (Livingstone, 1993, pp. 7–8)

FILM FOCUS 1.8: An oppositional and a dominant reading of *Disclosure* (1994)

Brewis (1998) rejects the dominant reading of the film *Disclosure* (1994) in favour of an oppositional, feminist Foucauldian reading of the text. A dominant reading of the film would involve Brewis accepting the message about the issue of workplace sexual harassment intended by the author, producer-director Barry Levinson. This reading suggests that the film's reversal of roles, involving

Continued

---

a woman as the harasser and a man as her victim, encourages men to define themselves as possible victims of sexual harassment which makes them more sympathetic to the issues faced by women in the workplace. Brewis challenges this reading on two grounds, first, because the film constitutes and consolidates understandings of working women as threatening and as having no legitimate claim to organizational success and second, by representing sexual harassment as highly erotic, the film encourages a reading which fails to see it as unwanted and abusive. Brewis further argues that the message about sexual harassment conveyed by the film does not correspond to research evidence, instead it reinforces 'the damaging stereotype that the recipient of harassment has some role to play in the harassing behaviour: that they in some way have invited it or at least failed to indicate that they do not welcome the advances' (Brewis, 1998, p. 96).

However, other writers in the management field have accepted the dominant reading of this film. For example, Comer and Cooper (1998) recommend *Disclosure* to educate students about gender relations and sexual harassment in order to reduce its prevalence in the workplace. Comer and Cooper do not read the message about working women conveyed by the film as particularly problematic, instead they focus on the under-examined issue of sexual harassment of men. They further suggest that their students are convinced by the message of the film, saying that students 'have asserted that the [film] is on target in its portrayal of gender relations and sexual harassment' (Comer and Cooper, 1998, p. 230).

However, because film audiences are so large and dispersed and their engagement with film often takes place in a private context such as the home, they are difficult to reach. Consequently, audience analysis has tended to focus on measurement techniques that are primarily quantitative and technologically driven (e.g. box office figures), thereby tending to overlook the meaning, salience or impact of a film (Ang, 1991). One way of gaining an impression of how a film is received is by analysing user comments on internet sites such as IMDb, www.imdb.com which also provides plot synopses, thumbnail reviews, cast and credit lists for over 825,000 films, or from message boards on internet sites such as Rotten Tomatoes, www.rottentomatoes.com which tracks and collates films reviews published in newspapers and magazines, or www.filmsite.org, which provides reviews and resources relating to classic American films. Wikipedia also has articles on many films http://en.wikipedia.org and lists of the '10 Best Business Movies' can also be found [www.american.com/ archive/2006/ November/10-best-business-movies – consulted 19.01.07]. Internet discussions of films provide a useful and readily available source through which to gain insight into audience responses (Deacy, 2005). What is more, the existence and popularity of internet forums related to film provides evidence to support the notion that 'audiences have profound investments in certain texts or groups of texts' (Hollows and Jancovich, 1995, p. 11) which, although they do not necessarily involve oppositional readings, neither are they entirely passive.

A deconstructive perspective

By now it should be clear that the structuralist approach offered by semiotics can only take us so far in our analysis. This is because one of the central problems with semiotics is that it assumes that texts have a unique essence which, as the discussion of audiences in the previous section illustrates, is highly problematic – since in principle at least there can be as many different readings of a text as there are readers of it. The theory and philosophy of deconstruction (Derrida, 1974) is helpful to us here.

Deconstruction is a methodological approach which seeks to uncover the multiple, hidden meanings within a text through exploration of relationships of inclusion and exclusion and the way that particular meanings are hidden or suppressed. Informed by structuralist semiotics and Saussure's (1966) ideas about the oppositional nature of signs, Derrida radicalizes their basic insights by calling into question the relationship between the signifier and the signified. Rather than seeing the signifier as inevitably leading to a signified, deconstruction calls into question the binary nature of this relationship, suggesting that the relationship between them is not definitive but elusive. The meaning of signs is thus located in the discursive context which is historically defined and changes over time. Derrida's writings are critical of what he refers to as 'logocentric' thinking which invites a view of texts as able to fix and capture meaning (Culler, 1982).

Central to Derrida's approach is the idea of oppositional linguistic dualisms which exist in a hierarchical relationship each containing a 'trace' of its opposite and depending for its existence on that which it is *not*. Invariably one term occupies a superior position relative to the other which is presented as somehow falling short or incomplete. The meaning of any sign is thus derived from a process of 'deferral' to other signs, defined relationally in terms of the way it differs from others. Signs can therefore be understood to be indeterminate because they contain 'their own opposites and thus refuse any *singular* grasp of their meanings' (Cooper and Burrell, 1988, p. 98, emphasis in original). Although Derrida was talking about written texts, his ideas can be extended to encompass film (Brunette and Wills, 1989). For example, a deconstructive perspective can be used to challenge the convention of film genres, suggesting them to be unstable and indeterminate. The deconstructionist notion of *difference* can also be used to explore how the meaning of a film depends upon absence as well as presence and to question realist perspectives which regard film texts as a reflection of pre-existing reality.

> Deconstructive thinking can lead us away from a conventional idea of cinema, and its relation to reality, as an *analogical* one based on similarity, to an idea of cinema, as Brunette and Wills (1989: 88) have put it, as an 'anagram of the real', a place of writing filled with non-natural conventions that allow us to understand it as a representation of reality. (Brunette, 2000, p. 91)

Deconstructionist analysis (Brunette and Wills, 1989) has been used in film studies to critique the discipline for its totalizing assumptions that encourage the view that individual films and the history of filmmaking can be treated as a comprehensive and coherent whole with generally agreed-upon boundaries. Hence when certain films are identified as 'typical' of a genre or an era a deconstructionist perspective would seek to expose the 'essentializing gestures' entailed in such an intellectual process. Rather than seeing film as the product of a single, intentional author, it invites a focus on 'dispersed intentionality', not as a characteristic that is endowed upon a text but instead as an important organizing principle in the construction of meaning. As Brunette and Wills argue, this gives rise to a different way of reading film, one which considers the text as '*fundamentally* incoherent' (1989, p. 62, emphasis in original). They go on to explain the implications of such an approach:

> From a deconstructive standpoint, analysis would no longer seek the supposed center of meaning but instead turn its attentions to the margins, where the supports of meaning are disclosed, to reading in and out of the text, examining the other texts onto which it opens itself out or from which it closes itself off. (Brunette and Wills, 1989, p. 62)

This gives rise to an approach that considers film as a form of *writing* which must be *read* in a way that invites a wider conceptualization of textuality than that enabled by structuralist analyses. Hence rather than being a narrative representation of reality, the meaning of any given film text is 'disseminated', characterized by internal fragmentation, instability, fluidity and disunity and therefore resistant to closure.

Conclusion

The approach adopted in this book is informed by the various approaches to film analysis that have been discussed in this chapter. However, there are some important ways in which it is different from previous approaches, one of the main ones being that rather than implying that films can *show* or *tell* you what management or organizations are really like. The approach taken here assumes that the meaning of film texts involves a process of interpretation on the part of the reader which is influenced by self-identity and by the time and place in which the particular reading takes place. The meaning of the text is therefore not fixed but open to an ongoing process of interpretation in the context of wider cultural and ideological meaning structures.

This approach also implies that representations of management and organization in film have the potential to inform how we understand and experience these activities in everyday life. From the point of view of someone who is interested in studying or practising management, reading film is an important way of gaining insight into the cultural ideology embedded within film texts. This can also stimulate the reader to reflect on the meaning that they attach to the practice of management, including the objects associated with it (such as tall buildings and smart suits), why they study and/or practise it and how these views have changed over time. This can provide a basis from which to develop greater reflexivity by questioning the meanings attached to management and organization based on a more informed understanding of where they come from and how they are formed.

Plate 2 Universal Film Studios Logo, 1950s–1960s
Courtesy of Universal Studios Licensing LLLP

2

The organization of film

Introduction

Chapter 1 introduced the main concepts and techniques that provide the basis for the analysis in the rest of this book. However, film texts cannot be understood without reference to the 'industrial and economic processes which shape their form, their content and the ways they are consumed by audiences' (Hollows, 1995, p. 16). Any attempted theorization of representations of management and organization in film must therefore take into account the processes of organization which help to determine its form; it political and economic features as well as its aesthetic or ideological aspects. This involves an analysis of the organizations that produce film and their managerial practices. This chapter therefore focuses on the institution of filmmaking, distribution and exhibition, this constituting the industry within which these texts are produced and consumed.

There are several other reasons for doing this. First, existing analyses of management and organization in popular culture have only limitedly sought to understand the material contexts of its production and consumption. Second, many of the readers of this book are already likely to be familiar with organizational analysis which they can apply in the context of this particular industry. Third, it is likely that the people who are involved in film production draw on their own organizational experience of the industry to inform the way their representations of management and organization are produced. For example, in the period 1920–1950, many Hollywood screenwriters were hostile towards managers of the studios because they felt themselves to be undervalued and exploited (Hollows, 1995). It is reasonable to assume that these sentiments filtered through to film texts, which although they needed to be commercially successful, did not necessarily have to communicate a message which was supportive of dominant economic interests. Finally, because the process of making, distributing and exhibiting film is embedded within power relations whereby dominant groups generally seek to impose meanings which subordinate groups may resist (Hall, 1980; 1981), it is important to understand how the industry is organized in order to be able to interpret these relationships.

In sum, the organization of film itself is important to the understanding of why it represents management and organization in various ways. While the organization of the industry does not straightforwardly determine the aesthetic and ideological content of film texts it does however set the constraints within which they are produced and provides a source of inspiration for their production. This chapter will explore how and why the organization of film gives rise to particular representations of organization. It also considers the relationship between the film industry and other organizations which are represented within this medium, thereby positioning the film industry relative to other forms of organization.

The American film industry

For almost its entire history the film industry has been dominated by the United States and Hollywood, both as a geographical centre of production and as a cultural influence on the organizational values of production (Gomery, 1998). Hollywood remains the home of the major film studio headquarters that control film production and worldwide distribution for exhibition in cinemas and people's homes. Although the American film industry is only the world's fourth largest film producer, after India, China/Hong Kong and the Philippines (UNESCO, 2000), it currently accounts for between 40 and 90 per cent of films shown in most parts of the world (Miller, 1998). To put this more precisely:

> American films now dominate around 70% of the French market, 85% of the Italian market, 90% of the German market and nearly all of the British market ... While Hollywood movies account for less than one-tenth of the world's annual production of feature-length films, American films account for more than 70% of box office receipts worldwide. (Sadar and Wyn Davies, 2004, p. 147)

Additionally, American films accounted for 92 per cent of the market in Australia and 75 per cent of the Russian market in 2003 (Miller et al., 2005) while Japan was the largest export market for US films in 1999 (Waterman, 2005). Although Europe produces more films each year than North America (17 per cent of the total number of films produced annually worldwide – UNESCO, 2000), they have in recent years become heavily reliant on government subsidies (Waterman, 2005) and despite relatively high levels of production in some countries, the success experienced by European film production industries during the 1950s and 1960s has waned considerably. The 'trend towards US dominance' therefore appears to be 'undubitable' (Miller et al., 2005, p. 17).

The current organization of film production owes much to the historical development of the American feature film industry and the success of the Hollywood studio system which took shape during the 1920s when the major film companies acquired large production facilities in and around Hollywood which provided affordable land, a wide variety of settings in which to shoot and a potential source of cheap labour (Sklar, 1975, cited in Belton, 1988). These corporations were organized on an industrial scale, managing hundreds or even thousands of contract workers in production lots and not only producing, but also distributing and exhibiting films, through their own chains of theatres. While undoubtedly creative, the process of film production was highly standardized and formalized, as 'each top studio developed a repertoire of contract stars and story formulas that were refined and continually recirculated through the marketplace' (Schatz, 1989, p. 7). The prevalence of this organizational system is attributed first, to its efficiency – being simply the most cost effective mode of organizing Hollywood film production; and second, because of its rent-seeking advantages, through enabling the studios to intercept 'some rents imputed to the stars and other filmmaking talent' (Caves, 2000, p. 92). This resulted in the production of a body of work with a house style and certain studios becoming associated with films of particular genres. While innovation was encouraged this was secondary to the imperative of making large amounts of money. This mass production process, sometimes described as a 'factory system', meant that films were produced on short, fixed schedules, often relying on the same actors from film to film employed on long-term contracts (Waterman, 2005) (see Film Focus 2.1). However, this was not a truly Fordist system such as the assembly line process for manufacturing cars as it did not entail the same level of deskilling as these other industries, labour was therefore not easily substitutable between tasks and manufacturing machinery did not provide a substitute for worker skills to the same extent (Miller et al., 2005).

Driven by technically and artistically oriented entrepreneurs (Jones, 2001) from a variety of social and cultural backgrounds, early film industry pioneers faced pressures associated with feature film production including the need for bigger budgets and longer production schedules (Mezias and Mezias, 2000). Centralized systems were set up to manage the distribution and marketing of films and this in turn led to the creation of larger, generalist companies, known as film studios or 'majors' that pursued a strategy of vertical integration which enabled them to control production, distribution and exhibition. 'The eventual result was the founding of the Hollywood studio system that persists in a somewhat altered form today.' (Mezias and Mezias, 2000, p. 308) First silent era films and later 'talkies' made for the domestic market were exported to other English speaking countries and 'by the 1930s foreign sales provided between a third and a half of industry returns' (Miller, 1998, p. 372). While imports initially also flowed in the other direction, France selling a dozen films a week to the United States at the beginning of the twentieth century (Miller et al., 2005), the international textual appeal of Hollywood combined with the aggressive dominance of its managerial, legal and technical methods meant that foreign competitors soon began to struggle to compete and the First and Second World Wars also significantly reduced Europe's ability to compete with Hollywood.

FILM FOCUS 2.1: Hollywood and the studio system in *The Player* (1992) and *The Bad and the Beautiful* (1952)

The organization of film production tends to be portrayed in film as a corrupt, money-grabbing world in which producers, actors and directors will stop at nothing to ensure their commercial success (Newitz, 2006). In *The Bad and the Beautiful* (1952), money and its relationship to individual and product success is of central concern to directors, actors, writers, and producers, as well as to studio bosses. The film represents the factory system of film production of the 1930s, mass produced films being made under the control of a studio boss who 'doesn't want to win awards', instead urging his team to make films that have 'a kiss at the end and put black ink on the books' ☉ [**approximate running time: 18.10–24 mins.**] *The Player* (1992) provides a more recent critique of the Hollywood film industry, representing film industry workers as subject to the financially driven calculations of management who are concerned only with the commercial, rather than the aesthetic, value of the product ☉ [**approximate running time: 7.30–9.30; 20.50–23.10 mins.**] In both films, the monster is the film producer who treats his co-workers as a financial resource, deceiving and manipulating them in order to maximize the value of their labour (Newitz, 2006).

By controlling the exhibition of films during their 'first-run' or initial period of release, through owning cinemas in urban centres across the United States, five corporations – Fox, MGM, Warner, Paramount and RKO – came to dominate the industry during the 1930s and 1940s, this constituting a mature oligopoly that worked together to restrict competition from the minors – Universal, Columbia and United Artists, as well as the smaller independents (Schatz, 1989). However, antitrust laws were used to challenge this oligopoly, in what came to be known as the Paramount case, and in 1948 the US federal government ruled that the majors had attempted to monopolize the industry to the exclusion of independent producers, distributors and exhibitors, ordering them to divest their interests in film theatres (Waterman, 2005). The 1950s and 1960s thus saw the end of what is referred to as the 'Golden Age' of Hollywood filmmaking as the industry faced a decline in cinema attendance suggested to have been precipitated by the arrival of television and a change in American lifestyles (Gomery, 1998). By the early 1970s, US cinema attendance was less than a quarter of its 1946 level (Waterman, 2005). The arrival of pay-television, video and DVD, however, proved to be considerably more effective in reviving the financial position of the studios than had been hoped. Moreover, rather than box office revenues being further eroded they have, since the 1970s, increased considerably. The 1980s gave rise to the 'corporate era' in Hollywood (Lewis, 1998), a period characterized by increased deregulation, reinterpretation of antitrust guidelines, leveraged mergers and acquisitions and the growing consolidation of assets and power by large corporations. This has led to the emergence of media conglomerates with interests in nearly all forms of mass media and popular culture, including book and magazine publishing, the music industry and theme parks (see Film Focus 2.2).

This process began in 1985–6, when Rupert Murdoch took over Twentieth Century Fox … at the same moment Michael Eisner began to transform and rebuild the Walt Disney Corporation. At the end of the 1980s Japan entered the fray; Sony took over Colombia Pictures, and Matsushita acquired MCA. Time and Warner merged. Viacom took over Paramount, and in 1995 Seagrams bought MCA from Matsushita. As a result the Hollywood industry today consists of but six multinational media conglomerates: Disney, Murdoch's Twentieth Century Fox, Seagram's Universal, Viacom's Paramount, Sony's Columbia, and Time Warner's Warner Bros. (Gomery, 1998, p. 251)

In 1998, Seagram sold Universal to Vivendi who, in partnership with General Electric, in 2004 created the wholly owned subsidiary NBC Universal. Between them these six companies own all of the main broadcast networks and many of the cable channels in the United States and also dominate worldwide film distribution (Epstein, 2005). Moreover, the trend towards corporate gigantism in the film industry is predicted to increase further in the future, as entertainment companies seek to develop strategic relationships with computer software providers and telephone hardware providers as a means of enabling the 'home box office' (Lewis, 1998). Not everyone involved in the film industry is comfortable with these developments. Barnouw (1993) suggests that filmmakers' have become increasingly concerned about the way that their domain is being transformed by 'merger mania', and the implications of this for censorship or self-censorship. Whether or not these concerns filter through to representations of organization and management in film texts is an issue we shall return to in Chapters 3 and 8.

This most recent wave of mergers has resulted in patterns of ownership that is more international than before, encompassing French, Japanese and Canadian interests but 'control over studio output remains in California and New York' (Miller et al., 2005, p. 92). The main advantages associated with conglomeration are suggested to be finance related, protecting the studio from serious fluctuations in income through the affiliation with a reliable cash cow business such as soft drinks or television stations (Waterman, 2005). One of the most striking things about these businesses is the extent of their stability, 'six of the seven major studios in business as of 2003 are the same companies that led the industry in the 1940s, or they are descendents of these firms' (Waterman, 2005, p. 20). However, unlike their predecessors which made their profits from worldwide exhibition to paying audiences in movie theatres, these companies routinely lose money on film exhibition. Instead, an increasing proportion of film revenues are derived from the home entertainment economy, through companies licensing their films for DVD sale, pay-television and syndication. What is more, films are no longer the product of a single organization, since studios outsource the making and financing of most of their films to equity partners and co-producers, thereby protecting themselves from potential financial losses (Epstein, 2005) through organizing according to a model of flexible specialisation (Caves, 2000).

FILM FOCUS 2.2: The impact of media conglomerations in *Outfoxed: Rupert Murdoch's War on Journalism* (2004)

Outfoxed (2004) considers the potential effects of a situation where a vast range of media interests including newspaper and book publishing, television broadcasting and film production, are owned by a few large and extremely powerful organizations. The film focuses on global media executive and owner of the Fox News Channel, Rupert Murdoch, who the film asserts has had a negative effect on freedom of expression and democracy in the United States through his influence on the political bias of news reporting. This includes the practice of sending internal memos written by media bosses to journalists in the run up to the Presidential election, telling them which issues to focus on and how to report them in a way which favours the Republican Party and presidential candidate George Bush. This is suggested to have resulted in the 'Fox Effect', whereby the commercial success of Fox's approach to broadcasting has influenced competitor news broadcasting organizations to imitate the organization's practices, thereby undermining professional journalistic principles of fair and unbiased reporting. Rupert Murdoch's interests also encompass the film studio Twentieth Century Fox which is a subsidiary of the Murdoch controlled News Corporation. ☺ [approximate running time: 1 hour 5.30–1 hour 9.10 mins.]

Film and the cultural industries

Film is a product of the cultural industries, sometimes also referred to as the creative industries since it entails the production of goods or services that have a cultural, artistic or entertainment value (Caves, 2000). Production is organized in a way that separates creative responsibility (led by the film director) from administrative responsibility (led by the film producer), creative workers having limited influence over budget setting and decision making which remains strongly hierarchical (Tashiro, 2002). In seeking to differentiate the culture industries from other forms of industry there is a tendency to imply that the values of creative entrepreneurs and artists who work in these industries are antithetical to those of business. Furthermore, it is suggested that creative workers value freedom of expression and have a commitment to the artistic product, while financially-driven managers impose an economic logic and seek to impose a formally organized production process. This sets up an opposition between those who are concerned with making money, what Bordieau (1984) terms *economic capital* – the narrow minded studio executives or Hollywood 'suits' – and those who are concerned with producing art or *cultural capital*, the former existing 'only to stifle the creative outpourings of the gifted and the bold' (Rothman, 2006, p. 149). However, these distinctions must be applied cautiously since it is dangerous to assume that the cultural industries are necessarily any more creative than other types of industry (Jeffcutt and Pratt, 2002). Moreover, in differentiating the cultural industries from other types of business organization, there is a risk of constructing essentialising dualisms which contrast creativity with management, implying that they are oppositional and incompatible with one another (Jeffcutt, 2000).

Having said this, film production does have specific organizational characteristics which distinguish it as a cultural industry. One of the main ones arises from the nature of film as a creative product of infinite variety which does not respond to a pre-existing identified consumer need in the same way that say a food item or a piece of agricultural machinery. It is therefore difficult to specify the 'use value' of specific products and hence to identify specific markets for them. Their success is therefore highly dependent on the way that those who experience the product respond to it which may be difficult to predict or even understand. This means there is a high degree of demand uncertainty associated with the industry and consequently the risks associated with the production of creative products are quite high in comparison to other industries (Caves, 2000). In this respect the film industry is suggested to be similar to the fashion industry (see Film Focus 2.3) where 'trying to judge what styles will sell next year – how to tailor an inventory, how much cloth to buy, how much to cut and so forth – is a bit of a guessing game' (Lederer, 2006, p. 162). Within the production and consumption of these symbolic goods, a crucial role is played by 'cultural intermediaries' (Bourdieu, 1984) whose role is to socially construct meaning in relation to creative products in a way that positions them as special and valuable. Cultural intermediaries, by virtue of their class position, social status and education, are able to produce narratives of distinctiveness in relation to cultural products which influence the meaning that other consumers attach to them (Wright, 2005).

FILM FOCUS 2.3: Fashion as a cultural industry in *The Devil Wears Prada* (2006)

While clothes are seen by Andy Sachs, personal assistant to the fearsome fashion magazine editor Miranda Priestly, as a product with a clearly identifiable use value in the film *The Devil Wears Prada* (2006), Miranda regards herself as part of a lucrative and powerful cultural industry, her role being to act as

Continued

a 'cultural intermediary', using her cultural capital, the embodied, institutionalized, and inherited cultural resources that she possesses, to bestow cultural products with differentiated value. In this scene, Miranda condescends to explain this to her assistant. 'I see … you think this has nothing to do with you. You go to your closet and you select, I don't know … that lumpy blue sweater for instance because you're trying to tell the world that you take yourself too seriously to care about what you put on your back. But what you don't know is that sweater is not just blue, it's not turquoise, its not lapis it's actually cerulean. And you're also blithely unaware of the fact that in 2002 Oscar de la Renta did a collection of cerulean gowns and then I think it was Yves Saint Laurent – wasn't it – who showed cerulean military jackets … And then cerulean quickly showed up in the collections of eight different designers and then it filtered down through the department stores and then trickled on down to into some tragic casual corner where you no doubt fished it out of some clearance bin. However, that blue represents millions of dollars and countless jobs and it's sort of comical how you think that you've made a choice that somehow exempts you from the fashion industry when in fact you're wearing a sweater that was selected for you by the people in this room from a pile of stuff'. ☉ [approximate running time: 20.20–23.30 mins.]

The culture industries are also characterized by the fact that consumers have limited time and money to spend on cultural activities. Jeffcutt and Pratt (2002, p. 228) describe the culture industries as 'chart businesses' because they 'live or die by the volume and success of their output being valued as "best" in the market place for a limited period'. Various strategies are used by the industry to manage this uncertainty including sinking high costs into a product in order to signal quality or creating a 'cultural repertoire' of products in order to spread their risks by balancing failures against successes. Even so, as Miller (1998, 371) notes, most film investments 'are complete failures, a pain that can only be borne by large firms'. Moreover, even if the product is sound, the timing of a release and what competitors release at the same time can significantly affect profitability (Waterman, 2005). Demand for creative goods like film can be enhanced by consumers (Caves, 2000) who play a role in evaluating film, for example by contributing to message boards on film websites, in a way that has the potential to influence demand for the product. As a result of these pressures there is a tension between trying to attract large audiences by limiting innovation and diversity and offering 'something for everyone' and still needing to preserve sufficient diversity to attract different audiences.

Garnham (1990) identifies three central characteristics of the culture industries; first, they use capital intensive technology as a means of mass production and distribution which makes the cost of entry into the industry high and restricts diversity. Second, they are hierarchical organizations with a complex division of labour. Third, their main aim is to maximise efficiency and profit. These characteristics provide the basis for an industry dominated by a small number of vertically integrated multinational conglomerates.

Capital intensive mass production and distribution

Film production is a capital intensive business. The average budget for a film produced by a major studio is approximately 60 million US dollars – theatrical distribution costs amounting to an additional 30 million, consequently, 'the average film has to generate a vast amount to break even' (Dekom, 2006, p. 101). Added to this the industry generates internal rates of return of between −20 per cent and 20 per cent, 'with the average (and mean) over the last five years somewhere in the −5% area' (Dekom, 2006, p. 102). In other words, the average film loses rather than makes money. While there are always exceptions in the form of a low-budget film that turns out to be highly profitable, in general, the more expensive the film and the higher paid the actors are who star in it, the more likely it is to make money. Moreover, in the period from 1975 to 2003, Hollywood has responded to market conditions by making more expensive films and fewer of them, in part to differentiate feature films from television productions and also to deal with the uncertainty associated with film production (Waterman, 2005). The studios spend an increasingly large proportion of their resources on marketing their products, in 2002 investing nearly as much in advertising and prints as on the movies themselves (Epstein, 2005).

Not only is this investment significant enough to create substantial and increasing barriers to entry but the time period in which studios recover the cost on their investment is also increasing because of changes in the way that products are consumed. Hence the success of the DVD format is such that 'it is not uncommon for the first week's gross in DVD sales of a highly popular movie to exceed its first-week gross in theatres and for video/DVD receipts to be greater than theatrical gross receipts' (Feingold, 2006, p. 412). This has led to a reduction in the time span, or 'window', between a film's theatrical release and its video release, in order to speed up the return on investment which in turn is suggested to have had a negative effect on box office attendance (Epstein, 2005). One of the most important aspects of the studios relates to their role as distributors (Waterman, 2005, p. 16), 'by controlling distribution, the studios act as gatekeepers: they decide which movies get produced and how they are made, and they also largely determine when and at what prices viewers get to see them on which media'. American dominance of international markets is suggested to be the result of the distribution system as studios rely on distribution arms under their control to ensure that their films are well positioned in international markets (Epstein, 2005).

> When *Jurassic Park*, *The Fugitive* or any other big film comes to Paris, the American distributors dictate the terms: 'You can have *Jurassic Park* for 10 to 15 weeks but to have it you must take another four or five American films to run along with it for two weeks each'. This is called a train – a locomotive film with cars that follow along. No matter how well the secondary films do, they stay for the number of weeks stipulated in the contract. Of course, the exhibitor agrees because he won't be able to get another *Jurassic Park* to pull in the audience. This means there is little room for French or other European titles in any given cinema. (Costa-Gavras, 1995, p. 5)

Another mechanism used to control the release sequence to segment markets is regional coding, a system which divides the world into six different regions, encrypting DVDs so that they only work on DVD players purchased in this region. Regional coding was developed to control the international distribution of film on a country-by-country basis so the timing of theatrical and video releases worldwide could be more effectively managed (Feingold, 2006). The system has been supplemented by the use of Regional Coding Enhancement to prevent US (Region 1) DVDs from being played on multi-region DVD players by some studios. In addition to enabling greater control over distribution of video releases worldwide, this gives the studios greater possibility of influencing the reception of a film.

FILM FOCUS 2.4: Film distribution, viral video and the Internet

Video sharing websites like *You Tube* [www.YouTube.com], a recently acquired subsidiary of *Google*, enable the internet distribution of film clips or 'viral videos' made by professional and amateur filmmakers typically through email. This could be seen as having removed some of the barriers to entry into the film industry by considerably reducing the costs associated with production and distribution. It is predicted that once business models that allow for a return on investment and profit have been developed, profitable cottage industries will emerge (Squire, 2006) as an increasing number of companies recognize the marketing potential associated with viral video. There are concerns that the digitalization of film has the potential to enable illegal internet file sharing similar to that seen in the music industry which some suggest has adversely affected industry revenues. Commercial internet film downloading services are already available in the United States, through the website *Movielink* [www.movielink.com – consulted 15.08.07] a joint venture between the studios that sources films from their libraries and other producers that enables them to be downloaded for viewing from a PC or television.

FILM FOCUS 2.5: Alternative distribution models

US Director/Producer Robert Greenwald has adopted a distribution model that relies on committed individuals, referred to as 'Brave New Friends', who host film screenings in venues such as universities, churches, schools and local theatres which they publicize themselves using materials provided by Brave New World Films, an organization which was set up to support the distribution of documentary films for social change following the success of films like *Outfoxed* (2004). In this way, they hope to reach a broader cross-section of people, as Greenwald explains, 'these are people who may not have an opinion and may not care, but certainly are not prepared to pay theater prices to see the film. We also know that we can get younger, more diverse audiences this way. The personal connection and recommendation to view a film like this is powerful.' The films also get high profile screenings, in cities such as New York, Los Angeles, San Francisco and Washington, D.C. and a limited theatrical run. This way, he explains, 'we create the excitement and interest that we can't afford to buy with national advertising, but which we can achieve through the energy and passion and voices of those seeing it around the country'. [http://www.walmartmovie.com/intro.php – consulted 05.06.07]. A similar strategy is also adopted by the filmmaker, Franny Armstrong director of *McLibel* (2005), who describes how independent filmmaking does not rely on the main channels such as the BBC and a wider audience can be reached. In an interview she estimates that her two films that produced by the small independent Spanner Films have been watched by 40 million people in 20 different countries. This is because the copyright belongs to the filmmaker this enabling it to be sold at a price that might not result in high profits but does enable more people to see the film. [http://www.spannerfilms.net/ – consulted 05.06.07]

Hierarchical organization and complex division of labour

Because creative products such as film are complex to produce, they require diversely skilled inputs. The division of labour is therefore complex, involving special effects, sound recording, editing, acting, directing, filming and film processing, scouting of locations, building sets, costume design and make up, music and dialogue coaching, catering, government relations and set publicity. The need for complex teams comprising many different types of creative worker, each with different skills and potentially conflicting priorities, is further complicated by the fact that creative industries involve a 'multiplicative productive function', i.e. 'every input must be present and do its job – or at least perform at or above some threshold of proficiency – if any commercially valuable output is to emerge' (Caves, 2000, p. 5), a characteristic which Caves refers to as the 'motley crew' property. Furthermore, because skills are vertically differentiated and creative workers ranked according to their skills, originality and proficiency, time is very expensive in relation to product development.

Up until the mid 1950s, the employment of the majority of production agents, including actors and producers, was on a salaried basis, individuals on long-term (usually seven year) contracts being assigned to work on different films over a period of time (Waterman, 2005). However, film production today is generally a project-based organization, resources being brought together for a single film production and then disbanded (Blair, 2001). Employment is often short term, highly skilled, casual, freelancing with serial short term contracts being common (Blair, 2001). Most film industry workers are employed on a freelance basis. These relationships are mediated in the United States by the main film industry union, the International Alliance of Theatrical Stage Employees, which regulates the recruitment and selection process, providing employers with information about potential employees and allocating employees to a project on the basis of seniority. However, the shift to flexible specialisation based on production tasks being undertaken by smaller and often transient enterprises poses a potential threat to union abilities to protect compensation levels (Caves, 2000).

There have also been changes in the skills required of workers as the mass production of relatively formulaic products by the studios has given way to the production of blockbusters, massively financed, special-effects laden films which require workers to undertake more complex and ill-defined tasks (Christopherson and Storper, 1989). Freelancing has given rise to a core-periphery distinction between a small group of highly skilled, successful workers who have greatest access to work hours and face lower employment insecurity due to their greater experience and better personal connections, and a larger number of lower-skilled workers who have more restricted access to work hours and thus experience longer periods of unemployment. Other analyses have adopted a human capital approach to the management of labour in the film industry suggesting that individual careers rely on the acquisition of a reputation based on successful performance which provides the basis for working together on a repeated basis with other successful individuals (Faulkner and Anderson, 1987) as a means of reducing uncertainty and risk. Blair's (2001) study of employment in the UK film industry suggests that gaining initial access to the industry relies on having contacts based on relationships involving friends or family as well as ex-colleagues and the establishment of semi-permanent work groups who move from project to project.

A distinction is made between 'above-the-line' and 'below-the-line' labour costs within the film industry. Writers, producers, film stars and directors fall into the category of 'proactive workers' or above-the-line, the costs of employment being borne by the film budget, whereas other workers, such as set designers constitute a below-the-line cost or 'reactive workers' (Miller et al. 2005). The salaries of above-the-line workers are set by agents, distributors and financiers and this has given rise to concerns about 'runaway production' costs wherein films that could be shot in the United States have been taken overseas, prompting film industry labour organizations to protest at the loss of jobs to counterparts in countries such as Canada. Runaway production is precipitated by tax incentives or subsidy programmes that are available in countries such as Canada and the United Kingdom which by directly or indirectly funding film production are intended to 'stimulate the local film industry and promote the country's culture' (Gerse, 2006, p. 485) (Film focus 2.6 provides an example). However, whether in some cases these do little more than provide incentives for American filmmakers to spend money on production or postproduction in a foreign country is debatable. Technological developments now enable a film to be shot in one location and edited almost instantaneously in another. Miller et al. (2005) argue that those who are most likely to be adversely affected by runaway production are below-the-line workers who constitute the flexible periphery. This, they suggest constitutes 'a form of "peripheral Taylorism", in that highly developed efficiencies are available from a skilled working class in places that nevertheless continue to import what is made on their "territory" but which is never under their control' (Miller et al., 2005, p. 137). Unlike the mass production of the studio system of the 1930s when film production tasks were undertaken in dedicated production lots where large numbers of employees were hired on a full-time basis, technological developments have enabled production to be disembedded from local contexts of social interaction and restructured across indefinite spans of time and space (Giddens, 1990). Hence, many studios no longer own production facilities and instead they rent studio space from other companies.

FILM FOCUS 2.6: State funding and *The Corporation* (2003)

Garnham (1990) suggests that although film production is a commercially driven capitalist activity, which treats film as a commodity the primary purpose of which is to maximize efficiency and profit, state funding and tax incentives may also be used to support the industry and protect it from the capitalist economic system. The makers of *The Corporation* (2003) describe how government programmes that support the local film industry provided a large proportion of the funding for the film. Canadian subsidies are allocated on the basis of a points system which involves calculating the number of Canadians who hold creative posts and the percentage of costs incurred in Canada, this being used to judge the extent to which it is a Canadian film (Gerse, 2006). [DVD extras, Q and A: 'Where Did the Money Come From?']

Maximising efficiency and profit

The drive to maximise efficiency and profit in the context of a relatively high-risk industry can also be seen to have contributed towards the development of a mode of production that reflects the principles of 'McDonalidization' (Ritzer, 1993). Ritzer argues that although McDonaldization started out by providing the bureaucratic ethos through which the fast-food chain McDonalds achieved market dominance, in recent years it has come to dominate all aspects of modern production and consumption in all sectors of American society and the rest of world. McDonaldization comprises four interrelated principles: efficiency, calculation, predictability and control. The first of these principles, efficiency, is about identifying the best and quickest means to achieving a goal. This can be identified in the studio system of the 1920s and 1930s involving the tightly managed production of films within the same genre, the same actors working on a series of products often based on recycled scripts with very minor changes. More recent examples of efficiency can detected in the trend towards investment in safe, relatively unimaginative products such as film sequels, prequels and remakes which carry less uncertainty than other products. The second principle, calculation, relies on the measurement of every aspect of process and product as a basis for ensuring consistency and an emphasis on product quantity rather than quality. Certainly, aspects of calculation can be seen in the Hollywood film industry, from the standardized conventions of scriptwriting and plot formation described in Chapter 1, to the employment of workers on a freelance basis to reduce studio overheads. In terms of product quantity versus quality, some would argue that the rise of expensive blockbusters has not resulted in films of better quality, much of the money being spent on special effects and stars' salaries that do not necessarily improve the quality of the product (Waterman, 2005).

The third principle of McDonaldization, predictability, is ensured by providing a narrow range of product items which are always available, a precise ordering process and an interaction with customers that is pre-scripted. Within the film industry, this principle is evident from the way films are marketed, as film trailers often cite other films that actors and directors have been involved in as a means of ensuring that consumers are familiar with the product even before they come to consume it. The fourth and final principle of McDonaldization is control – not only over the product but also over employees and customers, often involving the use of technology. The control over distribution historically exercised by the main players in the industry provides ample evidence of this principle. Future technological developments in distribution have the potential to further affect control. The transfer from analogue, 35 mm film, to digital projection will mean that studios will be able to send their latest film to the cinema in which it is going to be screened by satellite transmission or high-speed data link. This will enable exhibitors to manage films more effectively, for example it will be easier to move a film that is selling more tickets to a larger auditorium. While the principles of McDonaldization go some way towards explaining past strategies adopted within the film industry for maximising efficiency and profit, they do not effectively explain recent developments in the approach towards efficiency and profit in film production.

These are better explained through the parallel concept of Disneyization which, similar to McDonaldization, started out as a process developed in one industry and one organization in particular, Disney theme parks, but has come to affect other sectors of American society and the rest of the world (Bryman, 2004). Like McDonaldization, Disneyization has four dimensions: theming, merchandising, hybrid consumption and performative labour. It is unsurprising that these principles developed by Disney, the only new major studio to have become a distributor since the 1940s and a major industry player since the 1980s (Waterman, 2005), have been adopted throughout the industry. One of the clearest ways in which the film industry has sought in recent years to maximise its profits is through the combined principles of theming, merchandising and hybrid consumption. The application of these principles relates to the rise of the Hollywood blockbuster accompanied by a range of *merchandising* that is timed to coincide with the film's release date. The blockbuster is used as vehicle for promoting and selling all kinds of other film-related products and services, including music soundtracks, toys, video games, fast food and memorabilia of all kinds, either in the form of a character from the film or bearing copyright images from it. The related products are *themed*, clothed in a narrative derived from the film even if this is largely unrelated to the object being sold, such as a child's hamburger meal. This relates to the third dynamic of Disneyization, *hybrid consumption*, whereby forms of consumption associated with different organizational spheres become interlocked and thus increasingly difficult to distinguish. This form of brand extension is an expanding source of film industry revenue.

The final aspect of Disneyization, *performative labour*, involving frontline service work as a performance involving the display of certain moods, is less obviously apparent in the film industry. This can in part be explained by the nature of the product, which is in itself a vehicle for the communication of mood and emotion, acting being perhaps the original form of performative labour. Film actors are also constituted as stars through cultural intermediaries such as gossip columnists and talk show hosts who discursively construct them as systems of signifiers or texts (Dyer, 1979) and this suggests that we expect a high degree of performative labour from these creative workers both off screen as well as on. To summarize, what becomes evident from this discussion of McDonaldization and Disneyization is the extent to which these dynamics, the product of American culture, have affected the organization of film production and consumption. The next section takes this a step further in exploring the extent to which film provides a medium through which American ideas about management and organization are exported to other parts of the world.

Hollywood's global dominance

Filmmaking is a global business. More than half of a film's money is typically made outside the United States (Squire, 2006) and Hollywood's proportion of the world market is double what it was in 1990. In 1998 the most popular thirty-nine films across the world came from the United States. In 1996 the US cultural industries, comprising sales of film, music, television, software, journals and books, became the country's largest export (Miller et al., 2005). There are several explanations offered for Hollywood's global dominance of the film industry, summarized by Waterman (2005); first, that the size and value of the domestic market gives the United States a significant advantage over its competitors; second, that audiences have developed an Americanized consumer consciousness which predisposes them towards films that represent this culture. The third possibility is that the ethnic mix of the US population encourages a more universal approach to storytelling than is produced by other cultures (Miller, 1998). The fourth explanation relates to managerial differences, the studio system, which places greater emphasis on the bottom line and more control in the hands of business executives, is suggested to be a more effective form because it is more financially driven than approaches adopted by other film industries which are more strongly influenced by auteur theory (see Chapter 8). A fifth explanation relates to cultural imperialism suggesting that America has sought to impose its cultural and ideological dominance on other countries through the aggressive business practices adopted by the industry. Finally, it is argued that trade barriers used by other countries to restrict the import of American film and subsidies used to promote domestic production are in the long term counterproductive, being easily circumvented and insulating producers from the marketplace. Whatever the reasons for the economic and cultural dominance of the American film industry, it undoubtedly has significance for the nature of the texts produced by such a system and the way in which they represent management and organization.

One of the concerns to have arisen out of Hollywood's dominance of the global film industry relates to its cultural effects which are suggested to coincide with America's imperialistic efforts to influence poorer nations, film being used as a medium for the transfer of its dominant value system through the communication of discourses of modernization and progress and the creation of consumer demand for US goods and lifestyles. This is the type of argument pursued by Dorfman and Mattelart in their 1971 book *How to Read Donald Duck* where they argue that the United States has sought to communicate an ideological message to the Third World through stories told in Disney comic strips. The export of Disney cartoons during the 1970s enabled the communication of capitalist, imperialist values intended to counter the spread of socialism in countries like Chile. The authors suggest that an ideological thesis is promoted through the comics based on the notion that Disney is a world where work is an adventure undertaken merely as a contrast to leisure which enables consumption. Donald Duck, they suggest, represents the contemporary worker, promoting the concept of 'freedom of labour' – he is free to sell his labour to whomever he wants in a world where jobs abound. They suggest that the threat associated with the mass communication of this ideology of work 'derives not so much from their embodiment of the "American Way of Life", as that of the "American Dream of Life"' (Dorfman and Mattelart, 1971, p. 95). More recently, concerns have focused on Americanization as a force that induces cultural homogeneity on a global scale, threatening to overwhelm competing cultural traditions of filmmaking to such an extent that film directors from other countries tailor their films in a way which caters to 'American sensibilities in order to gain prestige and sales' (Ritzer, 2007, p. 29).

However, some commentators argue that the thesis of Americanization is overstated and that it promotes a view of audiences as needing protection from 'the United States as the source or epitome of all that is most debased and dangerous in popular culture' (Parker, 2002, p. 26). Instead, the cultural transfer enabled by film can be viewed as a two-way process. For instance, the success of the small handful of US-based companies that dominate the industry increasingly relies on their ability to appeal to cross-cultural audiences while also remaining sensitive to national cultural tastes and preferences. For example, in the case of the Indian film industry, where American films earn only 5–8 per cent of box office revenues, partly because of trade restrictions, Hindi or Bombay cinema, popularly referred to as 'Bollywood', exerts a significant influence on all aspects of Indian popular culture and constitutes one of the country's largest industries, 'eight hundred films a year are shown in more than thirteen thousand predominantly urban cinemas, viewed by an average of 11 million people each day, and exported to about a hundred countries' (Mishra, 2002, p. 1). Moreover, although Bollywood has drawn extensively on Hollywood storylines over several decades (an example is given in Film Focus 2.7), this use of texts does not necessarily imply the straight transfer of an American value system. Instead they may be reworked in a way which brings together some aspects of the indigenous culture with other cultural elements provided by Hollywood.

FILM FOCUS 2.7: Cultural imperialism or cultural fusion in *Aitraaz* (2004)?

Aitraaz (2004) is a Bollywood film that is based on the storyline of the film *Disclosure* (1994) (see Film Focus 6.4). Like the Hollywood film on which it is based, *Aitraaz* represents the issue of sexual harassment in a workplace situation where the gender roles are reversed, the woman becoming the harasser and the man her victim. However, the film also conforms to the storytelling traditions of Bollywood, as a melodramatic, sentimental romance which combines traditionalism with modernity (Mishra, 2002) and includes flamboyant song and dance routines. Many of the scenes are closely modelled on the Hollywood

Continued

storyline, as the chairman of Roy Industries introduces his new wife, Sonia, as the new managing director of the cellphone manufacturing company, thereby denying Raj the possibility of promotion and later when Sonia, calls him to a private meeting at her house where she seduces him, later accusing him of sexual harassment. Additional plot details are provided in the context of the former passionate relationship between Sonia and Raj, which is suggested to have ended because of Sonia's decision to abort an unwanted pregnancy, Sonia claiming that she did not want a child at this stage of her career because it would jeopardize her opportunity for power, prestige, status and money. 💿 [**approximate running times: 34.20–39.30; 1 hour 8.30–1 hour 10.50; 1 hour 16.30–1 hour 23.20 mins.**]

The film industry and other businesses

In addition to being a business in its own right, the film industry establishes and maintains relationships with other organizations that manufacture products and provide services. Film has long been regarded as a commercially significant medium of mass communication through its potential impact on the consumption of goods and services, one estimate being that for every foot of film sent abroad from the United States in the 1920s and 1930s, a dollar's worth of other goods was exported (Waterman, 2005; Miller et al. 2005). One way in which meaning is constructed in film is via a 'system of objects' (Baudrillard, 1996), consumable items through which characters are understood and differentiated from one another. Baudrillard (1996) argues that the value of such objects is relational. Each one can therefore be understood only in the context of the others. Organizations seek to exploit this principle through product placement, which involves the appearance of a company logo or product in a shot or its mention by one of the actors. Shots of a character's house, car, briefcase and shoes in combination can be used to paint a picture of his or her life in a way which signifies their status position within a particular cultural context. For example, American kitchens of the 1950s and 1960s in *Man in the Gray Flannel Suit* (1956) or *The Apartment* (1960) are used to communicate a message about the character's social status through the presence of modern technological innovations such as refrigerators and convenience food.

Product placement is a particular feature of Bond films, for example, the producer of *The Man with the Golden Gun* (1974) made a deal to use American Motors vehicles in all chase scenes in exchange for funds that were used to advertise the film [http://www.slate.com/id/2129112/ – consulted 01.02.08]. The most recent Bond film, *Casino Royale* (2006), contains prominent product placements for Gordon's Gin,

Sony Ericsson and Vaio, Omega watches, the Ford Group – including Ford, Aston Martin, Jaguar and Range Rover, and the Virgin brand which includes a guest appearance by Richard Branson walking through airport security. The value of such deals is estimated at over $30 million dollars (Epstein, 2006). Product placement is a highly developed business represented by its own professional body, the Entertainment Resources and Marketing Association whose mission is 'to engage in the business of branded entertainment, product placement, and product integration' [www.erma.org/web – consulted 16.08.07] using placement specialists and brokers whose job it is to ensure that logos, background advertisements and use of products is the result of a negotiated deal worth often worth many thousands of dollars.

FILM FOCUS 2.8: The role of product placement in *State and Main* (2000)

When the cast and crew in *State and Main* (2000) move their film shoot for 'The Old Mill' to a small town in Vermont after having had problems with their previous location, the community is exposed to the artistic peculiarities of these creative workers. One of the dilemmas faced by the film's director is how to deal with the film budget overspend, especially when the female lead actress demands an additional $800,000 for a nude scene. The opportunity arises for a product placement in the film worth one million dollars, the only problem being is that the product is made by a computer company, 'Bazoomer.com', which doesn't fit with a film set in 1895. 📀 [**approximate running time: 40.50–43.30; 56.30–58.30 mins.**]

However, there are some signs that companies are increasingly aware that audiences have become sophisticated readers of film, highly attuned to cultural references and expecting messages to be less direct and more ironic. Film focus 2.9 illustrates one company's attempts to develop a more subtle relationship between its products and film. This example demonstrates the importance of film as a form of cultural capital that bestows status on the reader, even if the reader of the text is an organization.

FILM FOCUS 2.9: The fictitious Orange Film Funding Board

UK telecommunications firm Orange has developed an advertising campaign comprising a series of trailers shown in cinemas before the start of films. The adverts feature short comedy sketches involving a series of famous film directors, producers, writers and actors as they pitch their ideas for a new film to the

Continued

fictitious Orange Film Funding Board, a panel of mildly eccentric business executives. The executives show little interest in the creative subtleties of the film pitch and even less concern for the artistic sensitivities of the presenter standing before them. Instead they suggest a series of modifications to the film involving crude product placements that are intended to promote Orange mobile phones to unsuspecting audiences. This campaign successfully parodies the encroachment of business interests into filmmaking, implying that such practices are crass and ludicrous. Orange thus seeks to represent itself as a business that is respectful of filmmakers' artistic and intellectual freedom; this image is reinforced through the company's sponsorship of British Academy of Filmmaking and Television Arts Awards (BAFTAs). The organization thus seeks to convey an image of itself as sympathetic to film as a cultural product.

Corporate films

Organizations also invest in the production of films intended to direct the attitudes of internal and external audiences towards a favourable view of the organization and its activities. Bennett (1983) takes the example of a film produced by the Cheesebrough-Pond Corporation, called *Family* which has the explicit purpose of convincing audiences 'that the corporation is one big, successful, happy family serving the nation and the "family of man" by serving its employees and its customers' (Bennett, 1983, p. 37). Other examples of corporate films include the short film *The Birth of the Robot* (1936) which proclaims the magical life-giving properties of Shell Oil in the modern industrial world and *Symphony in F* (1940) a film sponsored by the Ford Company and released four years after *Modern Times* (1936) that tells the story of how the 'Model T' is made. Both of these films draw on surrealism, making machines come to life as living beings. Because corporate films were not generally intended for public release they are quite difficult to obtain. However, if you are able to get hold of and watch one of these films, it will be apparent that they celebrate the achievements of modern organization. The example in Film Focus 2.10, which parodies corporate films of the 1950s, gives a sense of how the sensibilities surrounding the representation of business and management have since changed. In addition, corporate films are sometimes used within popular film to give the text a heightened sense of realism. Film Focus 2.11 gives two examples that represent corporate sponsored films within the text and the use of corporate sponsored film as a contrast to the everyday reality of lived experience.

FILM FOCUS 2.10: An ironic corporate film, *Your Studio and You* (1995)

Your Studio and You (1995) is a short film made to celebrate the acquisition of Universal Studios by the Canadian spirits company, Seagrams, and shown to employees of the company. It is the creation of Stone and Parker, makers of the television series *South Park*. A chirpy narrator accompanied by a 1950s light orchestra talks about how to improve the studio by incorporating 'modern, futuristic ideas' including initiatives such as the introduction of pastel coloured uniforms for security guards and redecorating the studios with kitsch porcelain deer. The narrator proceeds to interview a series of celebrities who sing the praises of Universal Studios. These include a 1950s-styled Demi Moore who claims that working for the studio is great because it gives her more time to bake ham for her family and also Sylvester Stallone, in the character of Rocky Balboa, whose garbled comments are subtitled for comic effect. The frequent product placement of Seagrams 'wine coolers' throughout the film provides the only reference to the acquisition of the film studio by the spirits giant. Although never publicly released, the film has attained something of a cult following and can be watched on *YouTube*. It can be read as an ironic commentary on the changing nature of the film industry and a critique of nostalgic visions of the 'Golden Era' of Hollywood filmmaking. 💿 [http://www.youtube.com/watch?v=tqMV90pnsZ4 – consulted 28.05.07]

FILM FOCUS 2.11: Corporate sponsored films within film in *The Full Monty* (1997) and *The Navigators* (2001)

In both of these films corporate sponsored films are used to represent a modernist discourse based on organizational progress and individual opportunity (see Chapter 4) which is contrasted with the everyday lived experience of industrial work. In *The Navigators* (2001) this is achieved by showing the reactions of the audience as they sit in the training room watching a corporate sponsored film. The camera focuses of the backs of the heads of a group of railway track workers as they watch a corporate sponsored film that is intended to explain the new methods of management. At this moment, the film audience is in an equivalent subject position to the employees, seeing exactly what they see. As images of fast, efficient trains speeding across the screen convey a message of modernisation and progress the female narrator talks about a 'new era of change' and the people who maintain the infrastructure as 'the foundation of the future'. The narrator explains the basis of the new internal market in which companies compete with each other to win contracts for maintenance of the

Continued

rail network. She goes on to say 'in the market environment we are entering the customer is the focus. Customers have to be won against fierce competition. Then they have to be kept by continuous improvement in service, which means continuous change'. This is followed by a shot of the new managing director who explains that these changes means a new organizational culture must be built. His vision, he explains is 'the end of "us" and "them" and the beginning of a partnership for progress'. However, we are also made conscious of audience's response to the corporate sponsored film. As the track workers chew gum, drink a can of Pepsi, fidget and doze, we become conscious of the gap between the film's message and the audience's response to it, the up-beat message of modernisation and progress contrasting with the railway workers' everyday experience. ☻ **[approximate running time: 19.30–24 mins.]**

Corporate sponsored films can also be used to promote a particular view of industry in society. The opening credits of *The Full Monty* (1997) shows a promotional film made in the 1970s which tells the story of Sheffield 'the beating heart of Britain's industrial North … built on Sheffield's primary industry' in which 'some 9,000 men' are employed 'to make the world's finest steel'. The film shows images of heroic industrial workers (see Chapter 5) and molten metal coming out of fiery furnaces. The narrator concludes by saying 'thanks to steel, Sheffield really is a city on the move'. This contrasts with the rest of the film set 25 years later, when the steel works have all closed and the unemployed workers spend their time hanging out on the street and feeling like 'yesterdays news' (Gibson-Graham, 2001). ☻ **[approximate running time: 0.45–2.20 mins.]**

Conclusion

This chapter has provided an overview of the organization of the film industry with a view to understanding the potential that this has to influence representations of management and organization within film texts. Creative workers in the film industry have had at best an ambivalent, and sometimes an outwardly hostile attitude towards the management of their activities, this being the result of an underlying tension that cultural workers perceive in relation to commercial versus artistic interests as being fundamentally incompatible. It is hardly surprising then, that that this opposition should shape not only the way that cultural workers, including the film directors, writers and actors who create the stories, depict their own organizations in film texts but also that it should influence their view of organizations more generally. By positioning themselves and their activities as antithetical to the values of business, creative workers construct management as distinct and separate and position managers as the enemy that undermines their creative efforts – a theme that will be pursued further in Chapter 3.

Ribstein (2005) suggests that negative representations of management and organization in film are made possible because of the agency relationship and the 'slack' in financiers' ability to control creative workers within the film industry. Rather than being driven by a concern for capital's exploitation of labour, he suggests that the main problem filmmakers have with capital being in control is that they – the artists – are not. Recent changes in film industry ownership, including the purchase of studios by massive global conglomerates, and changes in employment relations, precipitated by a desire to control costs by employing flexible labour and moving production to countries where employment is comparatively less regulated, are likely to mean that filmmakers are likely to feel in even less control over the product.

However, this chapter has also argued that the distinction between economic and cultural capital in the film industry tends to be overstated. Film is the result of collaboration between managers as agents of capital and creative workers, each depending on the other for the provision of knowledge, technologies and capital that transform ideas into cultural products. This chapter has sought to demonstrate that the production of meaning about management and organization within film texts is not the sole preserve of creative workers. Instead these representations form part of a complex circuit of communication that involves various kinds of business organizations which are not only positioned by others within the text but also seek to position themselves and their activities through strategies such as product placement. They thus have the potential to be *knowing readers* of film texts who are sensitive to the role of cultural capital and skilled in utilizing it in ways that are subtler than the binary divide between profit and creativity suggests.

Plate 3 Workers ascend the steps to enter the fiery jaws of the furnace machine in *Metropolis* (1927)

Rights: Friedrich-Wilhelm-Murnau-Stiftung; Distributor: Transit Film GmbH

The invisible enemy

Introduction

In many films employees are shown to be constrained or crushed by organization through the existence of monotonous work routines, technologies, bureaucratic rules and overzealous management. In some organizational life is suggested to be dreary and futile, often in contrast to more meaningful spheres of life such as those involving love and family. In others, the villain is the corporation and greedy big business is portrayed as the enemy of the people. The message conveyed is that organizations are uncaring, impersonal and amoral, in short, that they are capable of evil. Such representations can be seen as originating from a particular cultural perspective, satisfying the need within American cultural mythology for an enemy, a source of fear, insecurity and anxiety against which the nation's fragile identity must be defended (Sadar and Wyn Davies, 2004). The large corporation constitutes an appropriate motif of fear, a villainous system which can 'eat up the innocent little guys, the ordinary citizens beset by powers beyond their strength' (Sadar and Wyn Davies, 2004: 149).

Others have also observed the tendency for the organization to be represented as the enemy in popular culture, containing 'implicit or explicit representations of management and organizations that reflect a fair degree of ambivalence and often hostility' (Parker, 2002, p. 135). Similarly, Newitz (2006) argues that stories about capitalism turning people into monsters have circulated in American film since the late nineteenth century. It is the purpose of this chapter to consider why such representations exist and what potential effects they may have on the way we think about management and organization. Parker's comment on science fiction films is therefore applicable to film more generally:

> films represent the big corporation as being a problem in itself, as encouraging immoral and illegal practices, as being populated by hard-hearted utilitarians who seem not to care overmuch about the consequences of their actions ... It would have to be a wilfully

anti-contextual argument that then refused to acknowledge that these cultural products did not suggest something about contemporary anxieties. (Parker, 2001, p. 196)

It is also somewhat ironic that the majority of films, as highlighted in Chapter 2, are produced by large companies. Parker notes the contradiction created by this situation where film texts that represent the organization as evil are produced and disseminated by the corporations that constitute the focus of the text's critique, their producers conveniently ignoring 'the fact that their very art depends upon the management of organization and technology for its propagation' (Parker, 2002, p. 156). The authors of film texts could therefore be accused of 'biting the hand that feeds them'. He attributes this to the profit motive which means that entertainment corporations are principally interested in what sells even if this involves criticism of their own activities (see also Film Focus 3.1).

FILM FOCUS 3.1: The greedy organization in *Wall Street* (1987), *Other People's Money* (1991) and *The Corporation* (2003)

In *Wall Street* (1987) financial investor Gordon Gekko represents the ruthless, short-term organizational culture associated with the late-1980s where the only thing that counts is the relentless pursuit of money. His celebration of greed implies a harsh social Darwinist ideology in which organizational survival is a matter of the survival of the fittest. This is Gekko's message in his speech at the annual shareholders' meeting of Teldar Paper in which he justifies the actions of corporate raiders like himself through a critique of the wasteful bureaucracy of management. 'The point is, ladies and gentlemen: Greed, for lack of a better word, is good. Greed is right; greed works. Greed clarifies, cuts through, and captures the essence of the evolutionary spirit. Greed, in all of its forms, greed for life, for money, for love, knowledge – has marked the upward surge of mankind and greed, you mark my words – will save not only Teldar Paper but that other malfunctioning corporation called the USA.' ☺ [**approximate running time: 1 hour 12–1 hour 15.45 mins.**]

A similar theme is pursued in *Other People's Money* (1991) where 'Larry the liquidator' is a ruthless Wall Street investor who buys companies and strips their assets with no concern for the lives of the people who work there. His attentions turn to New England Wire and Cable, its debt-free status providing an attractive investment despite technological changes in the organizational environment which have made their products obsolete. His message when he addresses the company's shareholders is that the company is worth more dead than alive. ☺ [**approximate running time: 1 hour 25–1 hour 30.30 mins.**]

However, the greedy nature of organizations is suggested also to be a source of weakness. The filmmaker Michael Moore, one of the interviewees in *The Corporation* (2003), notes the irony of his own situation, using corporate money to make films that oppose the values that corporations believe in. This he suggests is because they have no values beyond making money, describing this as the 'greed flaw' in capitalism that dictates 'the rich man will sell you the rope to hang himself with if he thinks he can make a buck off it'. ☞ [**approximate running time: 2 hours 18.50–2 hours 21.40 mins.**]

A substantial part of this chapter is devoted to identifying and analysing how the signifiers of organization in film make explicit a vision of the organization as the enemy. The films included in this category are numerous and diverse. In addition to the films discussed in this chapter they include such recent titles as *The Constant Gardener* (2005), where the focus is on the corrupt business practices of the big pharmaceutical companies, *Syriana* (2005), where the enemy is the oil business which is manipulating terrorism, wars and social unrest to drive up the price of oil and *Thank You For Smoking* (2005), a satirical observation on the deception and lies associated with the tobacco industry. Because representations of organization as evil are so persistent throughout film history, this theme is a logical place to begin our exploration of management and organization in film. The chapter then moves on to consider the effects of these representations when, as Parker (2002, p. 134) notes, the average popular film 'reaches more people than even the most hyped academic "best seller"'.

Constructing an image of the enemy

However, this discussion raises another issue that we must consider which relates to the difficulty in representing such an abstract entity as an organization, its aims and motivations being very difficult to represent cinematically (Ribstein, 2005). Corporate immorality, as Parker (2002, p. 102) notes, has no clear victims, 'no one is left inspecting an empty wallet, a broken window or a pool of blood'. Because we are socialized into expecting criminals to have certain characteristics, the idea that a corporation could be criminal is more difficult to comprehend (Slapper, 1999). Cultural theorist Slavoj Žižek has suggested that the construction of an enemy relies on its opposite, for in order to treat one particular subject as having no value, something else must be invested with value to provide an alternative to it. 'The division friend/enemy is never just a recognition of factual difference. The enemy is by definition always (up to a point) *invisible*: it cannot be directly recognised because it looks like one of us, which is why the big problem and task of the political struggle is to provide/construct a recognisable *image* of the enemy' (Žižek, 2002, p. 5, emphasis in original).

Because of the difficulty in representing the organization as a protagonist, there is a tendency for film to reify and personify organizations, particularly when the narrative is influenced by the 'Hollywood system' described in Chapter 1 in which characters are represented as doing things to others. The use of certain signifiers enables the narrative development of the organization as a character like any other within the narrative. For example, in *The Corporation* (2003), the organization is represented metaphorically as a suit-wearing silhouette of a man wearing a trilby hat and carrying a briefcase, with the tail of a devil and an angel halo added. Similarly, in *Super Size Me* (2004), McDonalds is represented as a demonic clown. Further examples of representations that simultaneously reify and demonize the organization are given in Film Focus 3.2. Epstein (2005) suggests that such representations are the result of intertextuality, as filmmakers in the 1990s continue to work from images which are 'the recycled stereotypes from an earlier generation of directors, writers and producers' (Epstein, 2005, p. 329) working in the 1970s when representations of business and executives in popular culture were predominantly negative. This has given rise to frequent portrayals of the evil and even murderous business executive in films such as *The Devil's Advocate* (1997). Such representations also satisfy the need for film villains acceptable to a contemporary international audience, 'greedy executives of multinational corporations … in their expensive suits' are therefore cast as 'corporate terrorists' (Epstein, 2005, p. 336).

The extent to which such representations have an ideological function is further illustrated by Epstein (2005) who cites the example of Warner Bros. in the late 1990s which sold the rights to use short clips from the film *Wall Street* (1987) to the television-news network CNN (both organizations being owned by the same parent company, Time Warner), to use scenes from the film in which the immaculately dressed Gordon Gekko expresses the view that 'greed is good' (see Film Focus 3.1). The trend towards patterns of ownership of film production, described in Chapter 2, by conglomerates with interests in a variety of mass communication media implies that this ambiguity between entertainment and information is likely to increase, as the film *Outfoxed* (2004) suggests (see Film Focus 2.2).

FILM FOCUS 3.2: The murderous organization in *The Insider* (2000) and *Severance* (2006)

Many films represent a battle between good and evil, the organization being the malevolent character against which the hero or heroine must fight. The film *The Insider* (2000) is based on a non-fiction article by Brenner (1996) published in the magazine *Vanity Fair* which tells the story of corporate executive and scientist Jeffrey Wigand who was fired from tobacco company, Brown & Wilkinson, for threatening to blow the whistle on the company because they sought to prevent the release of research concerning the addictive effects of smoking and the company's efforts to enhance them. The film represents the 'Seven Dwarfs', the nickname for the CEOs of the leading tobacco companies testifying under oath before US congress that tobacco is not addictive, in a way that resembles historical images of the Nuremberg war crimes trial (Van Es, 2003). Wigand is portrayed as an individual of stubborn integrity with a whistleblowing personality who risks everything to tell the truth despite the efforts of the organization at deception and bullying. ⊙ [**approximate running times: 38–42.20; 1 hour 9.25–1 hour 12.40 mins.**]

The organization is associated with even more sinister and horrific acts in *Severance* (2006) where seven colleagues who work for the Palisade Defence Company go to Hungary on a team-building weekend. The lodge in which they find themselves stranded is an eerie deserted place where no phone signal can be received. Rumours circulate among the team involving the company's involvement in the Eastern European arms trade. The outdoor management-development activities that they have planned to improve teamwork skills and promote bonding include paint balling. However, this turns out to be more than just a game when they discover that someone out in the woods is trying to kill them, using the very weaponry that their company designs and sells. ⊙ [**approximate running times: 3.30–6.30; 27–31 mins.**]

The difficulty in representing organization in film is related to the question of what 'it' actually is, the answer to this question being highly dependent on how you understand the nature of a social entity like organization. Representations of organization encountered in film are founded on a specific set of epistemological assumptions concerning the nature of the entity that is being represented. Many of these texts rely on an objective realist view of organizations as tangible entities with distinctive properties which social actors who encounter them must confront and engage with. This assumes that organizations have a reality independent of the individuals who belong to it, thereby constituting a social order which acts on and inhibits them. As will be discussed further in Chapter 4, organizations are constituted in many films as formal and rational, comprising 'stable associations of persons engaged in concerted activities directed to the attainment of specific objectives' (Bittner, 1965, p. 239). However, this is somewhat complicated by the fact that film is also intensely concerned with representing informal characteristics of organization, those unplanned, non-rational characteristics of membership which accompany its formal, rational aspects, this latter aspect often being what makes film interesting and effective as a medium for representing organizations, as discussed in the introduction to this book. Such portrayals are based on a constructionist perspective which asserts that organizations are the result of ongoing social interactions between its members. Far from being a tangible reality that exists independently of the actions of its members, a constructionist viewpoint assumes organization has no existence independent of the sense-making processes through which its members construct meaning in relation to it.

What is interesting is that there is often a dual ontology implied in these representations. Objectivism is used to construct an image of organization as having an independent and stable identity and constructionism is applied to understand organization from the perspective of social actors. What is more, these perspectives are often present within the same film text, this providing a source of richness that is rarely a feature of academic analyses which tend instead to be founded on the assumption of 'paradigm incommensurability' (Burrell and Morgan, 1979), the idea that basic assumptions about the nature of reality result in the generation of different world views or 'paradigms' which develop separately and cannot be combined. Within film this dual ontology tends to be developed sequentially. Thus, objectivist representations tend to be used in the early stages of the film narrative to establish the organization as a protagonist whereas constructionist representations are introduced as the narrative develops in order to locate organization members as active agents who shape the meaning of organization through their own sense-making practices.

The remainder of this chapter is concerned with identifying the characteristics of objectivist representations of organization as a social order which acts on and inhibits the behaviour of its members, while Chapter 4 starts by focusing on representations of organization that constitute it as an objective reality but proceeds to consider representations that reflect a more constructionist viewpoint. Chapters 5, 6 and 7 are concerned with the meaning-making activities of social actors who belong to organizations in film, and are hence predominantly constructivist in orientation, while Chapter 8 calls these positions into question through reframing the debate about the nature of organizational reality in terms that challenge the relevance of this dichotomy.

The disciplined body

Many early, some might say 'classic', films such as *Metropolis* (1927), *The Crowd* (1928) and *Modern Times* (1936) can be read as a commentary on the potentially dehumanizing effects associated with the expansion of large-scale industrial capitalism. These film narratives are often driven by a concern with the way individuals cope, or indeed fail to cope with these changes, often suggesting them to be psychologically impoverished or deprived of their humanity as a result. The dehumanizing effects of organization are often conveyed metonymically through portraying individuals as lifeless, as more like machines than living, breathing human beings, the organization controlling their bodies as though they were mindless (Dale and Burrell, 2000). Such representations invoke the role of technology in enabling the rationalization of labour (see Film Focus 3.3).

The organization is thus portrayed as a *machine* whose parts, including human parts, ought to run like a machine (Morgan, 1997). Employee efficiency is suggested to increase the more that humans behave in a way that is machine-like in nature. Such portrayals are associated with the development of Fordism in the early 1900s and the rise of assembly line production, whereby the process of manufacture is broken down into a sequence of simple, routine operations, each performed separately by unskilled workers as a method of improving the efficiency of workers.

FILM FOCUS 3.3: Organization as machine in *Modern Times* (1936)

In *Modern Times* (1936) the dehumanizing effects of industrial production can be read in the early scenes of the film where Charlie Chaplin plays an assembly line 'factory worker' in the Electro Corporation. The film conveys the message that human beings are reduced to robots in the service of the organization as machine. Newitz (2006) argues that the robot or cyborg often provides a metaphor in film for the use of humans as obedient tools of industrial production, being quite literally manufactured for this purpose. She cites the example of *Modern Times* (1936) as illustrative of the romantic cyborg, being both the product of and the solution to problems of work in industrial society. Through his gradual incorporation into the industrial system the factory worker becomes like just another machine part, assuming an objectified status which affects his behaviour to such an extent that he becomes hybridized, as betrayed by his jerky repetitive movements and obsession with tightening bolts. In this context, the role of management is to sustain the efficient operation of robotic humans through use of technologies that treat the worker as an assembly line product. This can be read in the scene with the 'Billows Feeding Machine' which is intended to improve productivity by feeding workers whilst they work. All human needs, including that for food, become secondary to the needs of the machine. However, when management and the machine's inventors test the machine on the factory worker the machine malfunctions in a way which gradually turns into a brutal assault, forcing food and metal bolts into his mouth. While the consequences of this treatment are mental instability, (the factory worker has a nervous breakdown) this offers him only a temporary reprieve from industrial work rather than permanent escape (see Chapter 7). Ultimately the factory worker becomes caught in the cogwheels of the machine, becoming part of the machine itself, just another cogwheel. Conversely, at the same time that humans are treated as machines, the technology takes on a human voice in contrast to the human beings who remain voiceless. *Modern Times* was one of last silent films to be made, 'talkies' being an innovation which Chaplin resisted. Although the characters in the film communicate through inter-titles, limited use is made of spoken words which are always filtered through machines – the orders of the factory boss, the spoken instruction manual of the eating machine, the radio. ✆ [approximate running time: 1.10–13 mins.]

Disciplinarity is also conveyed through the obverse logic of representing non-living objects such as factory machines or technologies as having human qualities like facial characteristics or the ability to speak. The second metaphor is of organization and its constituent elements as a *living organism*, adapting to its environment much like an animal species and having certain needs which must be satisfied to ensure its survival (Morgan, 1997). The metaphor of organization and its constituent parts as a living organism is a recurrent theme in many films, from *Metropolis* (1927), in which workers must constantly work to feed the furnace machine by entering its fiery jaws which threaten to burn them alive (see Film Focus 3.4 and Plate 3.1), to *The Matrix* (1999), where virtual-intelligent computers have taken over the human body, keeping human beings alive in suspended animation as living batteries that generate electricity for the computer system (Boje, 2001). A further example can be read in *Desk Set* (1957), in which the narrative revolves around a group of female employees' fears of being replaced by 'EMERAC', an 'electronic brain machine' that is rumoured to be able to do their jobs. Eventually, the women start to apply the organic metaphor in their own relationship with the machine, referring to her as 'Miss Emmy', asking the machine's operators what 'she' can do and speculating as to how 'she' is feeling. Rather than representing the organism as a relatively benign entity, living and working through the unity of its constituent elements in relative harmony with its environment, these films tends to reflect a harsher, social Darwinist ideology wherein organizations and the machines and technologies that support them must deny human beings their humanity, making them more like machines in order to ensure their own survival.

The two metaphors of organization as machine and as organism express the character of the organization as a disciplinary social entity which requires individuals to give up their identity, becoming anonymous drones in order to provide the organization with what it needs in order to survive. For example, in the opening scene of *Modern Times* (1936), we see a flock of sheep all moving in the same direction which acts as a metonym for a crowd of industrial workers. Among them is one lone black sheep that can be read as a metaphorical representation of the factory worker, unwilling or unable to comply with the demands of the large industrial workplace. Another example is given in Film Focus 3.4. Whether by representing the organization as a totalizing machine or as a fearsome fire-breathing monster, the end result involves the production of the disciplined subject.

FILM FOCUS 3.4: Loss of humanity in *Metropolis* (1927)

In *Metropolis* (1927), we see ranks of identical workers wearing drab uniforms shuffling in lockstep with their heads downcast and shoulders hunched into enormous elevators to descend to the industrial Lower City where they toil for ten hours a day. Their job is to run the machines that provide power to the Upper City which is inhabited by planners or thinkers who live a life of ease and luxury. In a later scene we see Freder, son of the ruler of the corporate city-state Metropolis, entering the Lower City and seeing the terrible conditions suffered by the people whom work there. Freder witnesses an explosion of a furnace machine that resembles a monster with huge fiery jaws into which workers must descend. The theme of loss of humanity is communicated by the metaphor of machines as living things. The immense power of the machines relative to human beings is also connoted in this film, and in *Modern Times* (1936), by their immense size in relation to the people that maintain them. ☉ [**approximate running times: 2.30–6; 12–16 mins.**]

The nature of these metaphorical representations can also be understood as a reflection of what Jacques (1996) describes as the 'manufacturing' of the employee, a process whereby a new social contract was developed based on a different vocabulary of objects and a set of concepts for speaking about work. Jacques argues that not only did these changes introduce the possibility of management at the beginning of the twentieth century (an issue we shall return to in Chapter 4) they also led to the production of the concept of the 'universal worker' or employee. Through historical analysis of the etymological origins of the term which came into English usage in the late nineteenth century to refer to railway workers, eventually replacing words like 'hired labourer' or 'worker', Jacques suggests that the entrance of the word 'employee' into contemporary language signified a shift in the social contract that shaped future social action. Furthermore, the term presumed certain things about the subject's abilities, motivations, rights and duties that influenced the development of managerial knowledge and continues to affect managerial action today.

The characteristics of the manufactured employee which Jacques (1996) identifies tend to be reflected in representations of the modern worker in several early films about management and organization. For example, Charlie in the early scenes of *Modern Times* (1936) can be read as representing 'the good worker' who is an ally to the employer rather than a threat, displaying no apparent sense of collective identity in relation to his fellow workers at the Electro Corporation and therefore not being a part of labour even though he is one of them. Similarly, the inhabitants of the lower city in *Metropolis* (1927) represent 'the permanent worker' and 'the organization's worker', satisfying the need for a stable workforce in an era of mass production through employment on a permanent rather than a temporary basis and thereby making concepts like turnover or absenteeism meaningful. What is more, these representations suggest that workers belong to the organization in the form of a human resource to be used like coal or iron. The hierarchical division between the lower and the upper city in *Metropolis* (1927) creates a sub-ordinate, super-ordinate distinction which Jacques suggests provided a transitional ordering principle in the decades 1910–1920 based on military distinctions between officers and men, this new boundary being translated into a basic distinction between manager and employee. The manufactured employee in *Modern Times* (1936) is also essentially a 'task worker', this reflecting the economies of mass production which precipitated a shift from the social division of labour based on products to one based on highly mechanized and routinized tasks under Fordism. As Braverman (1974) argues in his thesis on deskilling, employees lacked bargaining power, since they lacked the skills of the craftsperson and any skills that they did possess could only be utilized within the organization.

The factory worker in *Modern Times* (1936) is also based on the characteristic of 'the ignorant, childlike (and encoded) self' (Jacques, 1996, p. 28), which in many ways is similar to F.W. Taylor's portrayal of the Pennsylvania Dutch immigrant Schmidt, the subject of his writings on scientific management. Taylor portrays Schmidt as industrious but lacking initiative or originality, suggesting that he is transformed through the application of the principles of scientific management into working four times harder for slightly more pay. However, this depiction relies upon an infantilized representation of the subject since it is assumed that workers like Schmidt and the factory worker in *Modern Times* (1936) can be 'developed' through analysis and control by professional managers who play the role of knowledgeable adults (Jacques, 1996). Films like *The Crowd* (1928) also articulate the rhetoric of equality through representing the 'typologized worker', an employee who endorses the American Dream (see Chapter 4), assuming everyone to have an equal chance to succeed and being able to do work which they are best suited to. As the narrative in *Modern Times* (1936) develops, it also becomes clear that the factory worker is based on the notion of 'the divided self' his working life being antithetical to his romantic life with his Gamine, with whom he eventually escapes from his life as an industrial worker.

The final aspect of the 'manufactured employee' in many films that represent management and organization involves 'the wage worker', this reflecting a shift away from labour tied to outputs, towards labour that is tied to clock time, as a measure of inputs and a device used to enforce the effort-bargain between worker and organization (Jacques, 1996). Representations of the wage worker are reliant on the technology of the clock as a means of signifying the imposition of temporal discipline. Clocks are everywhere in films about management and organization, from the imposing corporate clock towers with their ominous chimes in *Patterns* (1956) and *Executive Suite* (1954), the ubiquitous office clock in *The Apartment* (1960) and *Clockwatchers* (1997), the gold pocket watch carried by the President of Hudsucker Industries in *The Hudsucker Proxy* (1994), to the deco clock with its ten digit face in *Metropolis* (1927). Time is inextricably linked to power in these organizations through the imposition of time rules which are made visible and explicit through this technology (Hassard, 1991). The clock is a metonym for organizational time reflecting a Newtonian concept of time as uniform, infinitely divisible and continuous and implying that organizations and employees can work like clockwork (Butler, 1995), thereby reinforcing the machine metaphor of organization. The measurement of time as a concrete, objective, and managerially controlled phenomenon is a crucial aspect of this logic which Parker

(2002) refers to in the following terms, 'all members (but particularly those at the bottom) were subject to the disciplines of work study and time and motion. Attendance was ensured by the pay-packet, obedience by the threat of dismissal and efficiency by the man in the white coat with the stop-watch and clip-board' (Parker, 2002, p. 51). The films in Film Focus 3.5 represent these ideas.

FILM FOCUS 3.5: Time measurement and efficiency in *Spotswood* (1991) and *I'm Alright Jack* (1959)

While both of these films represent scientific management they do so in a way which calls its logic and efficacy into question. When management consultant Mr Wallace in *Spotswood* (1991) is called into to an outdated factory that makes moccasin slippers to improve efficiency he is confronted by workplace practices which seem to him to be of an earlier generation. The lack of shared understanding between Mr Wallace's agenda and the workers impression of him as someone who is there to help them is discovered when Wallace takes on a young assistant to help him conduct a time and motion study, the aim of which is to erode patterns of social contact between employees in order to ensure that their working time is spent more efficiently. The response of factory workers to these changes and Wallace's discomfort in his managerial role can be read as a critique of Taylorism that draws on the findings of the famous Hawthorne studies (1927–1932) which emphasized the importance of social relationships as a basis for motivation and meaning in relation to work (see also Chapter 7). [**approximate running times: 11.20–13; 16.30–17.30; 32.30–35.40 mins.**]

I'm Alright Jack (1959) is set in the political context of 1950s industrial Britain where powerful unions resist the efforts of management to improve efficiency through time and motion study, rigidly protecting job demarcation and threatening to strike at the first signs of any dispute. However, the factory owners are equally self-interested, deliberately orchestrating a situation in an ammunitions factory that has won an important arms deal which leads to a workers' strike so that they can personally benefit from transferring the contract to another company. Meanwhile the government makes no intervention to resolve the dispute and the general public continues to suffer. Stanley Windrush is the comic hero of this narrative, an Oxford graduate from a wealthy family who wants a career in industry, but is manipulated by everyone. In this scene, Stanley seeks to expose the extent of these corrupt vested interests on a television programme which ends in chaos as he reveals the bag of money that the corrupt capitalist bosses have bribed him with. [**approximate running time: 39.50–44.20; 1 hour 30–1 hour 36 mins.**]

These representations also suggest that organizational time is a resource which is sold by the employee and bought by the organization. The time of the worker is represented in many films as a currency, the value of which must be optimized through mechanisation and rationalisation in pursuit of profit (Thompson, 1967). The anxious employees watch the clock waiting for 5 o'clock when time once again becomes their own to spend as they like. The capitalist system is suggested in many films to monopolize not only the worker's labour time but also their self-identity, such that 'the worker feels dead while working, for nothing he does at work enriches his life in any way' (Newitz, 2006, p. 34). For example, in *Metropolis* (1927) the ten digits on the face of the clock in the Lower City represent the ten hour work day which Freder endures as he becomes sympathetic to the plight of the workers. His task involves continuously moving the hands of the clock back and forth in erratic and apparently random sequences despite his growing exhaustion. In addition, these films suggest that organizations are intensely greedy in relation to their consumption of employee time. For example, in *The Apartment* (1960) the organization not only controls Baxter's time at work but also his personal time, by forcing him to submit to the demands of his superiors who wish to use his apartment for their illicit affairs. Similarly, in *Office Space* (1998), Peter must fight to protect his weekend time from a boss who wants him to work on Saturdays and Sundays.

In sum, one of the ways of coming to know the invisible enemy is through the representation of the disciplined subject whose unhappiness and suffering indicates the existence of a large and powerful organization which manipulates and controls their activities from behind the scenes. The work of Foucault (1977) can be used to understand the formulation of subjectivities in relation to the identity of the manufactured employee within these representations. In many films the employee is portrayed as the subject of 'hierarchical observation', enabled by the clock and a bewildering variety of technological surveillance devices through which manufactured employees are able to be monitored by management, as can be read for instance in *Brazil* (1985), *Modern Times* (1936) and *Metropolis* (1927). The worker is further constituted as an 'object', about which management collects and records knowledge, in the form of bureaucratic records such as personnel files, often allocating a number to each individual in place of their name (see Film Focus 1.3). The modern employee becomes the focus of 'normalizing relationships', involving the apparently neutral objectivity of rules and practices which have been scientifically tested by experts such as time and motion study (Film Focus 3.5). Finally, through *techniques of examination* the manufactured employee is governed by an apparently neutral and objective authority which is based on a system of differentiation, correction and training and measured by periodic examination.

The mad organization

To make the organization visible as the enemy within film it must be constituted as different from us, the characteristics that it displays and the actions it takes sometimes seeming so bizarre, callous or aggrandizing that the only way that we can make sense of them is as a kind of madness, akin to a person having a serious mental illness. Not only does this depiction involve an objectivist construction of organization as having an identity independent of its members, it also relies on anthropomorphization, attributing human qualities to a non-living thing. This is sometimes achieved through the representation of mad organizational leaders, fanatically crazed individuals with idiosyncratic habits who harbour desires to dominate or destroy the world, such as in the futuristic portrayal of corporate leadership in *Blade Runner* (1982). A focus on the mental state of the organization and its leaders also provides the basis for Kets de Vries and Miller's (1984) argument that organizations, like individuals, can develop neurotic disorders, such as depression, paranoia or compulsiveness, which result in dysfunctional behaviour. This psychoanalytical approach to understanding organizations argues that there is often a link between the pathological behaviours of organizations and the mental conflicts and neurotic disorders experienced by its senior managers, the latter providing the initial stimulus through which certain patterns of behaviour become collectively entrenched. Film Focus 3.6 provides an illustration of how these ideas are represented in film.

FILM FOCUS 3.6: Psychoanalysing the organization in *Rogue Trader* (2000)

Stein's (2000) analysis of the collapse of Barings Bank, the United Kingdom's oldest investment bank, uses concepts from psychoanalysis and applies them to the organization as a means of understanding the group mind or mentality (Stein, 2000, p. 1227). He argues that anxieties associated with the deregulation of the UK financial sector led senior members of the bank to collectively generate the shared idea that they needed to find a 'saviour' who was a direct opposite or 'shadow' of themselves in order to prevent the bank's collapse. These collective anxieties fostered an assumption of dependency within the group who were looking for someone who could uniquely satisfy the organization's needs. The young derivatives trader Nick Leeson, who joined the bank in 1989, was an extreme risk taker who lacked formal education, had a tendency to lie, and exhibited a lack of behavioural and emotional restraint that was distinctly 'un-English'. He thus represented a saviour who was the direct opposite to the conservative approach of the bank. These dynamics are illustrated in a scene from the film *Rogue Trader* (2000) where at the company's annual dinner the chairman explains the new recruitment strategy and the organization's shift away from the 'old school tie' approach. ✐ [**approximate running time: 14.20–15.20 mins.**] A psychoanalytic approach helps to explain why, even though Leeson left considerable evidence, fuelled by his

Continued

unconscious sense of guilt, the company failed to recognize what was happening for a long period of time. Stein (2000) suggests that if the bank had been more aware of its fear of failure due to conservatism in a rapidly changing market it might not have made this mistake. He concludes that the problem is organizational and not the fault of an individual 'rogue trader'.

The idea of the mad organization is also pursued by Bakan (2004) in his book *The Corporation* (on which the film of the same name is based), who argues that the corporation exhibits psychopathic traits which make it incapable of moral obligation and protects it from punishment. He suggests that this stems from the nature of the corporate form which generally protects the human beings who own and run corporations from legal liability.

> Directors are traditionally protected by the fact that they have no direct involvement with decisions that may lead to a corporation's committing a crime. Executives are protected by the law's unwillingness to find them liable for their companies' illegal actions unless they can be proven to have been "directing minds" behind those actions. Such proof is difficult if not impossible to produce in most cases, because corporate decisions normally result from numerous and diffuse individuals' inputs, and because courts tend to attribute conduct to the corporate "person" rather than to the actual people who run corporations. (Bakan, 2004, p. 79)

What is more, he argues, a corporation is unable to exercise moral responsibility, since it cannot make judgements on the basis of rational consideration of alternatives and consequences of its actions. Neither, he argues, is the corporation capable of respect, or concern for the effects on others, since it only regards others as instrumental to achieving its own purposes. This is what gives rise to issues such as the 'free rider problem', no individual business organization having the incentive to incur costs associated with use of public goods, such as water or air, or what economist Milton Friedman terms 'externalities'.

The psychopathic corporation

Bakan (2004) further suggests that the characteristics of the modern corporation are remarkably similar to those of a person who has a psychopathic personality. The first of these characteristics is that they are singularly self-interested, unable to feel genuine concern for others; second, they are irresponsible and in attempting to satisfy corporate goals they will put everybody and everything else at risk; third, the psychopathic corporation has a tendency to manipulate everything, including public opinion. The fourth characteristic is an orientation towards grandiose notions, in other words, insisting that they are 'number one'; fifth, they lack empathy and exhibit asocial tendencies, being singularly unconcerned with their victims, sixth, psychopathic corporations refuse to accept responsibility for their own actions and are unable to feel remorse. Hence, if they are caught engaged in some form of wrongdoing they will pay the penalty and continue to do what they were doing before. Finally, they tend to relate to others superficially, the way they represent themselves may not accurately reflect how they are. These characteristics can be seen in films such as *The Insider* (2000), (Film Focus 3.2), *Erin Brockovich* (2000) (Film Focus 1.4) and *A Civil Action* (1998) in which a company is found guilty of polluting the local environment and causing the deaths of a number of children from leukaemia. Further examples of the psychopathic organization are given in Film Focus 3.7.

FILM FOCUS 3.7: The psychopathic organization in *Class Action* (1991), *Fight Club* (1999) and *Tucker: The Man and His Dreams* (1988)

All of these films represent the mad organization by focusing on the way that auto companies calculate risks associated with their products. This relates to the 1970s case of the Pinto, where it has been argued that Ford knew there was a serious flaw in product manufacture which meant there was a danger of petrol tank explosion in crashes and yet the company did not voluntarily recall the vehicles. The films make reference to the corporate practice of conducting cost-benefit analysis, placing a financial value on death, including $10,000 for 'pain and suffering', and weighing the costs associated with recalling the vehicle against the probable number of deaths if the product is not recalled. In *Fight Club* (1999) Jack is employed as a recall coordinator working for a car company. In this scene he describes the rational process whereby the organization calculates risk, while inspecting the interior of a burnt out vehicle. ☉ [**approximate running time: 18.30–21 mins.**] *Tucker: The Man and His Dreams* (1988) is the story of one man's heroic struggle against Detroit's 'Big Three' automobile manufacturers in seeking to realise his dream of producing an innovative new car design. In this scene, Preston makes a presentation to government officials in which he accuses the auto companies of having wilfully neglected the issue of consumer safety in pursuit of greater profits. ☉ [**approximate running time: 17.20–19.40 mins.**]

The criminal charges of homicide brought against Ford in 1978 were the first ever brought against an American corporation (Hoffman, 1984). A guilty verdict would have required that the company be shown to have engaged in conscious and unjustifiable disregard of harm that might result from its actions.

Continued

The key phrase on which the trial hinged was 'acceptable standards' and whether Ford knowingly prioritized profit above product safety in their decision over the placement of the gas tank. This raises an interesting issue about whether it is ever possible to know if a corporation intends harm. Other writers (De George, 1981) have focused on the lack of action taken by the company to voluntarily recall the Pinto or to offer customers the possibility of modification to the vehicle which would make the gas tank safer. This they argue provides sufficient grounds to support the charge of recklessness. These issues form the basis for *Class Action* (1991), a legal drama about a case brought by an injured man against a car company. Ford's handling of the Pinto case in the 1970s provides evidence for asserting that organizations have psychopathic characteristics, including lack of empathy and asocial tendencies, refusal to accept responsibility for their actions and an inability to feel remorse.

Obedience and conformity

However, while madness is helpful as a means of characterising representations of organization in film as the enemy, they do not help us to understand how the people who work for mad organizations respond to situations where they are expected to behave in ways that are supportive of its psychopathic tendencies, or indeed whether they see these demands as legitimate or ethical. Milgram's (1963) studies of obedience to authority are relevant here, since they explore the effects of group norms on behaviour to try and find out how and why individuals can be induced to cause harm to others by virtue of being instructed to do so. Milgram's well known experimental study involved assigning groups of volunteers the role of 'teachers' and giving them the task of punishing 'learners' by giving them electric shocks of increasing voltage each time the learner gave an incorrect answer to a question. In each case, the teacher was placed in a separate room where she or he could not see the learner, who was in fact an actor, and they could only speak to each other using a microphone. This whole affair was overseen by a third person, who instructed the teacher that they continue with the test, assuring them that they were not responsible for anything that might happen, even when cries of pain could be heard from the learners in the next room. The experiment found that a large proportion of people display obedience to authority, continuing with the electric shocks even if this apparently causes considerable pain and injury to others. Milgram concludes that when they see themselves as an instrument for carrying out someone else's wishes, people cease to take responsibility for their own actions (see Film Focus 3.8).

FILM FOCUS 3.8: Obedience to authority in *Enron: The Smartest Guys in the Room* (2005)

Enron: The Smartest Guys in the Room (2005) is a documentary film which tells the story of the downfall of Enron. This particular scene focuses on the company's move from the supply of gas to electricity and the strategy which they adopted of targeting the state of California's deregulated power market. Evidence is provided to suggest that Enron instructed the temporary shut downs of power stations in the area in order to stimulate energy shortages and push up the price of power. The film includes recordings of actual telephone conversations retrieved after the company's collapse involving Enron's West Coast traders laughing about the effects of these tactics which coincided with a heat wave causing distress and ill health and forcing many people to leave their homes. The main message of the film involves asking why more people within the organization did not question what was going on sooner. In explanation, the film makes reference to the Milgram experiments as evidence of how the traders could apparently find what they were doing amusing. ☻ [**approximate running time 1 hour 0.30–1 hour 14 mins.**]

The extent to which organizations can induce a high degree of conformity in their members can also be understood with reference to Goffman's (1968) study of total institutions, in which he argues that individuals take on roles and act out performances that affect how they are perceived by others, this forming the basis for what Goffman terms the 'interaction order'. The total institution is one in which all human activities, including working, eating and sleeping, are conducted in the same place and under the same authority. What is more, these activities are carried out in the presence of a large group of others who are treated in the same way. The organization of these activities is planned and formally ordered, certain tasks being carried out at specific times of day. 'Finally, the various enforced activities are brought together into a single rational plan purportedly designed to fulfil the official aim of the institution' (Goffman, 1968, p. 17). While Goffman focuses principally on types of organization such as mental hospitals and prisons, he suggests that these elements can also be found in other kinds of organization. The level of conformity engendered within total institutions is, Goffman argues, achieved by removing the things and relationships that sustain an individual's sense of self in a process of identity 'stripping', exposing them instead to physical and psychological subjugation and humiliation. Such findings are reinforced by Zimbardo et al.'s (1973) study of conformity pressures in 'total situations' which involved constructing a mock prison environment and recruiting a group of volunteers to participate in an experiment. Some of the male volunteers, all of whom were classed as emotionally stable, middle class, well educated, and with no criminal record, were randomly assigned the role of prisoner or guard. The two groups were allocated different uniforms and the guards were instructed to enforce the prison rules. While the experiment was intended to be a fourteen day study, it had to be stopped early because the guards began to subject the prisoners to psychological cruelty and some of the prisoners began to show signs of mental breakdown. Representations of organization in films like *One Flew over the Cuckoo's Nest* (1975) emphasize aspects of conformity and obedience to authority, implying that organizational membership is a totalizing experience. Film Focus 3.9 provides a further example.

FILM FOCUS 3.9: The organization as a total institution in *Fight Club* (1999)

Tyler embarks on the process of recruiting members to 'Project Mayhem' a militaristic organization which he establishes as a means of promoting his anti-consumerist ideology the purpose of which is to carry out acts of sabotage, vandalism and attack directed at businesses. Unquestioning obedience to authority constitutes the foundation of membership of Project Mayhem, as indicated by the rules of membership which include: 'You don't ask questions' and 'You must trust Tyler'. However, it is the method through which conformity to the organization is engendered that bear's closest relation to Goffman's analysis of 'identity stripping'. As a test of their commitment to the cause the prospective recruits are required to stand outside the house that constitutes the headquarters of Project Mayhem for several days where they are subject to periodic verbal intimidation. They are instructed to arrive with various items of kit and their membership entails shaving their hair and wearing a uniform. As the organization becomes progressively more powerful, all aspects of the members' former selves are apparently erased, leaving them parroting certain key phrases associated with the organization in a robotic manner. [**approximate running time: 1 hour 21.20–1 hour 30 mins.**]

The dead hand of bureaucracy

While these analyses reveal much about the way that individuals who find themselves in positions with relatively little power are induced to comply with the demands of the mad organization, it does not adequately explain how individuals with greater responsibility and higher organizational status, who could be argued to have much greater choice in how they respond to organizational demands, become active participants in the construction of the mad organization. Such explanations rely more on understandings of collective rather than individual behaviour.

The dead hand of bureaucracy that stops constructive progress from being made is a recurring theme in film. Hierarchical structures with complex divisions of labour are frequently signified in film by the numerous floors of a tall building and by employee names and job titles etched on office doors and corporate information boards. Individual characters are assigned to specific roles and tasks, written guidelines proscribe the actions they can take for which they are rewarded through security of employment and incremental salary rises achieved by their following regularized procedures for job promotion (see Film Focus 3.10 for an example). Such representations find their origins in sociological theory, in particular the work of Weber (1947) who suggested that bureaucracy was coming to replace traditional and charismatic authority in contemporary society as a system of organization which was highly efficient, reliable and precise. Bureaucracy relies on a legal-rational form of authority, the people who make decisions within such a system doing so on the basis of their formal position in the administrative hierarchy rather than because of any personal advantages they might possess over others. Its rise over the course of the twentieth century is associated with the growth of large organizations (see Chapter 4) and the shift of the labour force from farm and factory to administrative hierarchy. Indeed, bureaucracy has moved into every corner of the organization, including:

> into the great shipping offices permeated with the smell of carbon paper; into the sprawling, chaotic floors of stock exchanges and the busy but orderly banking halls; into the cavernous windowless rooms, guarded by mantraps and armed guards, that house hundreds of blinking computer consoles; into honey-combed government bureaus with desks piled nearly on top of one another, separated by Plexiglas windows; into the "rabbit warrens" of advertising and public relations firms; into the antiseptic, pastel or blanch-white, Muzak-filled corridors of suburban corporate headquarters; or into the designer-decorated private executive suites. (Jackall, 1988, p. 10)

Bureaucracy provides a system of power, privilege and domination as well as a technical system of organization. What is more, Weber was ambivalent about bureaucracy which he saw as giving rise to a form of being that was impersonal, emotionless and hence devoid of passion and sensitivity, the individual being reduced to a 'single cog' in a vast machine over which he or she has no control (Gerth and Mills, 1948; cited in Parker, 2002, p. 19). Such ambivalence is further reinforced by Merton's (1940) depiction of the 'bureaucratic personality' which is characterized by a tendency towards 'goal displacement', a pattern of behaviour where organization members become more concerned that rules are followed than whether rule-following is conductive to the achievement of organizational goals. The representation of the bureaucratic personality is evident in many films, often being embodied through the portrayal of one or more minor characters whose rule-following behaviours obstruct the goals of the protagonist. This can be read in the film *Brazil* (1985) when Jill

Layton tries to report a typing mistake to state officials that had led to the wrong man's arrest but she is prevented from doing so because she has the wrong form (see also Film Focus 3.10).

FILM FOCUS 3.10: Impersonal bureaucracy in *The Apartment* (1960) and *Brazil* (1985)

The Apartment (1960) represents bureaucracy as a technically efficient, reliable and precise mode of organization. This can be read at the beginning of the film when the central character, Bud Baxter, explains: 'On November 1st 1959 the population of New York City was 8 million, 42 thousand, 783. If you laid all these people end to end, figuring an average height of 5 feet 6 ½ inches it would reach from Times Square to the outskirts of Karachi, Pakistan. I know facts like this because I've worked for an insurance company, Consolidated Life of New York. We're one of the top five companies in the country. Our home office has 31,259 employees, which is more than the entire population of Naches, Mississippi. I work on the nineteenth floor, Ordinary Policy Department, Premium Accounting Division, Section W. Desk Number 861. My name is C.C. Baxter, C for Calvin C. for Clifford. However, most people call me Bud. I've been with Consolidated for 3 years and 10 months and my take home pay is 94.70 a week. The hours in our department are 8.50 to 5.20'. A bell rings. All the employees rise from their desk together to leave. 'They are staggered by floor so that 16 elevators can handle the 31,259 employees without a serious traffic jam'. ☺ [**approximate running time: 0–3.10 mins.**]

The futuristic film *Brazil* (1985) represents the dysfunctions of bureaucracy in an industrial world somewhere in the twentieth century. The unintended consequences of bureaucracy, and the way in which rule-following can become an end in itself are represented through the incident of a typing mistake that leads to the arrest and charging of 'Mr Buttle' as a terrorist, rather than 'Mr Tuttle' – the letter 'B' having been typed incorrectly on the form, rather than the letter 'T', that leads to his arrest. Sam Lowry's boss, Mr Kurtzmann, is relieved to find that this mistake is not his department's responsibility and having done so, he has no interest in correcting it in order to save the wrongly accused man. ☺ [**approximate running time: 13.30–15.20 mins.**]

Films which portray the organization as the enemy imply that bureaucracy has dehumanizing effects on organizational members, this echoing Adams and Balfour's (2004) suggestion that complex organizations give rise to administrative evil, situations in which ordinary people in professional roles do evil things without even realising that they have done anything wrong. They suggest that the culture of technical rationality is to blame for this because it provides a language which may be used to create emotional distance from the actions that are being carried out. Such sentiments echo the views of Bauman (1989) who argues that the characteristics of modern, bureaucratic organization, including complex hierarchy, rational problem-solving, rule-following behaviour, clear delineation of responsibility, narrow focus on tasks and separation of personal feelings from efficient role performance, have contributed towards the erosion of moral responsibility. He argues that a rule-following, bureaucratic mentality encourages obedience and conformity which results in the abdication of individual ethical agency. In its place, bureaucratic organizations subscribe to a form of collective ethical responsibility based on a set of rules that neutralizes the moral capacity of the individual. Bauman refers to three ways that the moral impulse of the individual may be neutralized; first, through the 'denial of proximity', the organization creating a distance between itself and those who bear the consequences of its actions; second, through the 'effacement of face' whereby the objects of action are not seen as worthy of moral consideration; and third, through 'reduction to traits', through which the moral self is dissembled into a collection of attributes associated with particular roles such as 'the customer' or 'the employee'. Three examples of films in which the denial of proximity is provided as evidence of the existence of evil in organization are given in Film Focus 3.11.

FILM FOCUS 3.11: Obedience and denial of proximity in *Fun with Dick and Jane* (2005), *Rogue Trader* (2000) and *Boiler Room* (2000)

These films are founded on the assumption that organizations seek to inculcate a bureaucratic mentality based on rule-following behaviour which encourages obedience and conformity. In this scene from *Fun with Dick and Jane* (2005), a comedy with a plot loosely based on the Enron scandal, Dick gets a lucky break and is promoted to Vice President of Communications at Globadyne. Almost immediately he is asked by his boss to make a live TV appearance on 'Money Live' to announce the firm's quarterly projections. However, when he is asked to explain why his CEO has unloaded a considerable share of his stocks in the company and why Globadyne portfolio documents are being subpoenaed, he is entirely ignorant of these issues. After giving a terrible interview he returns to the office to find his colleagues furiously shredding paperwork. When he asks what is happening to the organization he is told by his drunken boss 'we took our shifting losses and we put them into businesses that we actually own. And then the balance sheet it showed profit but actually there was debt'. Dick realizes that his narrow focus on tasks within the hierarchical structure have left him in the position of apparently being the last one to know what was going on. ☉ [**approximate running time 11.15–16.10 mins.**]

Continued

FILM FOCUS 3.11: Continued

The films *Rogue Trader* (2000) and *Boiler Room* (2000) illustrate how physical distance between the character perpetrating an immoral action and those affected by it can help neutralize the moral impulse. For example, in *Rogue Trader* (2000) although the derivatives trader working for Barings Bank, Nick Leeson, is able to maintain the deception entailed in covering his trading losses while he is based in Singapore, when he returns to the London office the consequences of his actions start to place him under increasing psychological pressure. As he notes, 'it was one thing to con people over the phone ... quite another to do it to their face'. ☺ [**approximate running time: 45.30–49.30 mins.**] In *Boiler Room* (2000), narrator Seth expresses a similar view when he compares the illegal gambling business he ran from his apartment to the legal but morally corrupt business he is working for as an investment broker. 'You know it's funny looking back, the illegal business I was running was the most legitimate thing I had going. I looked my customers in the eye and provided a service they wanted. Now I don't even look at my customers and I push them something they never asked for'. ☺ [**approximate running time: 1 hour 28–1 hour 29 mins.**]

Conclusion

So how do we account for the frequency and extent of portrayals of organization as the enemy in film? Some writers have taken a pragmatic view, suggesting that these representations provide a convenient scapegoat that is acceptable to global audiences and provides an outlet for creative workers' frustrations about their lack of autonomy with respect to their cultural product (Epstein, 2005; Ribstein, 2005). Others have argued that they are a reflection of the cultural context from which they originate, serving to articulate collective concerns about the sacrifices that individuals have to make in a nation that is economically and morally devoted to capitalism (Sadar and Wyn Davies, 2004; Newitz, 2006). Yet others, such as Parker (2002), regard them as evidence of a backlash against management, arguing that there is significance in the 'coincidence of ideas' between negative representations of organization in popular culture and the emergence and growth of a broader societal critique of management since 1975.

These representations can also be read as a commentary on the inevitability of organization as an inexorable force in our midst. The consistent representation of organization in film as an objectively knowable entity with a highly specific set of negative characteristics – bureaucratic, dehumanizing and all consuming – implies that these are necessary or unavoidable evils, an unfortunate consequence of modernist, technological progress. Interestingly, Gouldner (1955) suggests that social scientists are guilty of a similar thing, in assuming bureaucracy to be an inevitable consequence of organizational size and technological sophistication they help to 'bury men's hopes' [sic] (Gouldner, 1955, p. 507) rather than leaving open the possibility that organizations could exhibit different characteristics. It could be, therefore, that while these representations help to confirm what we collectively suspect organizations, especially those that are extremely large and powerful, to be like, they simultaneously invite our acceptance of them as things that the individual must endure, finding happiness despite them rather than through them. This reading is supportive of an ideological approach (discussed in Chapter 1), in that it assumes film to be a device the purpose of which is to support the status quo of capitalist interests by encouraging audiences to accept things as they are rather than to question or challenge them.

What these interpretations all tend to overlook is that the purpose of rendering the enemy visible is to distinguish it as separate from ourselves. It is, as Žižek (2002) says, through the enemy that we come also to know the friend. Take, for example, the film *Fast Food Nation* (2006) which provides a critical analysis of the American fast food industry. This film clearly depicts the mad organization, in this case the fictitious Mickey's burger chain, showing it to possess many of core characteristics described in this chapter. Yet the hero in this story is the company's marketing executive, a 'nice-guy' manager who seeks to investigate claims about the organization's unethical practices while also seeking to continue to provide for his family. The film represents the organization as an abstract entity that can be distinguished from its members even, as in this case, a relatively senior one. This positioning of the enemy enables the actions of the organization to be distanced from those its members, in particular the hero or 'organization man' who constitutes the focus of the following chapter.

Plate 4 Executives assemble in the boardroom on the 40th floor of Ramsay and Company, New York in *Patterns* (1956)

Organization man

Introduction

The films in this chapter represent the world of executive work in the large, bureaucratic, male-dominated corporation where narratives about power, reward and success dominate. The chapter explores the iconographic conventions used to represent this type of workplace, such as the executive boardroom and the corporate elevator, as well as signifiers like the dark suit, white-collar and tie and trilby hat that signify the sombre, unemotional and responsible nature of the central subject – the organization man. Organization man is a discursive category used to celebrate the corporate managerial values of hierarchy, bureaucracy, loyalty and authority. Representations of organization man, and the large, corporation which he is suggested to inhabit, have helped to establish some highly influential concepts that continue to inform the way we continue to think about work and the workplace today. Hence, although the attitudes and behaviour represented in these films may seem initially remote from contemporary workplace practices, closer examination reveals the underlying concepts, relating to progress, success and career ambition, that connect them to contemporary practice.

The classical corporate executive film is defined as commencing in the decade following World War II and ending by 1958 (Boozer, 2002) partly as a reflection of values which flourished in the decades between 1930 and 1960 (Boltanski and Chiapello, 2005). This temporal definition is useful in contextualising many of the films reviewed in this chapter which reflect socio-economic conditions in the post-war era when big business 'began to look like a hierarchy of opportunity, an arena where one could make a contribution to society as well as develop a lucrative long-term career' (Boozer, 2002, p. 18). As America was lifted out of the Great Depression by a manufacturing boom the expansion of large industries throughout the 1950s combined with rising consumer demand created a managerial 'revolution' involving the creation of 'a new breed of formally educated and carefully groomed corporate executives' (Boozer, 2002, p. 19). These films reflect the construction of management as a legitimate, respected social grouping in the post-war period, a reputation that was cemented through technology and bureaucracy in the 1950s and 1960s (Scarbrough and Burrell, 1996). In addition to glorifying organization man by celebrating and mythologizing his experience, this chapter argues that these representations reflect a degree of scepticism about the rise of modern management and the effects of bureaucracy and instrumental rationality on the human spirit.

The process of constructing meaning in relation to the white-collar worker in the large organization further relies on establishing oppositions between organization men – as white, male, middle class conformists, and the women – secretaries and wives, who constitute the other through which the meaning of organization man is made explicit. This gendered conceptualisation is based on a perspective that regards masculinity and femininity as socially constructed labels which are the result of discourses about how males and females should behave in organizations. Organization man is a gendered stereotype, the idealized form of a particular kind of organizational subject, the film representations that constitute the focus of this chapter being an ideological formation of what it means to be a man in this context.

Setting the scene: the large corporation

Developments in the United States in the early decades of the twentieth century provided the foundations for the emergence of the key phenomenon of our time – the large organization (Perrow, 1991). One of the most significant factors underlying the rise of the large, publicly traded industrial corporation in the period 1890 to 1905 was the creation of 'socialized property' which involved a change in the form and organisation of property that altered relationships between owners, workers, managers, suppliers and consumers and transformed the organization of ownership as economic entities came to be owned by many individuals (Roy, 1997). This coincided with the corporation's acquisition of many legal rights and responsibilities, resulting in a situation where it had 'its own identity, separate from the flesh-and-blood people who were its owners and managers and empowered, like a real person, to conduct business in its own name, acquire assets, employ workers, pay taxes, and go to court to assert its rights and defend its actions' (Bakan, 2004, p. 16).

An explanation of the emergence of the modern business enterprise as the archetype of today's modern corporation is provided by Chandler (1977) who argues that technological changes at the beginning of the twentieth century created economies of scale which meant significant efficiencies were able to be gained by establishing larger productive units. Improved transport and communications combined with population growth stimulated the expansion of national and international markets, which in turn made it necessary to vertically integrate production and distribution and to coordinate activities through the creation of bureaucratic, managerial hierarchies to meet rising demand. Administrative coordination provided the basis for the emergence of a profession of salaried managers, originally trained as civil engineers, who replaced individual proprietors and partnerships and became a source of continued growth. This is what Chandler sees as the rise of the 'visible hand' of management, which he argues came to replace the 'invisible hand' of the market, referred to by Adam Smith. This historical analysis leads Chandler to conclude that as large business enterprises grew they came to alter sectors of the economy in which they operated.

However, critics of Chandler have suggested that this analysis positions managers as far-sighted heroes 'seeking efficient solutions to technically induced problems of coordination' (Roy, 1997, p. 176), implying that the survival of large, modern organizations provides a validation of their superior productivity, efficiency and success. Chandler's analysis explains change 'as the rational adaptation to asocial exogenous forces like technology and markets' (Roy, 1997, p. 259) rather than being shaped by social relations and a framework of power within which actors were embedded. What is more, Roy suggests Chandler's emphasis on the technocratic role of the rational salaried manager overlooks other social actors who played a part in the rise of the large corporation, including investors, bankers, workers, lawyers and governments.

Whatever the historical explanation for the rise of the large organization, its significance is such that it has transformed our experience of all aspects of social life by absorbing activities that were formerly carried out by small informal groups. Perrow (1991) cites the importance of 'factory bureaucracies' in enabling the rise of the large organization, the development of methods of continuous production based on centralized control and the establishment of hierarchy which gradually extended into all forms of organization.

> The creation of large-scale organizations with multiple levels of authority, the adoption of the line and staff system, the functional form of organization, the vertical integration of production, and the rise of middle management as a new stratum in the occupational structure are vital consequences of the rise of the large industrial corporation. (Roy, 1997, p. 263)

Modernist organization

The representation of organizations as large, pyramid structures can be read as a celebration of modernism, as a project or intellectual movement and an era or phase of capitalism dominated by industrial organization. Modernism advocates a break with history and tradition and a rejection of mythical and religious aspects of humanity. The modernist project relies on the conviction that rational, scientific reasoning leads to the discovery of absolute forms of knowledge, which in turn leads to human progress. The period of 'high' modernism, after 1945, is characterized by the belief in linear progress, absolute truths, and rational planning of ideal social orders under standardized conditions of knowledge and production (Harvey, 1990). Aesthetic modernism of this period, constituted through art, architecture and other aspects of high culture, is located within the urban environment which provides the image of rationality, the machines, skyscraper dominated landscapes, contemporary technologies, including transport and communication systems, which constituted the city as a living machine and provided the material practices on which intellectual modernism drew (Harvey, 1990). In films like *The Apartment* (1960) and *Executive Suite* (1954), as well as *Metropolis* (1927), *The Crowd* (1928) and *Modern Times* (1936), modernism is strongly encoded through the representation of the urban environment which denotes the values of intellectual modernism.

The skyscraper is key aspect of iconography and source of recurrent symbolic meaning in films about large organizations. Even the names of the fictitious organisations represented in these films, the 'Federal Broadcasting Company' (*Desk Set*, 1957), 'Consolidated Life' (*The Apartment*, 1960), the 'World Wide Wicket Company' (*How to Succeed in Business without Really Trying*, 1967), denote a sense of scale, global reach and uniformity. 'Tall office buildings signify the permanence and scale of the large organization through the density of human occupation that they afford. Skyscrapers and big corporations grew up together, and the buildings dramatized the separateness and stratification of the new commercial power' (Sampson, 1995, p. 39). They are the apotheosis of corporate culture of the twentieth and twenty-first centuries, playing an important role as 'representational strategies of financial and political elites to endow their city or nation with a projected self-consciousness (McNeill, 2005, p. 46).

Large buildings were used by large American companies in the early part of the twentieth century to denote the values that the organization wanted to be known for among its customers and the public. Moudry (2006) argues that skyscrapers provided symbolic markers for financial institutions in the 1920s, such as the Metropolitan Life Insurance Company, which in 1909 completed the construction of a 700-foot tower to accommodate its corporate headquarters in New York. The Met Life Tower, which was then the tallest building in the world, signified a corporate ideology that celebrated traditional values of responsibility, dependability and family which were intended to unify employees and policyholders dispersed across the country. Moreover, the tower provided a physical manifestation of the organization's paper-intensive clerical, bureaucratic activities which, unlike those relating to product manufacture, could not readily be seen by the consumer. The height of the tower presented architectural challenges whose innovative technical solutions were presented as components in the physical and symbolic construction of the 'Tower of Strength'. Images of the tower were also used extensively by other companies to market their products, 'as the newest of New York's skyscraper wonders, the tower served as a symbol, not only of the company, but also of the entire working world' (Moudry, 2006, p. 208). Moreover the symbolic meaning of the building was not confined only to its external aspects. The internal work space was designed in a way that emulated the design of a factory, its network of elevators, corridors and offices like an enormous filing system (Mills, 1951), signifying standardization, systematization and efficiency, features that can be clearly identified in films like *The Apartment* (1960) (see Film Focus 3.6).

Not only is modernism communicated through the environment in which the large organization is located, it can also be read in the representation of material organizational practices which confirm them as rational entities. The modernist organization is identifiable by its clear boundaries which separate it from its external environment (Clegg, 1990). In many films, signifiers of buildings, walls and doors convey meaning that is related to the general signified of the organization as a distinct entity that is separate from its environment. Characters are represented entering and exiting the entity through these points. For example, in *The Hudsucker Proxy* (1994), Norville Barnes enters the organization, through the revolving glass doors which separate the building from the street, at the same moment as Waring Hudsucker breaks through the plate glass window of the boardroom exiting the organization and falling to his death. Similarly, in *How to Succeed in Business without Really Trying* (1967), Ponty Finch enters the organisation through a window he is cleaning in his job as a window washer, sings a song and asks the company president for a job. Another example is given in Film Focus 4.1.

FILM FOCUS 4.1: Penetrating the boundaries of the modernist organization in *Time Out* (2001)

An example of the impermeable nature of modernist organizational boundaries can be read in *Time Out* (2001). When Vincent loses his job as a financial consultant he is not able to face telling his wife, friends and family. Instead, he constructs an elaborate fictional work life for himself involving the possibility of a promotion in Geneva. Then he fills his days by driving around and pretending to be working. On one occasion this entails following a group of office executives into a modernist chrome and glass office building where, wearing a suit and carrying a briefcase, Vincent wanders around pretending to be a member of the organization by looking efficient and preoccupied. Despite his attempts to blend in, his lack of office space or obvious activity means that after a few hours he is noticed by security guards and politely asked to leave the building. ◉ [**approximate running time: 53.45–55.20 mins.**]

The rational manager

Further evidence of the modernist organization is found in relation to the themes of purposive action and instrumental rationality. The Hollywood system, described in Chapter 1, invites a modernist view of organization through its construction of characters who behave rationally and self-interestedly in ways that link formal means with intended ends. Managerial discourses are also significant in providing a convenient vehicle through which such narratives can be effectively developed. It is therefore worthwhile tracing the origin of these discourses in order to understand how and why they impact upon film texts.

Managerial rationality is a mode of thought which is suggested to have been invented and developed in the United States at the beginning of the twentieth century (Shenhav, 1999). Hoskin and Macve (1998) trace the genesis of managerial thought to the West Point military academy in the United States which provided training in civil engineering and produced the professionals who supervised the building of the railroads. The training of these early engineers was based on a 'human accounting system' which enabled the discipline of the trainees based on linguistic-numerical measurement of their performance, involving technologies of 'objective' accountability and 'meticulous hierarchical structure' (Hoskin and Macve 1998, p. 94). They suggest that this system, which was more powerful and comprehensive than any other system of its time, was successful because the engineers implemented the disciplinary system that they themselves had internalized through their training. This resulted in the creation of 'new breed of knowledge and power experts' based on a 'generalized accountability system' and a 'clearly articulated management structure' (Hoskin and Macve, 1998, pp. 82–86). Locke (1996) defines the American post-war model of management as a hierarchical command and control system built on principles of scientific management and human relations which he argues do not fit well with the experience of management as an art. He argues that education was the cornerstone of this American 'invention', through the university education of business undergraduates and MBAs in the 1950s and 1960s, produced with the intention of professionalizing management as a 'properly credentialed, highly paid elite of experts' (Locke 1996, p. 29), by teaching them supposedly scientific approaches to management (see Film Focus 4.2).

It is unsurprising that these dramatic social changes provided the basis for representations of large organizations and the professional manager in film, especially when we consider that their emergence in these film texts followed similar patterns of organization within the American film industry (see Chapter 2). However, while these films in some ways represented the professional manager as a technically-minded hero solving organizational problems, they also contained rather more ambivalent messages about the underlying meaning associated with the role of the manager.

FILM FOCUS 4.2: Business school education in *The Hudsucker Proxy* (1994) and *Human Resources* (1999)

Many of the films in this book represent their central characters in a way which makes explicit that they are graduates of business schools as a means of signifying their professional, managerial status. In the opening of the film

Hudsucker Proxy (1994), we discover that Norville Barnes is a graduate from the Muncie College of Business Education. Having a business education but no experience makes it difficult for him to get a job. In *Human Resources* (1999) Frank, a recent graduate from a prestigious business school in Paris, tells his boss about a 'case' that he studied at university, in which the company was facing similar issues to those encountered by the managers of the factory where he is doing his industrial placement. He suggests the possibility of conducting an employee survey to assess employees' individual views and to use this to respond to the unions' position. Frank's boss is interested and he encourages Frank to pursue his ideas within the company. Frank's status as a graduate of a business school provides a differentiator of organizational status and power, positioning him above factory workers, including his father and sister, who participate in the survey. ☉ [**approximate running time: 28.13–32 mins.**]

Organization man

The central construct discussed in this chapter is 'organization man', the product of a society which specialized not only in the mass production of goods and services but also in manufacturing a standardized managerial persona. The term is also the name of a book, written by *Fortune* magazine journalist William H. Whyte (1956), describing changes in the American workplace that had resulted from the growth of large organizations – one of his interests being in the way that these changes had been represented in popular culture, including novels, magazines and films. Indeed, when Whyte (1956) wrote about the 'modern corporate executive' who not only worked for the organization, but also belonged to it, he could have been describing many of the central characters in the films reviewed in this chapter.

The rise of organization man can be located historically in terms of discourses of normality and social uniformity which were popular following World War II, when many large organizations not only drew on military disciplines, such as long-range planning and logistics, as the basis for organization but also looked to men with military experience to provide managerial leadership (Mills, 1951; Sampson, 1995). A crucial signifier of this identity was the gray flannel suit, which 'could effectively disguise the inconsistencies and inequalities of the people beneath it, so that the postwar middle class could be perceived – and could perceive itself – as normal, as unified, as uniform' (Creadick, 2006, p. 278), this helping to erase prior identities and allow its wearer to become part of a collective, an indistinguishable member of the social group. Organization man argues Creadick (2006) represented the desire for a return to normality, in contrast to the social, economic and emotional upheaval associated with depression and war, themes which are deliberately juxtaposed in *The Man in the Gray Flannel Suit* (1956).

Writing at the mid-point of the twentieth century, C. Wright Mills (1951) described a pattern of demographic expansion of the middle class which he saw as caused by 'the rise of big business and big government' and the 'steady growth of bureaucracy' (Mills, 1951, p. 68). At the core of his analysis was the view of managers as a powerful force but his focus was on lower-level employees within the 'new office', a newly-created cadre of personnel who were employed in monotonous, routine jobs that involved little discretion or creativity and brought little prospect of promotion. This white-collar employee was, he argued, a victim of the growth of business, his depiction of these individuals implying that they were consumed by work, to such an extent that their entire identity, both inside and outside the workplace was defined according to these corporate values. Organization man was:

> pushed by forces beyond his control, pulled into movements he does not understand: he gets into situations in which his is the most helpless position. The white-collar man is the hero as victim, the small creature who is acted upon but who does not act, who works along unnoticed in somebody's office or store, never talking aloud, never talking back, never taking a stand. (Mills, 1951, p. xii)

Mills was preoccupied with the structure or 'white-collar pyramids' which characterized these hierarchical organizations, and the subtleties of skill, function, class, status and power that differentiated individuals within them. The metaphor he used to describe this was the 'enormous file', each office being part of a giant filing system. Revolutionized by new technology such as the typewriter and the electronic calculator, Mills saw the modern office as like a factory, both in terms of scale and as a result of the mechanized, standardized nature of its procedures where tasks were carried out by interchangeable clerks and 'the drag and beat of work', the 'production unit' tempo, required that 'time consumed by anything but business at hand be explained and apologized for' (Mills, 1951, p. 204).

The changing work ethic

Principal among the changes in the American workplace described by Whyte (1956) was a shift from the Protestant ethic to what he described as the 'social ethic'. Over fifty years earlier, sociologist Max Weber (1930) had argued that the religious values associated with Protestantism had helped to influence the growth of capitalism in Western Europe in the nineteenth century. Protestants believed that individual salvation and the assurance of an afterlife in God's Kingdom could be achieved through the experience of hard work and being cautious with money or exercising thrift in their everyday life. Consequently, Weber argued, they were more inclined than followers of other religions, such as Catholicism, to undergo these tribulations, which also happened to support the accumulation of wealth and property, thus ensuring their greater success in the capitalist system. The Protestant ethic was so successful it continued to exist as a set of cultural values which eventually spread throughout the capitalist world in a way which ceased to be confined to followers of the religion and instead came to be defined as societal values in countries like America.

However, Whyte (1956) argued that the former dominance of the Protestant ethic had been usurped in American society. This he claimed was due to the growth of large, complex organizations which had precipitated a shift in American social values, stimulated by a change in public perspective that regarded suffering as a means of gaining salvation as unnecessary. Moreover, he claimed, the Protestant ethic did not fit with the vision of work that large, bureaucratic corporations represented because those who worked their could see that individual success was not necessarily the result of hard work, instead 'those who survived best were not necessarily the fittest but, in more cases than not, those who by birth and personal connections had the breaks' (Whyte, 1956 [2002], pp. 16–17). It was impossible, he argued, for members of these organizations to exercise thrift, since part of their job, through advertising and marketing functions, was to persuade other people to consume more rather than less. His central thesis was that the Protestant ethic had been superseded by the social ethic in which the individual was subjugated to the group.

The social ethic is based on three propositions: first, the belief in the group as a source of creativity; second, the belief in belongingness as the ultimate need of the individual; and third, the application of science as source of belongingness. All three of these propositions were fulfilled through becoming a member of a large, bureaucratic corporation. Together they provided an ideology which supported this form of organization more effectively than the Protestant ethic because it provided a moral imperative to self-adaptation to ensure conformity to the social norms of the organization. Fitting in was the key to organizational success, a skill which resulted in the production of a 'pervasive form of dull conformity' (Parker, 2002, p. 19), through the suppression of individual initiative and imagination.

Writing several years later, in Men and Women of the Corporation, Kanter (1977) describes a remarkably similar situation. Her analysis charts the rise of the career manager in the United States who sought to achieve legitimacy through professionalization as the ideological basis through which a relatively small and exclusive group of men were able to exercise control over a large group of workers. Kanter focuses on the 'masculine ethic' on which these career managers relied, identifying the traits that this celebrated, such as tough-mindedness, abstract analytical ability, and a capacity to set aside personal and emotional considerations in the interests of task accomplishment. 'For most of the twentieth century a "masculine ethic" of rationality dominated the spirit of managerialism and gave the manager role its defining image. It told men how to be successful as men in the new organizational worlds of the twentieth century' (Kanter, 1977, p. 25).

These managerial elites shared 'the same social and class assumptions, much like a private club' (Boozer, 2002, p. 23) whose members dress and act similarly (Film Focus 4.3).

Kanter argues that such practices reflect a desire for 'social certainty' based on peer acceptance and ease of communication. In all three analytical accounts provided by Mills (1951), Whyte (1956) and Kanter (1977), organization man is portrayed as a loyal, rule-following individual who exists within a rigidly hierarchical, bureaucratic system.

FILM FOCUS 4.3: Social conformity and the managerial club in *The Firm* (1993) and *Patterns* (1956)

The powerful disciplinary effects associated with organizational membership are represented in these two films, where the pressure to conform prevents individuals from acting in accordance with their moral principles or even the law. In *The Firm* (1993) when top Harvard law graduate Mitch McDeere is offered jobs with various firms all with attractive employment packages, he eventually accepts the generous offer made by a small Memphis firm. The Firm hosts social events for its employees who are treated as part of an extended family and lays down various tacit rules for its partners; for example, although it does not forbid partners' wives from paid employment it 'encourages' them to have children. The Firm also ensures that its newest employee's material needs are well catered for, providing Mitch and his wife with a beautiful, fully furnished house complete with a Mercedes coupe on the drive. However, the stability which this organizational culture promotes turns out to have a sinister purpose, Mitch discovers that The Firm is engaged in money laundering for the Mafia and becomes suspicious of the deaths of its former partners. The Firm's intent is to establish such a high level of dependency among its employees that they are unable to betray the organization even when they discover the full extent of the corruption. ☻ [**approximate running time: 9.20–14.30 mins.**]

A similar message is conveyed in the opening scenes of *Patterns* (1956) when Ohio engineer Fred Staples arrives on the first day in a new job on the 'executive corridor' on the 40th floor of Ramsay & Company in New York, it becomes clear that he has joined an elite group and that this paternalistic organization has considered his every need, including decorating his new office with painted friezes and furnishing it in the 'early American' style which they have found out Staples favours. As he explains to his colleague Briggs, he found his new house to be 'furnished like a magazine', complete with fresh milk in the refrigerator and a bottle of bourbon on the bar. Staples declares 'You know, you think of big business, you think of it as being very impersonal, you know? But it's really not true with your Mr Ramsey'. However, the paternalistic culture is not entirely benign as indicated by the statement given by Mr Ramsay at the start of the boardroom meeting when he announces that 'the issue of executive diets' is of concern to him because 'a healthy executive is an efficient one'. ☻ [**approximate running time: 6.40–14.05 mins.**]

The American Dream

From the seven-year old Johnny Sims' proud declaration in *The Crowd* (1928) that his daddy says he is going to be 'somebody big', to Ponty Finch's concern to 'get someplace' in *How to Succeed in Business without Really Trying* (1967), or Brantley Foster's desire to make it to the top in *The Secret of My Success* (1987), many of the characters in films that represent management embody and articulate the American Dream, an ideology which 'views America as a land of opportunity in which individuals by hard work and self-improvement can achieve the highest measure of success' (Legge, 2005, p. 124). As Boozer (2002, p. 11) notes, these films are often about 'the basic ambitions, methods, and ethics of an individual's career quest, in relation both to a particular company of employ and to America's larger success myth'. They are a reflection of the pioneering narrative of the American journey in which the individual sets forth into the wilderness in a project of remaking the self (Sadar and Wyn Davies, 2004). Mills (1951) describes career success in America as 'an engaging image, a driving motive, and a way of life' (1951, p. 259) that is linked to a liberal ideology of expanding capitalism, wherein everyone is rewarded according to their ability and effort. Within this system, career success is a matter of climbing the ladder of the bureaucratic hierarchy, rung by careful rung, step by step, up to the top. The working lifetime is measured in a series of stages and the individual worker in constant motion at a certain pace – where going either too fast, like Ponty in the film *How to Succeed in Business without Really Trying* (1967), or too slow, like Mr Twimble, carries the risk of failure (Film Focus 4.4).

FILM FOCUS 4.4: The company way in *How to Succeed in Business without Really Trying* (1967) and *The Secret of My Success* (1987)

How to Succeed in Business without Really Trying (1967) is a musical film which features the meteoric rise of young, ambitious former window washer Ponty Finch from the bottom to the top of the corporate hierarchy, thanks to the advice he reads in a self-help book bought from a newsstand entitled 'How to Succeed in Business'. Ponty's first job is in the mailroom of the World Wide Wicket Company. While he is there he receives some advice from head of the mail room, Mr Twimble, who has just been promoted after working for the company for 25 years, in the song 'The Company Way'.

> *Twimble:* I play it the company way; wherever the company puts me there I stay.
> *Finch:* But what is your point of view?
> *Twimble:* I have no point of view.
> *Finch:* Supposing the company thinks …
> *Twimble:* I think so too.

Continued

> Finch: Now, what would you say … ?
> Twimble: I wouldn't say.
> Finch: Your face is a company face.
> Twimble: It smiles at executives then goes back in place …
> Finch: So you play it the company way?
> Twimble: All company policy is by me OK.
> Finch: You'll never rise up to the top.
> Twimble: But there's one thing clear: whoever the company fires, I will still be here.

The career seeking Finch is thus signified in opposition to Twimble, who is everything he is not – risk averse, unquestioning, and lacking in ideas or opinions. ☻ [**approximate running time: 13.10–17.45 mins.**]

A similar message is conveyed to the ambitious young Brantley Foster in *The Secret of My Success* (1987). When Brantley, a College graduate from Kansas who comes to New York in search of a business career, is given a job by his uncle in the post room of the Pearson Corporation, his colleague warns him not to 'converse with the suits' unless they speak first. Brantley, like Ponty, disregards this advice, cutting through the rules and conventions of the organization and assuming a more senior position within the company. ☻ [**approximate running time: 17–19 mins.**]

The American Dream is also predicated on the development of a science of organizing which involves predicting and explaining workplace behaviour using theories of motivation (Guest, 1990; Jacques, 1996). Theories which 'capture the values of middle America' and emphasize 'opportunities for progress and growth, based on individual achievement' (Legge, 2005, p. 124). Films about management and organization reflect an ideology that is informed by motivation theories such as Maslow's (1943) hierarchy of needs, McGregor's (1960) Theory Y and Herzberg's (1966) motivator-hygiene theory which had wide currency at the time many of these films were released. These ideas are represented in the film *Executive Suite* (1954) when Don Walling makes his speech to the executive board (see Film Focus 4.7), stating that by helping people 'to rise to their fullest' in their work and enabling them to 'fulfil themselves' the executives of Tredway Furniture Corporation could 'make happiness'.

Career as progress

The career path of the central character is often extremely important in these films as a means of constructing a narrative that conforms to the norm of 'classical Hollywood cinema' (Bordwell and Thompson, 2004) by showing a series of organizational events that affect the goal-governed protagonist as he or she strives towards the achievement of status, power and financial rewards that accrue from career success. The concept of career is also related to the idea of the modernist organization discussed earlier, through its conception of a working lifetime as linear and the creation of a formalized relationship between age and career progress in a way which allows us 'to chart our passage through socially recognised and meaningful sequences of related events' (Hassard, 1991, p. 112). Hassard explores the organizational process whereby we are socialized into rigid time disciplines, focusing on career as a construct whereby this is achieved. The traditional concept of career as a ladder to be climbed or a predictable path to be journeyed along provides an organizing device for defining an individual's status and progress in organized society. Moreover, the highly formalized relationship between age and organizational status means that 'increasingly, success or failure is judged on one criterion, the timing of personal accomplishments' (Hassard, 1991, p. 111). Career time is a cultural construct which organizational members are socialized into accepting as a necessary aspect of their organizational existence. Grey (1994) describes professional accountants' careers as a self-disciplinary project of the self in which techniques such as performance appraisal and ratings schemes are seen as benevolent processes through which individuals can manage their careers more effectively. As the trainee accountants get nearer to the 'top' of the career ladder, more and more aspects of their non-work lives are affected by it, 'friends become transformed into "contacts", and social activity becomes "networking"' (1994, p. 492). Even choice of marriage partner is affected by career because, in the words of one interviewee, 'it's important to have a well-packaged wife' (Grey, 1994, p. 493).

The struggle for upward job mobility is also evident in these films from the numerous metonyms that symbolize career progress and promotion, such as getting the key to the executive washroom in *The Apartment* (1960) (see Film Focus 4.5), being invited into the executive dining room in *How to Succeed in Business without Really Trying* (1967), riding the elevator up to the top floor of the building in *Patterns* (1956) and *The Apartment* (1960), or even going on a mission into space in *Gattaca* (1997) (Film Focus 4.5). These films relate to what Mills (1951) described as 'the status panic' wherein individuals, differentiated from one another by minute gradations of rank, are subject to increased status competition. Moreover, striving for success is not specific to a single temporal period, for as Jackall observes in relation to the 1980s, 'perceptions of pervasive mediocrity breed an endless quest for social distinctions even of a minor sort that might give one an "edge", enable one to "step out of the crowd", or at least serve as a basis for individual claims to privilege' (Jackall, 1988, p. 197).

It is not simply the job that individuals strive for but the symbolic manifestations of power and status associated with it, such as the private office with their name on the door in *The Apartment* (1960) or the reserved parking space in the car park in *Office Space* (1998).

FILM FOCUS 4.5: Career progress in *The Apartment* (1960) and *Gattaca* (1997)

In *The Apartment* (1960) Bud Baxter is an office worker who lends his apartment out to his bosses so they can have extramarital affairs with their secretaries. In exchange, they write glowing reports about him that recommend his promotion. When Baxter is called up to the 27th floor he suspects that he is going to get his promotion. However, the excited Baxter is disappointed when it becomes clear that Personnel Director, Mr Sheldrake, suspects that the managers' recommendations conceal an ulterior motive. Just as Baxter thinks he is going to be sacked, Sheldrake announces he would like to use the apartment. In return, Sheldrake offers to promote him to Second Administrative Assistant, a position signified by having a private office. Later in the film, Sheldrake rewards Baxter again for lending him his apartment, this time making him Assistant Personnel Director. However, at this point, love gets in the way of Baxter's career ambition since he cannot face the idea of Sheldrake using his apartment to meet elevator operator, Miss Kubelik, whom he has fallen in love with. When Sheldrake asks for the key to the apartment, Baxter instead gives him the key to the executive washroom, explaining that he won't need it any longer because he is quitting. ☯ **[approximate running times: 23–31; 1 hour 51.40–1 hour 54 mins.]**

Gattaca (1997) is a futuristic portrayal of a world where genetic profiling provides the basis for 'genoism' a form of social discrimination which pervades in all spheres of life including employment. Entry to the Gattaca Aerospace Corporation is restricted to those with the right genetic make up who are known as valids. While those who do not have a suitable genetic profile constitute part of a new underclass of 'invalids' who must clean the offices of the elite suit-clad workers. By impersonating a valid Vincent manages to gain entry to the organization where his efforts are ultimately rewarded by being assigned to a space mission. ☯ **[approximate running time: 4–5.40 mins.]**

Social advancement through individualist enterprise, therefore, may be recognized as an impulse that is aligned with the very definition of film character identity and plot structure in the age of Hollywood studio cinema and in American film generally. But it is the business career film that most directly represents the nature and practice of American economic ambition. (Boozer, 2002, p. 5)

Equating height with status and power is a metaphorical device that is also used in *Metropolis* (1927) to distinguish the underground workers from the above ground capitalists. The root metaphor of 'up-down' is suggested by Tolliver and Coleman (2001) to be a fundamental part of an implicit ideology that governs how we think, feel and behave in organizations. Success is defined by moving upwards in the organizational structure relative to others, whereas failure is defined by movement downwards. They further argue that the continuing popularity of Maslow's (1943) hierarchy of needs, despite the theory's inconsistencies and lack of empirical support, can be attributed to the centrality of the 'up-down' metaphor, the individual moves up the need hierarchy to achieve a full state of human completeness through self-actualization. Jackall (1988) argues that advancement within the large organization relies on being perceived as a 'team player'. The most important characteristics of this role involve not being seen as standing out from the group through having strong convictions or distinctive characteristics. Jackall's study of large corporations in the 1980s leads him to conclude that the vocabulary of team play derived from the game of American football is invoked to discipline others into conforming and to cast suspicion on individuals who pose a threat. Similar dynamics can be read in the film *Boiler Room* (2000) where financial brokers use language based on gendered sporting metaphors, explaining that the job involves 'playing the numbers' and describing working for the organization as 'a contact sport' and they refer to successful brokers as 'top dogs'. Sporting metaphors fulfil a disciplinary purpose in *The Apartment* (1960), for instance when Bud Baxter is accused by his colleagues of not being a team player.

However, we may question the relevance of the linear model of career as a journey up the organizational hierarchy in an era where there is much greater emphasis on a more fluid identity project of 'boundaryless' career (Handy, 1994). Yet it can also be argued that individuals are still governed by certain social rules that proscribe what constitutes a career (Barley, 1989). Hence just as films must 'tell a story' about the life of a character, so employees have to construct a narrative about their organizational life that draws on certain established and socially agreed upon scripts in order to be accepted. The importance of career narratives can be read in *Time Out* (2001) where Vincent goes to extreme lengths not only to conceal the fact that he has been sacked from his job but also to construct an elaborate narrative involving the possibility of a promotion (see Film Focus 7.2). He constructs an ideal career narrative even though he knows it is not a genuine account of events. When eventually, due to the efforts of his father, he is interviewed by a prospective employer for another job, Vincent allows the interviewer to construct a narrative that explains the gap in his employment in a way that is acceptable. He knows that if he does not he risks being seen as socially unacceptable and hence is unlikely to get the job. However, he looks distant and uninterested in the narrative that is being constructed on his behalf.

Rewards and success

A further dynamic associated with the pursuit of success in film is that the central characters tend to be engaged in the pursuit of extrinsic rewards of status and money but then discover that intrinsic rewards, such as social recognition and self-actualisation Maslow (1943) are more important. This relates to what Mills (1951) describes as the rise of 'a literature of resignation' in the form of fictional tales which strive 'to control goals and ways of life by lowering the level of ambition' (1951, p. 282) and replacing the goal of external success with internal goals. Career ambitious, externally successful people are represented as 'obnoxious, guilt-ridden, ulcerated people of uneasy conscience' (1951, p. 282), their organizational success having been achieved at the expense of internal virtue and spiritual happiness. The 'literature of resignation' that Mills describes resolves the central tension created by the American Dream in setting up the desire for success, yet deals with the frustrations of those who fail to achieve their ambitions. For example, in *The Apartment* (1960), Bud Baxter's actions initially seem to suggest that a worker can progress more quickly through the corporate hierarchy through unethical behaviour (a puzzled colleague noting that he has been working in the organization for twice as long as Bud and not been promoted). However, by the end of the film it becomes clear that Bud is not fulfilled by this method of advancement. The message of the film is that achievement through hard, honest work is more satisfying (Denzin, 1990).

The organization is also represented as requiring total commitment. This is demonstrated by spending long hours at work, as a way of measuring a manager's loyalty, trustworthiness and performance (Kanter, 1977). Not only is marriage seen as precluding women from these roles but it also precludes men who are not willing to submit to these organizational demands. As Jackall (1988, p. 43) notes, in the 1980s, 'not everyone has or sustains a burning desire for getting ahead' in the large, bureaucratic corporation. They may be unwilling to sacrifice family life or free-time activities to put in the extraordinarily long hours at the office required in the upper circles of their organizations. For example, in *The Man in the Gray Flannel Suit* (1956) success in the corporate world is represented as entailing significant personal sacrifice (Film Focus 4.6).

Film characters signified as successful in business tend to be depicted as treating the organization as though it was their home. Their offices may be decorated and furnished like a living room or an apartment, having all the things necessary to be inhabited on a permanent basis, including a well-stocked bar and a change of clothes (Film Focus 4.3). More recent films such as *Working Girl* (1988) depict successful businessmen getting changed in their office, having no need to return home to perform such a task thanks to the provision of a regular supply of freshly laundered shirts. This message invokes the distinction introduced in Chapter 3 between the domains of working time bought by the organisation, as distinct from time which is owned by the individual. The use of signifiers of home in a workplace context can be read as signifying the erosion of boundaries between public and private lives, a theme which will be returned to in Chapter 5.

Film Focus 4.6: Reward and sacrifice in *The Man in the Gray Flannel Suit* (1956) and *Patterns* (1956)

The Man in the Gray Flannel Suit (1956) follows the fortunes of ex-soldier, husband and father Tom Rath who joins a large advertising corporation to earn more money so his family can afford a bigger house and better lifestyle. However, his actions come at some personal cost as he finds the hostile, political environment of his employing organization to be at odds with his family values. In an attempt to fit in and get ahead, Tom applies some of the principles he learned as a soldier, explaining to his wife 'I've got to protect myself, haven't I?' However, she doesn't agree, accusing him of turning into a cheap, slippery 'yes man'. In a later scene, Tom's boss, Hodges, urges him to spend time with his kids, saying 'Big successful businesses just aren't built by men like you, nine to five, and home and family, you live on 'em, but you never build one. Big successful businesses are built by men like me. You're everything they've got. You live it, body and soul. Lift it up regardless of anybody or anything else. Without men like me there wouldn't be any big successful businesses ... My mistake was in being one of those men.' The turning point for Tom Rath is when he is given the opportunity to accompany his boss on an important business trip. He declines in favour of spending the time with his family. This determines his position in the organization as a nine-to-five man, rather than a corporate climber. ☯ [**approximate running times: 1 hour 41–1 hour 46; 2 hours–2 hours 4; 2 hours 25–2 hours 28 mins.**]

In *Patterns* (1956) the effects of organizational commitment are powerfully represented through the character of vice president Bill Briggs who has been with the firm for over 40 years. The 62 year old Briggs, who suffers from a heart problem and a stomach ulcer, is unceremoniously pushed aside by president of the corporation, Walter Ramsey, in favour of younger executive who has recently joined the corporation, Fred Staples, whom Ramsey hopes will be more compliant in implementing his ruthless HR practices. Following the second boardroom confrontation, Briggs collapses and dies in hospital. Staples later confronts Ramsey about his treatment of Briggs, telling Ramsey that he 'hates his guts', Ramsey retorts 'I'm not a nice human being, what else?' to which Staples responds 'you drive your people to peak efficiency if they can make it. Or a grave if they can't.' ☯ [**approximate running time: 1 hour 2–1 hour 11; 1 hour 16–1 hour 22 mins.**]

The pursuit of success within these films is also based on 'micropolitical action' (Mangham, 1979). Modern organizations are inhabited by small groups of managers who are engaged in contests over who is to hold power acting in self interest in order to further their own careers (see Film Focus 4.7). In these white-collar workplaces,

FILM FOCUS 4.7: Motivation and micropolitics in *Executive Suite* (1954)

Mangham's view of organization as comprising coalitions of 'real flesh-and-blood managers' (1979, p. 96) interested in their own careers rather than the success or failure of the organization is represented in several corporate executive films of the 1950s. A key site of power struggles between managers is the boardroom where characters struggle to 'set the scene' by imposing their interpretation of the situation on other participants. In *Patterns* (1956) these power struggles take place in the conference room (see Plate 4.1 and Film Focus 4.6). In *Executive Suite* (1954) the members of the executive board of the Tredway Furniture Corporation must vote to elect a new company president following the sudden death of their former leader. The first part of the film traces the micropolitical tactics of board members as they prepare for the all important meeting where the new president will be elected. In this boardroom scene, the rational organizational purpose of protecting the stockholder interests is juxtaposed against the importance of motivating the workers, the latter perspective being articulated by young, energetic family man, Don Walling. Walling argues that corporate success is instead reliant on employees having a sense of pride in the product, dramatically emphasizing his point by taking a small table and demonstrating its poor workmanship by ripping off one of its legs. He declares 'business is people and when you help people to rise to their fullest, you make them fulfil themselves, you create more and better goods for more people, you make happiness!' His idealistic rhetoric is rewarded by board members who elect him president of the company. [**currently unavailable on DVD**]

'the stress is on agility, rather than ability, on "getting along" in a context of associates, superiors, and rules, rather than "getting ahead" across an open market' (Mills, 1951, p. 263). Commenting over thirty years later, Jackall (1988) challenges the notion that hard work, ability and dedicated service leads to success in the large, modern American corporation. He argues that bureaucratic work causes people to bracket their private moralities in favour of the organizational situation. Notions of fairness and equity are abandoned in favour of 'keeping one's eye on the main chance, maintaining and furthering one's own position and career' (Jackall, 1988, p. 202). Moreover, hierarchical authority, rather than being an abstract principle of organizational membership, is embodied in personal relationships, wherein the subordinate learns to accept subordination and protects their boss so as to allow their face to 'shine more brightly' (Jackall, 1988, p. 19) as a means of gaining rewards and advancement. The bureaucratic ethic erodes morality because rather than meaning being derived from the link between economic success and morality as measured by God, as under the Protestant ethic, it is derived purely from personal fate, as defined through the capriciousness of one's supervisors and the market.

Positioning the other: secretaries and wives

Organization man is also defined relationally through the oppositions between male corporate executives and female roles, predominantly secretaries and wives who are constituted as the other. Organization man is given greater definition through comparison with what he is not, through various markers of difference (O'Sullivan and Sheridan, 2005) which run through the text. For example, he is suggested to be heroic and ambitious because she is nurturing and supportive; he is dispassionate as she is emotional; he is grey and tall just as she is colourful and curvaceous. These binary differences provide the basis for a logocentric (Derrida, 1974) system of meaning in which organization man is discursively constructed as a superior sign through a process of opposition and deferral involving other signs in the overall sign system.

Mills (1951) wrote about the role of the 'white-collar girl' within the hierarchy of the large organization, typically a secretary or female clerk. While the organization man is signified by the gray flannel suit or trilby hat, the female white-collar worker is represented by a series of tightly defined signifiers such as the typewriter or the stenographer's pad. What is distinctive about these signifiers is that they are closely linked to the office workplace, to the extent that she is almost a part of the office, blending into the background as she is absorbed into its daily functions and routines. To illustrate, Mills quotes the editors of *Fortune* magazine.

> The male is the name on the door, the hat on the coat rack, and the smoke in the corner room. But the male is not the office. The office is the competent woman at the other end of his buzzer, the two young ladies chanting his name monotonously into the mouthpieces … the four girls in the class coop pecking out his initials with pink fingernails on the keyboards of four voluble machines, the half dozen assorted skirts whisking through the filing cases of his correspondence, and the elegant miss in the reception room recognizing his friends and disposing of his antipathies with the pleased voice and impersonal eye of a presidential consort. (Mills, 1951, p. 200)

Kanter's (1977) study of secretaries at a large corporation in the 1970s suggests that they did not have careers independent from their bosses. Instead the secretary-boss relationship is subject to 'patrimony' the personal preferences of the ruler. A secretary's formal rank was derived from that of her boss, if he got promoted, she followed. Kanter argues that women in organizations are judged not only by how they carry out their occupational role but also by how they live up to images of womanhood. Similarly, Jackall suggests:

> the corporation stimulates the natural impulses of the erotic sphere through its gathering together of an abundance of attractive and energetic men and women and through its continual symbolic celebration of vitality, power and success. At the same time, the managerial ethic of self-control imposes solemn rules for self-abnegation, at least in public. (Jackall, 1988, p. 48)

Pringle (1988) argues that secretaries are defined and identified as a gendered category – they are assumed to be women, and relationally – the meaning of their role being derived from the other category, bosses, to which their work relates, the relationship between boss and secretary being 'the most sexualized of all workplace relationships' (Pringle, 1989, p. 158). Based on an interview study of office workers she argues that these ideas reflect cultural understandings of secretaries as representing everything that bosses are not. This helps to explain the general vagueness that surrounds the nature of secretarial work, what it involves, the status of those who undertake it and the difficulties encountered by women who defy these normative conventions, for example by trying to become a boss. The vagueness surrounding what a secretary *does* means that, unlike most other occupations, the secretary is represented in film in a way which draws attention to what she *is*. Images of secretaries thus emphasize the sexual nature of the role.

Pringle (1988) identifies three competing historical discourses surrounding understandings of what a secretary is that have sometimes coexisted and at other times been in competition with each other. The first is the 'office wife', a middle-class, serious secretarial figure who is deferential and loyal to her boss. The second is the 'sexy secretary' who is working-class, portrayed as a potentially disruptive presence in the workplace and caricatured as the 'mindless Dolly bird' who has no interest in serious work at all; this discourse became dominant in the 1950s and '60s. The third discourse arises from the previous two and relates to the 'career woman' who resists sexual and familial definitions and plays down the special relationship between boss and secretary, instead emphasizing the skill and experience associated with her role. This discourse, which has become more dominant since the 1970s, is associated with the emergence of the 'office manager' (see Film Focus 4.8).

FILM FOCUS 4.8: Competing discourses of secretarial work in *How to Succeed in Business without Really Trying* (1967)

Competing discourses of secretarial work can be read in the film *How to Succeed in Business without Really Trying* (1967). Secretaries are represented

---

as objects of sexual desire, the film showing them sitting at their desks in the typing pool painting their fingernails or preening their elaborate hairstyles, in contrast to the asexual representation of their male bosses. These representations reinforce the notion that they do little work and their interests and priorities lie outside work, hence they are not 'real' workers (Pringle 1988). Additionally, the discourse of the 'office wife' can be identified in the song 'A Secretary is not a Toy' where the secretaries acting in a ladylike manner chastize their male co-workers for treating them as sex objects, singing 'gentlemen, gentlemen, a secretary is not a toy, no, my boy, not a toy, to fondle and dandle and playfully handle, in search of some puerile joy'. Relationships in the film are based on bosses and secretaries operating in pairs, each secretary working for and relating to one boss at a time. For instance, Rosemary is an intelligent and serious woman who becomes Ponty's girlfriend, then secretary and then his wife. She is a typical 'office wife', loving, honouring and obeying her boss, being trustworthy, loyal and devoted in her task of mediating his relations with the rest of the organization. The 'sexy secretary' is represented by the character of Hetty, a former cinema cigarette girl who is given a job as a secretary through the patronage of the company president. Hetty is represented as a 'mindless Dolly bird', a dangerously seductive and disruptive presence in the workplace, having a potentially negative influence on the career of her boss and displaying no interest, skill or ability related to her job. The absence of the 'career woman' may be related to the historical period in which this film and the musical on which it was based, were made, when this discourse was still relatively underdeveloped. ☺ [approximate running time: 28.20–36 mins.]

The 1950s also began to give rise to representations of 'girls in gray flannel suits' (Davis, 2006), in films such as *Desk Set* (1957), this reflecting the dramatic increase in women's participation in the labour force and the emergence of a growing number of middle-class, university educated women who, increasingly frustrated by the domestic ideal assigned to them, wanted to build careers rather than just get a job, and to be able to keep it after they married. Yet their employment options remained significantly constrained by the narrow range of working roles available to them, encompassing clerical, nursing and service work. Such characters are represented in film of the decade as incomplete despite their career success, either looking for a man, or unconscious of their lack, only made happy when they were paired with a man.

These representations were the focus of popular feminist writer Betty Friedan (1963), whose account of the 'problem with no name' sought to identify the basis of the mystique that promoted domestic femininity and constrained women's position in American society at a time when women were highly educated yet choosing to marry at a younger age and take on the role of the housewife. Using women's magazines and advertising from the late 1930s to the 1960s, Friedan argues that the image of the happy housewife in popular culture constrains women's choices in favour of domestic fulfilment rather than paid employment. Within these texts she identifies a shift in the 1950s away from love stories involving career women as independent, confident and adventurous, towards narratives which suggest femininity and happiness relies on not becoming an aggressive career woman who, through prioritising career over marriage, ultimately chooses celibacy and loneliness. Although Friedman's argument implies that female audiences are socialized into accepting these false images and that this is what prevents them from becoming full participants in organizations (an assumption that will be critiqued further in Chapter 6) her analysis provides valuable insights into how working women are constructed as the other in popular culture.

In addition to female clerical workers, secretaries and career women, Kanter (1977) suggests another category of women whose lives were bound to the corporation – the wives of men employed by the organization (see Film Focus 4.9). In her 1970s study of the 'Indsco Corporation' she argues that wives, though they do not enter the door of the organization, play a powerful role behind the scenes furthering the careers of their husbands. Through social events outside the business boundaries, such as dinner parties, the company plays a role in these women's lives, influencing how they spent their time and their relationships with their husbands. As one woman explained 'If Fred was doing well, I felt *I* was doing well. I'm the woman behind the man, I could take some pride in his achievements' (Kanter, 1977, p. 105). Rejecting the label of corporate wife as victim, 'swallowed up by a greedy organization' (Kanter, 1977, p. 111), Kanter argues that the corporate wife's career comprises three phases, the technical phase, the managerial phase and the institutional phase. The principal dilemma faced by wives during the technical phase of their husbands' careers, when the main challenge for husbands is whether they can carry out the technical requirements of their jobs, is exclusion/inclusion; should they seek involvement in their husband's job, or pursue interests and activities independent of it? As the husband moves higher up the managerial ladder the challenge for wives involves 'charting a course between instrumentality and sentimentality' (Kanter, 1977, p. 116). Wives must tread a path between acting politically within the corporate social network to further their husbands' careers and acting authentically, which could reduce the possibility of forming genuine friendships and lead to loneliness. Through their handling of this managerial phase, wives could have significant influence on their husband's careers, influencing the chances of them reaching higher levels within the corporation when the wife enters the institutional phase, becoming a public figure whose behaviour is judged alongside that of her husband.

FILM FOCUS 4.9: Representing wives in *Patterns* (1956) and *Woman's World* (1954)

These films highlight the role of wives in supporting the careers of their husbands. In *Woman's World* (1954) three company executives who work in the auto industry are short listed for the position of general manager. It is the view of their boss that an executive's wife is of crucial importance to his success and so he brings the three men to New York with their wives to observe their behaviour. The message of the film clearly positions the wives as subordinate to their organization men, not least through the film's tagline, 'It's a woman's world ... because men are in it!' The behaviour of the three women and the outcome of the selection process confirm the dangers of having a wife who is overambitious and insufficiently nurturing, through the character of the childless wife Carol who is prepared to seduce other men in order to further her husband's career. She is ultimately punished for her actions by losing both her husband and the possibility of being the wife of a wealthy New York executive. **[currently unavailable on DVD]**

The perils of an overly ambitious wife are also represented in *Patterns* (1956) when Fred Staples hosts a social event at his home to which he invites his new boss, Ramsey. Unknown to Staples, Ramsey engages his wife in conversation about her husband's career. Anxious to enhance her husband's success and ensure he gets the recognition he deserves, she gives Ramsey a copy of the report her husband has been working on with a colleague named Briggs, little knowing that Ramsey intends to use this as a means of getting rid of Briggs. When Fred discovers that his wife has been seeking to support his career in this way he is extremely angry, accusing her of misrepresenting him in his relationship with his colleagues but she retorts that his greater contribution to the report should be recognised. To which he declares that he doesn't want to step on another human being to get into the next capital gains bracket. ☉ **[approximate running time: 38–50 mins.]**

Conclusion

Although organizational life has undoubtedly changed since the period represented by the majority of the films reviewed in this chapter these characters and conventions continue to have an impact on understandings of managerial work in large, modern organizations. Through their signification of glamour and excitement, echoes of which continue to be found in many more recent films, they convey a message of desire in relation to the possibility of building a successful career as a professional manager within a specific type of organization. However, what is contained inside or included within the representation of organization man relies to an extent on what is left outside or excluded. The organizations inhabited by organization man are nearly always located in a major American or international city, (typically though not exclusively New York), thereby signifying organizations located in non-urban, non-Western contexts as less desirable. They also tend to be highly successful profit-making enterprises which display their substantial financial wealth somewhat ostentatiously, often having a global reach which extends far beyond their spatial location, thereby excluding smaller, public sector or not-for-profit organizations. Furthermore, the organizations and characters depicted in these films are typically not directly involved in any form of manufacturing or productive labour, thereby physically and conceptually separating professional managerial work from its opposite in the form of labour. In seeking to understand the message of desire that these films represent in relation to managerial work these other possibilities of organization are suppressed and hidden.

The approach adopted here has sought to emphasize that the meaning of these texts is located in historical and cultural contexts which change over time. Evidence of the indeterminate nature of organization man can be read in more recent film texts which involve the redefinition of certain key signifiers that point towards the changing meaning of the sign. For example, *Trading Places* (1983) and *The Pursuit of Happyness* (2006) revisit many of the same themes of the American Dream and managerial career success in the large male-dominated organization using many of the same signifiers, including dark suits, elevators and tall, modern buildings, established in earlier films. While organization man continues to be positioned as the heroic figure within this narrative, there are also some important differences in the way the central subject is represented, one of the most significant being the absence of organization man's 'whiteness' which, according to Creadick (2006), was so much a part of the definition of this subject in the 1950s it was barely acknowledged. Similarly, films such as *Working Girl* (1988) and *The Devil Wears Prada* (2006) reconstruct the gendered nature of the central subject. However, while the character of organization woman in these films is signified in many of the same ways as her male predecessor, see Chapter 6, the overall effect of the representation is somewhat different.

While the subject of the narrative in these films has been redefined in ways which reflect an increased cultural sensitivity, the meaning of the subject and the context of its representation has remained relatively static since the 1950s. Any changes that have arisen are less significant than they at first seem, since they can be understood as entailing the incorporation of aspects of otherness into the category of organization man, rather than a reformulation of it. Furthermore, while some space is left within the narrative for opposition to these dominant discourses, for example through construction of characters who do not conform to the codes of organization man or otherwise contravene the norms of the organization, this provides only a temporary diversion. Even if the central character ultimately decides to leave the organization, such as in *The Man in the Gray Flannel Suit* (1956), *Baby Boom* (1987) or *The Devil Wears Prada* (2006), it is only after they have proven their ability to become a successful organizational member. These representations thus confirm the desirability of certain membership roles and the undesirability of others within a highly specific location.

Plate 5 Office co-workers smash the fax machine to pieces with a baseball bat in *Office Space* (1998)

Deconstructing the worker

Introduction

The category of 'organization man' presented in the previous chapter comprises a set of clearly defined characteristics that together constitute an ideal type or an 'anagram of the real' (Brunette and Wills, 1989). This ideal type celebrates the corporate managerial values of conformity, hierarchy, bureaucracy, loyalty and authority – values associated with the membership of large organizations in the decades between 1930 and 1960. This chapter will argue that changes in the discourses surrounding management in the 1980s and 1990s gave rise to a reconstructed vision of organizational membership based on a critique of the values associated with organization man as dehumanizing, alienating and fundamentally repressive (Boltanski and Chiapello, 2005) (see Film Focus 5.1 for an example). Many of the films in this chapter are indicative of these changes, in seeking to deconstruct the image of the visible hand of management depicted by Chandler (1977) as comprising an elite group of respected professionals who orchestrate the productive activities of the organization.

A significant aspect of this critique entails drawing attention to those on the receiving end of management – the workers, who constitute the target of managerial initiatives and are subject to its changing priorities, including those which ultimately involve their exclusion from the organization, for example through redundancy in *Office Space* (1998), *Human Resources* (1999) and *American Beauty* (1999), organizational closure in *The Full Monty* (1997) and *Brassed Off* (1996), or being fired in *Norma Rae* (1979) and *Philadelphia* (1993). They thereby depict the alienation associated with organized work and the various strategies of resistance adopted by employees in the face of corporate management. These representations also seek to portray the human effects associated with transition from industrial to post-industrial, and modern to postmodern forms of organization as a difficult process that threatens what it means to be a worker in late capitalism, see for example *Human Resources* (1999) and *Startup.Com* (2001). Central to this portrayal is the representation of the loss of masculine work identities associated with traditional or 'standard' employment and a critique of the flexibilization and feminization of labour. Such depictions of loss are reliant on romantic representation of the heroic worker in the context of industrial organization in films such as *Norma Rae* (1979) and *Bread and Roses* (2000). They are also reflective of a perceived shift from collectivism to individualism in employee relations as depicted in films like *I'm Alright Jack* (1959) and *Saturday Night and Sunday Morning* (1960).

The films in this chapter focus on the way that managerial discourses have reconstructed the self-identities of working people by invoking an alternative set of values to those associated with organization man. The values of individualism, autonomy, self-actualization and self-development form the basis for this new 'spirit of capitalism', as Boltanski and Chiapello (2005) describe it. This constitutes the basis for many of the narratives in this chapter, particularly in films of the 1980s such as *Trading Places* (1983), *Wall Street* (1987), *Working Girl* (1988) and *Dealers* (1989) which celebrate the qualities of individual enterprise and business initiative (Williamson, 1991). However, more recent films like *Fight Club* (1999) reveal increased scepticism towards the discourses that underpin these changes in the organization of contemporary work. This chapter explores the contradictions and tensions entailed in representing the self-identity of the postmodern worker.

This chapter will also explore the role of humour in enabling the representation of corporate managerialism and the characters associated with it as objects of derision and a source of comedy. Many films represent organizations as contexts in which opportunities arise for workers to engage in humour. Indeed it is comparatively rare for a film not to present organization in a way that does not somehow parody its practices, often by representing workers as knowing subjects who are the only ones able to see the ridiculous nature of management. The question thus arises as to whether these representations act as a safety-valve for audiences, providing an outlet for tensions and diffusing conflict without necessarily challenging the organizational power structures that prompted them, or whether they act as a medium for communicating more serious messages of resistance, including cynicism, alienation and disenchantment in a way which has the potential to impact on everyday workplace practices.

FILM FOCUS 5.1: Organization man becomes the enemy in *The Matrix Revolutions* (2003)

The extent to which organization man has become the target of negative representations in film can be read from texts which use signifiers of the white male in a dark suit to signify the enemy. Whereas earlier films such as *Men in Black* (1997) used these signifiers to indicate heroism, in the Matrix trilogy the suit signifies the enemy, in the form of a computer system. In *The Matrix*

Revolutions (2003) the few remaining humans must battle against a vast army of duplicates of Agent Smith. 'Row upon row of white men in suits, all with the same face, stand shoulder-to-shoulder in countless office buildings, menacing in their ties and tastefully polished leather shoes. One is reminded simultaneously of a military dictatorship and a huge business conference' (Newitz, 2006, p. 178). No longer is it the dirty machines of industry with their cogs and chimneys which are presented as a threat to humanity but the organization man who constitutes part of a worldwide, disembodied technological computerized system 'whose "logic" is sensed in the process of programming our outer and inner worlds, even to the point of colonizing our former "unconscious"' (Jameson, 1992, p. 84).

The heroic industrial worker

In many films, including *Metropolis* (1927) and *Modern Times* (1936) as well as more recent texts, the culture of manufacturing industry is represented as a harsh, aggressive, masculine environment in which manual work is portrayed as distinct from mental work and has its own worth based on a 'cult of toughness' (Roper, 1994). These texts tend to project an image of the industrial worker as a physically powerful figure whose commonsense and practical experience provides him with the resources that equip him for his daily confrontations with the machinery of production and his encounters with management and unions. In films such as *Norma Rae* (1979) and *Bread and Roses* (2000) workplaces are characterized by a culture of 'us and them' (Collinson, 1992) communicated through gestures, movements and expressions as well as verbal interaction between workers and managers, these latter two films presenting the actions of workers heroically in their struggle against oppressive, exploitative management (see Film Focus 5.2). In other films such as *Blue Collar* (1978), *I'm Alright Jack* (1959), *The Angry Silence* (1960) and *Hoffa* (1992) unionization is portrayed more ambiguously, as a political force that provides a parallel to management in threatening to undermine the efforts of the heroic worker (see also Film Focus 3.5).

FILM FOCUS 5.2: A culture of 'us and them' in *Blue Collar* (1978) and *Bread and Roses* (2000)

The three Detroit auto plant workers in *Blue Collar* (1978) are caught between the demands of a corrupt union which fails to represent them effectively

Continued

and the racial harassment and poor working conditions imposed by management. Industrial relations in this context is summed up by one of them as a situation in which 'they pit the lifers against the new boys, the young against the old, the black against the white – everything they do is to keep us in our place'. Facing financial pressures and feeling the injustice of their situation they come up with a plan to rob the local union branch. However, rather than finding money in the safe, they find a notebook detailing the union's illegal money-lending practices. When they try to blackmail the union into giving them money in exchange for keeping quiet about the notebook, the stakes are raised further and one of them gets killed in an industrial 'accident'. ☾ [**approximate running time: 1 hour–1 hour 5 mins.**]

Bread and Roses (2000) is set in the context of service rather than manufacturing work. It is based on the 'Janitors for Justice' campaign for fair working conditions and focuses on events in Los Angeles in 1990 when workers staged a strike in protest against the routine exploitation of unskilled immigrant workers hired by the cleaning contract companies used by major corporations. The strategy of the union organizers involves helping the workers to assert their employment rights while also confronting the building occupiers, including those prestigious banking and legal firms which have sought to disassociate themselves from the dubious employment practices of their cleaning contractors whilst also driving down their prices. ☾ [**approximate running times: 15–19.50; 54.30–56.20 mins.**]

Representations of the heroic worker suggest an instrumental engagement with work based on its clear separation from other, more meaningful domains of social experience. This characterization is particularly evident in *Saturday Night and Sunday Morning* (1960) where the hero, Arthur Seaton, is portrayed as viewing his labour purely instrumentally, as a means of economic subsistence and as a means to an end, experiencing it as a constraint on his freedom to pursue other more enjoyable activities. In this respect, Arthur is suggested to be similar to the UK truck manufacturing workers studied by Collinson (1992) for whom 'the obligatory eight hours of "daily slog" conjures up images of sacrifice, imprisonment and boring routine', paid work being an activity which is 'undertaken with reluctant acceptance' (Collinson, 1992, p. 4). This characterization further relies on representation of the strategy of 'resistance through distance' which involves avoidance, withdrawal and instrumentalism (Collinson, 1994) as tactics which subordinates use to try to escape or avoid the demands of authority by distancing themselves either physically or symbolically from the organization (see Film Focus 5.3). However, as the conclusion to the film

Saturday Night and Sunday Morning makes explicit, the strategy of 'resistance through distance', as Collinson (1994) notes, is only partial since it involves the exercise of limited discretion around the edges of a formally commodified position. It therefore only offers a short-term escape from reality which effectively endorses managerial power rather than challenges it.

Arthur's attitude also reflects an ethos of individualism, implying that workers have become less collectivist in their orientation towards paid employment (see Film Focus 5.3). This appears to fit with the view of writers like Storey (1992) who assert that employment relations in Britain have in recent decades drifted away from a collectivist orientation towards more individualistic employer-led initiatives. Arthur Seaton appears as a forebear of such changes, expressing his rejection of employee-led collectivism combined with a deep mistrust of paternalistic management. He thus represents the archetype of the self-interested worker.

Saturday Night and Sunday Morning (1960) also draws attention to the potentially subversive effect of humour (see Film Focus 5.3). Collinson (2002) suggests that even though humour might not always be consistently directed towards management, it is often far from manageable or supportive of it. He further argues that humour has the potential to be subversive by keeping dissent alive and providing an alternative evaluation of official, managerial action (Collinson, 2002). Furthermore, within organizations it is often one of the safest ways of expressing an alternative point of view. The attempts of Arthur's supervisor to manage humour through practices of suppression are supportive of Collinson's argument that those in power are concerned with ensuring that humour is stopped. The example given by Collinson (2002) is of the Ford Motor company in the 1930s and 1940s where laughter was viewed as a disciplinary offence, this included humming, whistling, and even smiling. Such control also serves to reinforce the division between the domains of work where humour is not permitted and non-work where it is.

FILM FOCUS 5.3: Industrial labour and 'resistance through distance' in *Saturday Night and Sunday Morning* (1960)

This film is part of the tradition of British social realism (1959–1963), led by a group of socially committed film directors who wanted to produce populist cinema that would reconnect with the traditional working class, rather than provide escapist fantasies for audiences. The films tended to depict working class activities as heroic. *Saturday Night and Sunday Morning* (1960), based on a book by Alan Sillitoe achieved unexpected box office success attributed to audience identification with the main character, Arthur Seaton, who embodied and reflected social change in British society. Set in the streets and factories of

Continued

the industrial town of Nottingham. Arthur spends his days at a factory bench, his evenings in local pubs and with his girlfriend Brenda (wife of a fellow factory worker). In the first scene we see the young Arthur Seaton travelling on his way to work. Arthur is scathing of his older male colleagues at the factory whom he regards as pathetically unchallenging of the labour process. Speaking to the camera, he urges the audience 'don't let the bastards grind you down' 'What I'm out for is a good time, all the rest is propaganda'. In the second scene Arthur is on the banks of a river on a Sunday afternoon, fishing with a friend. Their conversation turns to marriage. Arthur complains that it costs too much to get married, 'a lump sum down and your wages a week for life … I work for the factory, the income tax and the insurance already … they rob you right left and centre.' To which his friend replies, 'that's how things are Arthur … all you can do is go on working and hope that summat good'll turn up'. 'Maybe' replies Arthur 'but you've got to be as cunning as them bastards' … The scene ends with Arthur saying 'work tomorrow', and the friend replies 'aye, me an' all'. From this we read that Arthur views his job as nothing more than a means of economic subsistence which he believes he has little power to change. His employment is characterized by oppositional relations between workers and management as 'us and them'. This causes him to resist managerial attempts to impose workplace discipline by adopting a strategy of 'resistance through distance' in the form of joking and horseplay. This is illustrated in the scene that immediately follows where we see Arthur back at work again on Monday, playing a practical joke which entails placing a dead rat in the workstation of a female co-worker. The foreman's response to this act is illustrative of the perceived threat to managerial authority that is entailed by such a gesture.

☙ [**approximate running times: 0–5; 19.44–27 mins.**]

Similar to the industrial workers in Beynon's (1975) study of the Ford car manufacturing plant in the 1960s who 'knew what they would be doing each week, when they would begin and end work, which people they would see at work and roughly how much they would be earning' (Bradley et al., 2000, p. 52), workers depicted in films like *Saturday Night and Sunday Morning* (1960) and *Gung Ho* (1986) are represented as experiencing a high degree of predictability associated with their employment. While the existence of standard employment has been revealed to be the exception rather than the rule, only ever being enjoyed by a privileged minority of typically white, male, skilled workers for three decades between 1945 and 1975 (Pahl, 1984), this provides the basis for a highly specific representation of the heroic industrial worker in film based on a post-war certainty about the nature of work as involving full-time, waged employment for men and a long-term commitment to one organization (McDowell, 1997).

The enterprising post-industrial worker

In recent decades, however, representations of stable, predictable industrial work have given way to alternatives that reflect the shift in advanced industrial nations in the late twentieth century away from labour-intensive manufacturing contexts towards service work, and from production to consumption (see Film Focus 5.4). These changes are associated with the concept of post-industrial society wherein the industrial era concerned with controlling labour and the mass production of goods gave way to a post-industrial era comprised of organizations which are concerned with the creation of knowledge and use of information. Evidence of the shift from production of goods to knowledge can even be found in the filming location used for *Saturday Night and Sunday Morning* (1960), the workplace scenes which were shot in the Nottingham Raleigh bicycle factory are now the site of Nottingham business school (where some readers of this book may even be studying). Post-industrial organization also implies abandonment of the large, rigid, hierarchical organizational structure associated with modernism in favour of a more fluid and flexible structure that is more responsive to the rapidly changing needs of consumers.

FILM FOCUS 5.4: The shift from production to consumption in *Roger and Me* (1989)

Roger and Me (1989) is a Michael Moore documentary that traces events following the closure of the General Motors plant in the town of Flint Michigan as the loss of manufacturing jobs earns the town the dubious award of becoming the unemployment capital of the country. In this scene, local government officials try to promote the attractions of the town which include a luxury hotel, a shopping mall and Auto World, a Heritage centre dedicated to commemorating Flint's industrial history, thereby hoping to turn it into a tourist attraction with the aim of generating jobs based on the consumption of services rather than the mass production of goods. However, the narrative concludes that the hotel, pavilion and heritage centre all fail after only six months, since 'tourists don't seem to want to visit Flint'. ☉ [**approximate running time: 59–1 hour 7.40 mins.**]

Films that trace the shift to post-industrial work often focus on the reconstruction of self-identity that such societal transitions can be seen as having precipitated. Films like *The Full Monty* (1997), *Brassed Off* (1996) and *Mondays in the Sun* (2002) narrate the decline of traditional working class male manufacturing work in advanced industrial nations such as Britain and Spain. These transitions are suggested to be multiple and complex, encompassing the decline of life time employment for a single employer in a fixed geographical location and its replacement by forms of work that are more flexible, feminized and based on knowledge, service and consumption. The self-identity of workers is shown to be fundamentally challenged by these changes, their heroic identities undermined by the decline of industrial organization, particularly in traditionally masculine heavy industries like ship building and coal mining (see Film Focus 5.5). The significance of this loss is represented relationally its meaning dependent on the establishment of oppositions which provide the conditions of possibility within which the identity of the heroic, male worker exists. However, as Bradley et al. (2000) argue the 'female takeover', comprising the feminization of the labour force, the proportion of employed women increasing in comparison to men, and the feminization of work, whereby the nature of jobs changes in a way which makes women more suited to them than men, is overstated. 'The feminization of the labour force does not mean an end to the distinction between "men's work" and "women's work" since cultures of work organizations continue to be deeply gendered in ways that persistently disadvantage women' (Bradley et al., 2000, pp. 82–91).

FILM FOCUS 5.5: Deindustrialization and loss in *The Full Monty* (1997), *Brassed Off* (1996) and *Mondays in the Sun* (2002)

The Full Monty (1997) and *Brassed Off* (1996) represent the loss of masculine identity as a result of deindustrialization in Britain. They represent work as an important source of working-class male identity and lack of employment as invoking painful and powerful feelings of loss. The deserted unused space of the steel factory in *The Full Monty* 'mirrors the dilapidated masculinities of the men: now they must steal steel rather than produce it' (Farrell, 2003, p. 120). The men's efforts to find work are represented as futile and the power relations between men and women are reversed as the women who are more able to obtain paid employment in the new service economy have money to spend on entertainment through the objectification of male bodies. Hence the feelings of redundancy experienced by these workers are not confined to their paid employment, one of them noting that 'a few years and men won't exist, except in a zoo or summat. I mean we're not needed no more, obsolete, dinosaurs, yesterday's news'.

Westwood (2003) observes the tendency in the United Kingdom to mourn the passing of traditional manufacturing jobs while viewing new forms of employment in the service sector with distain. This can be read in *The Full Monty* in the scene where Dave takes a job as a security guard for the supermarket chain ASDA. The job of the security guard (of which there are two in the film, guarding the abandoned steel factory and guarding the supermarket) 'indicates the relative security or safety of the traditional male occupation' (Farrell, 2003, p. 124). When Gaz visits Dave in the store where he is working he follows him into the suit section, takess a suit off the nearest hanger and heads for the door at speed, saying 'well come on then Mr Security do your job!' Dave pleads with Gaz not to steal the suit, to which he retorts 'you've got a job, do it!' As they run through the doors out of the store the alarms go off but rather than stopping Gaz's theft, Dave runs out with him, rejoining the striptease act that the men have been practising. Westwood reads from this that 'working at ASDA seems not only to have less value than the traditional steelworking jobs formerly undertaken by these men, but also less value than stealing or stripping' (Westwood 2003, p. 5). ✆ [**approximate running times: 9.40–11.45; 58.20–1 hour 1.50 mins.**]

Mondays in the Sun (2002) also explores the decline of industrial manufacturing. The film is set in the Spanish city of Vigo, following the closure of the local shipyard through characters such as Lino, who dyes his hair to try to make himself look younger in an effort to increase his chances of getting another job, and Amador who has become an alcoholic living alone in a squalid apartment since his wife left him. While *Brassed Off* and *Mondays in the Sun* are fundamentally pessimistic films about the end of a particular masculine working class identity, *The Full Monty* can be read as encoding a more optimistic message about the development of new masculine identities in post-industrial society (Gibson-Graham, 2001).

Du Gay (1996) argues that these changes in the organization of the global economy have problematized the patriarchal hierarchies through which the fixed, stable, identity of the modern worker was established. Consequently, he argues, there is little doubt that 'what it means to be a worker is no longer as certain as it once was' because of technological and structural changes within the global economy which have undermined the predominance of manufacturing industries in Western societies, calling into question their image as an 'engine of growth' and provider of 'real jobs' (Du Gay 1996, p. 3) (see Film Focus 5.6 for an example). These changes in the nature of employment involving the breakdown of traditional hierarchies are suggested to have enabled and encouraged working people towards greater self-definition of identity. In this context of rising individualism and social mobility, high priority is placed on achieving self-realisation. Gone are the rigid and predictable social structures and processes upon which work identity was founded, instead the post-industrial worker must construct a self-identity based on 'shifting and non-absolute foundations' (Bendle, 2002, p. 6).

FILM FOCUS 5.6: The shift from industrial to knowledge work in *Human Resources* (1999)

In the film *Human Resources* (1999) the relationship between father and son provides a device for representing the changes in the identity of the worker and the shift from production to knowledge work. When Franck returns from business school in Paris to his provincial home-town he takes up a placement as a management trainee in the HR (Human Resources) department of the steel factory where his father has worked on the shopfloor for 30 years. While admired by his family for his academic success, Franck is shunned by former school friends, many of whom are manual workers at the factory. On his first day, Franck sees his father working his machine on the shopfloor and is introduced to some of his co-workers before being taken upstairs to the offices. His brief within the HR department is to assist in the implementation of the 35-hour week and help to manage relations between unions and management. However, Franck's suggestions are simply used as a distraction by management who, Franck discovers, intend to make 12 employees redundant as part of the reorganization of working time, despite having made assurances to the union that an agreement will not result in job losses. Franck's position places increasing strain upon his relationship with his father whose approach to work is quite different from Franck's. In a scene following an argument with his parents, Franck meets a worker from the factory in a bar. The worker explains his motivation to work and his relationship with Franck's father, Jean-Claude as fellow worker and role model. In a later scene Franck, who eventually quits his management job and joins the union-organized protest at the job losses, challenges his father's unwillingness to take a stand against management. ☻ [**approximate running times: 5–12.20; 56.30–59.20; 1 hour 29.10–34.30 mins.**] The relationship between father and son provides insight into the impact of the shift from industrial to post-industrial work and the impact that this has on the self-identities of working people.

Film represents post-industrial work also as a project of enterprise. The 'entrepreneur of the self' is a construct used by Du Gay (1996) to suggest that no matter what the circumstances, individuals are continuously engaged in shaping their life by being an enterprising consumer with needs, desires and preferences which the market must satisfy. They are 'driven by the desire to optimize the worth of his or her own existence' (Du Gay, 1996, p. 181) towards taking absolute responsibility for their own self-optimisation and become 'entrepreneurs' of their own lives. Du Gay traces the changes in discursive formations used to construct and maintain identity from the modernist, bureaucratic and permanent to the postmodern, fluid and temporary. He charts the rise of the entrepreneur of the self that has arisen since the 1980s from the discourse of 'excellence' which positions the employee as a highly individualistic, self-determining individual who is in charge of his or her own destiny and in search of fulfilment through their work. The entrepreneurial employee is self-governing according to certain rules of conduct that comprise energy, initiative, calculation, self-reliance and personal responsibility. This discourse of entrepreneurialism promotes a vision of the ideal employee as someone whose behaviour reflects the values of quality, efficiency, competition and performance rather than loyalty to a particular social group or an organization.

The discourse of enterprise can be identified in films of the late 1980s and early 1990s such as *Wall Street* (1987) and *Other People's Money* (1991) which celebrate individual self-gratification as the basis for economic success (see also Film Focus 3.1). Williamson (1991) suggests these films represent the capacity for entrepreneurialism as an innate, commonsensical property possessed by those who come from outside the system. For example, the street-hustler and beggar, Willie-Ray Valentine in *Trading Places* (1983), the working class secretary from the Bronx in *Working Girl* (1988) or the child who finds himself in an adult body and gets a job in a toy company in *Big* (1988). What is more, they imply that the process of building an entrepreneurial identity does not just commence at the point an individual joins a work organization. For example, *Baby Boom* (1987) represents the construction of entrepreneurial identity as a process that commences even before the individual is born. In one scene a group of mothers sitting in a play park coordinate their children's diaries. Pre-school children have 'resumés' and references just like a prospective employee to get them into the right educational institutions. Such narratives serve to locate everyone whether employees or not within a discourse of cultural excellence in the context of the enterprising organization. In addition to celebrating the enterprising post-industrial worker Williamson (1991) argues that many of these films also dramatize the social indignation associated with moral corruption in business. Films such as *Wall Street* (1987) and *Rogue Trader* (2000) can be read as reflecting concerns about the new opportunities for business deviance created by deregulation of markets and a renewed belief in the need to ensure their effective, legal functioning (Stein, 2000).

Films representing the post-industrial worker often seek to locate this discursive category in the context of an organizational culture that shapes the employee's identity and experience and exerts a powerful influence on their values and actions. To this end, the narratives often trace the process whereby the individual is socialized into becoming a member of the organization, made aware of the stories and legends that define its values and disciplined into behaving in ways that conform to its norms through rites and rituals. The importance of culture stems from the shift from coercive to normative control (Etzioni, 1961) associated with the rise of knowledge-intensive companies that rely on the attitude and commitment of their employees rather than their instrumental compliance within the mechanistic, disenchanted, modern, bureaucratic system described in Chapter 3. Film tends to represent the dark side of organizational culture as 'a subtle and frequently penetrating form of power' which counteracts 'questioning and independent thinking' (Alvesson, 2002, p. 118) by forcing individuals to subordinate themselves to the organization's norms, values and social patterns (see for example Film Focus 5.7).

Representations of organizational culture in film appear to reinforce studies like Kunda's (1992) ethnographic analysis of an American high-technology firm, in which he argues that management uses normative control to create a strong organizational culture based on values such as informality and trust. Kunda explores the way in which this culture is managed through rituals such as ceremonial dinners and training programmes and artifacts, like annual reports, used to tell employees about the culture and ensure their commitment to its goals. Through the construction of an organizational identity or 'self', this anti-bureaucratic culture is internalized to the extent that management does not have to discipline workers into fitting in with it because they enforce it upon themselves. Casey (1995) explores similar issues in her study of the large American Hephaestus Corporation, as an example of a post-industrial organization which has constructed a 'designer culture' based on discourses of 'team work' and 'corporate family' to promote an ideal character type of the post-industrial worker that embodies a new form of individualism and rejects collectivist affiliations. The purpose of organizational culture for Casey, is as a mechanism for controlling employees by shaping their identities in ways that involve emulation of this ideal. Willmott (1993) argues that a parallel can be drawn between 'corporate culturalism' and the disciplinary techniques described by George Orwell in 1949 in his fictitious futuristic portrayal of Oceania in *Nineteen Eighty-Four*. Willmott (1993, p. 517) argues that corporate culturalism promotes employee commitment to 'a monolithic structure of feeling and thought' which is inherently ideological and totalitarian. As in the Orwellian world of *Nineteen-Eighty Four*, corporate culturalism relies on 'doublethink', which acts as a mechanism for controlling workers by suggesting that corporate culture provides them with stability, a sense of belonging and security whilst simultaneously offering them the promise of autonomy and freedom.

FILM FOCUS 5.7: Socialization and corporate culture in *Fear and Trembling* (2003) and *Gung Ho* (1986)

Both of these films depict the clash between Japanese and Western corporate cultures. *Fear and Trembling* (2003) tells the story of a Japanese-born Belgian woman, Amélie who gets a job as an interpreter in a large Japanese corporation. Her acculturation into the organization involves all kinds of menial tasks, including making the coffee, changing the dates on desk calendars, delivering post and photocopying the rules of the golf club for her boss over and over again until the copy is perfect. When one evening she bumps into Mr Tenshi in the photocopy room and he asks her to help him by doing some market research and writing a report while his boss is away on a business trip. She is extremely pleased to be doing something interesting and challenging. However, when senior manager Mr Omochi discovers what these two junior workers have done he is furious with their violation of the cultural rules of the organization, accusing them of the 'despicable pragmatism' and 'individualism' associated with Western cultures. ☻ [**approximate running time: 29–37.30 mins.**]

In *Gung Ho* (1986) when Japanese company Assan Motors comes to Hadleyville Pennsylvania to take over a recently closed auto plant and re-employ its workers, Hunt Stevenson is appointed employee liaison manager, his role to mediate the relationship between American industrial workers and the new Japanese management. The clash of cultures rapidly becomes apparent, management becoming increasingly dissatisfied with the American work ethic and employees increasingly frustrated with the expectations of their new bosses. In this scene, Hunt confronts his Japanese boss Oishi Kazihiro who says 'I was beginning to think like an American … everybody in this country thinks they are special, nobody wants to be part of a team, they are all too busy getting personalized licence plates, none of you would last two days in management training … because you are all selfish and that's what makes you weak!' Yet the tables turn when Oishi at a late evening meeting, having assimilated various aspects of American culture, confronts his own boss with the realization that there are things they could learn from the Americans claiming, 'our friends, our families should be our lives, we are killing ourselves!' The solution comes by fusing the two cultures together, Japanese and American workers employed side by side harmoniously. ☻ [**approximate running time: 1 hour 13–1 hour 15; 1 hour 21.30–1 hour 23.45 mins.**]

As might be expected in the context of corporate culturalism, organizational misbehaviour tends to involve power struggles over symbolic, rather than material resources (Ackroyd and Thompson, 1999). For example, in *Clockwatchers* (1998) and *Office Space* (1998) the employees battle over objects such as a coveted stapler, pencils and personalized coffee cups. The importance of these items is such that when some of them start to go missing the magnitude of their significance is apparently no less than if a valuable piece of machinery or a wallet had been stolen (see Film Focus 7.9).

The cynical postmodern worker

Postmodernism can be understood as a periodizing concept used to refer to an era coming after modernism and a theoretical perspective that involves the rejection of modernist beliefs in the existence of fundamental truths based on reason and observation (Hassard, 1993). The concept of postmodernism has important implications for the representation of time and space within film. Harvey (1990, p. 240) suggests that 'the history of capitalism has been characterized by speed-up in the pace of life' and this has led to the compression of spatial and temporal worlds. Hence time is longer measured in ways that are uniform and consistent for large numbers of people. Instead our experiences of time are fragmented and multiple. In this context, time is bound up with the spatial organization of work in ways that involve 'desynchronization' (Glennie and Thrift, 1996) whereby the use of particular spaces at particular times is becoming less and less predictable and space is displaced by time so local conditions are no longer important. This in turn is linked to globalization and the rise of an economic order wherein capitalism relies on rapid simultaneous access to pooled information.

Postmodernism draws on the notions of fragmentation, of family, community and society, which leads to ambiguity and threatens self-identity 'when individuals are called upon to play multiple roles with little temporal or spatial separation between them' (Hatch, 1997, p. 44). An example can be seen in the film *Startup.Com* (2001) (see Film Focus 5.8) which depicts a fragmented view of the life of the postmodern worker. Whereas it may have seemed easy for some, mainly male industrial workers, to know where work stopped and leisure began, for the postmodern worker the boundaries between work, leisure and family have become blurred. Du Gay (1996) suggests that the overlapping nature of relations of production and consumption within this new mode of organization make it impossible to maintain a division between the two spheres of work and non-work identity. Consequently he suggests it is becoming harder and harder to distinguish between when one is or is not working 'activities at work become preparation for turning the family into a family enterprise that absorbs all leisure; leisure activities become preconditions of employability. Anticipation of these possibilities undermines the distinctions between *work*, *leisure*, and *family*' (Du Gay, 1996, p. 183, emphasis in original).

Postmodern theory is oriented towards understanding a computerized, mass-media-dominated world where information technologies define what is real

FILM FOCUS 5.8: Fragmented identity and blurred boundaries in *Startup.Com* (2001)

Startup.Com (2001) is a fly-on-the-wall documentary drama about two child-hood friends who have an idea for an internet business and set up a New York based website to enable people to pay their parking penalties online. The film covers the time period from August 1999 when Kaleil and Tom set up their business to November 2000 when it goes into bankruptcy. The film represents the hype and ambition associated with the Dot Com Bubble, the period from 1997–2001 when stock markets rose because of the potential envisaged in the development of new, internet technologies. Many of the so-called 'Dot Coms' were started by 'Generation Xers' (see Film Focus 7.1), funded by venture capitalists who saw the potential enabled by the new technologies and their strategy of going for rapid growth. In many ways 'Dot Coms' embraced the business opportunities enabled by time-space decompression in post-industrial society, as indicated by Tom and Kaleil's statement in the opening scene, 'We have the right …'

The first scene shows Kaleil and Tom leaving their jobs, obtaining venture capital, deciding on a name for the company and celebrating its launch. In the second scene, dated January 2000 when the company has 120 employees, there are issues about company strategy and division of responsibility between the partners. For Tom, there are also tensions as a result of the blurred boundaries between work and leisure; the expectation that he should work weekends conflicts with his desire to spend time with his young daughter. The film also documents the deterioration of Kaleil's relationship with his girlfriend who is fed up with the demands of the business. In the third scene, dated April when the company employees 200 people, Kaleil questions Tom's ability to lead the technological development of the company. Kaleil takes security measures to ensure Tom cannot enter the business premises and the partners enter a legal battle with each other to protect their interests. The film represents Tom and Kaleil's friendship overlapping with their business relationship in a way that is congruent with the concept of the 'entrepreneur of the self'. Through exploring the tensions entailed in eroding the distinction between personal and organizational lives, the film challenges the popular entrepreneurial discourse which suggests that new companies are founded by friends who happen to enjoy spending time together, sharing their ideas and work harmoniously together. 👁 **[approximate running times: 0.30–5; 54.20–57; 1 hour 15.30–1 hour 28.30 mins.]**

(Denzin, 1991). The postmodern world of investment banking in *Rogue Trader* (2000) is based on the story of Nick Leeson whose fraudulent trading led to losses which eventually forced Barings Bank into liquidation (see Film Focus 3.6). The film depicts Leeson's manipulation of the imaginary political economy of signs as so successful he was able to conceal his immense trading losses in an account that he created and named after the lucky Chinese number, the '88888' account. The film contrasts the modernism of Barings Bank with the postmodernism of the financial markets Leeson operates in where 'symbolic proxies', pieces of paper or electronic impulses, are used as a substitute for tangible property or real commodities (Shapiro, 1990). The postmodern worker exchanges symbolic proxies, such as bank statements, stock certificates, mortgages, commodities and futures contracts, for tangible property. What is more, Shapiro (1990) argues, it is easier to hide, fabricate or distort such symbolic proxies than the commodities they represent, as the examples in Film Focus 5.9 illustrate.

This relates to Baudrillard's (1983) suggestion that the postmodern condition entails the consumption of signs, messages and images which are not defined by

FILM FOCUS 5.9: Symbolic proxies in *Dealers* (1989) and *Rogue Trader* (2000)

Both of these films represent the fast-paced environment of the London Stock Exchange in the 1980s following the 'Big Bang' caused by the deregulation of financial markets under a Conservative government and the arrival of 'yuppie traders', (Stein, 2000). Tangible property is signified purely by flickering numbers on electronic screens which indicate the rise and fall of financial fortunes. *Dealers* (1989) opens with the suicide of a city trader in the corporate boardroom, one of a group of fast-living, risk-taking individuals addicted to cocaine, fast cars, alcohol and cigarettes who expect to burn out by the age of 35. In this scene the traders take a risk on the market that pays off, enabling their company to recover its losses on the dollar account which had caused their former colleague's suicide. ☺ [**approximate running time: 1 hour 17.20–1 hour 20 mins.**] *Rogue Trader* (2000) is based on the story of derivatives trader Nick Leeson who joined Barings Bank in the late 1980s when the conservative values of the bank that reflected the British aristocratic establishment were being challenged. In this scene, we see Leeson setting up a trading position in Singapore. Leeson was permitted by the bank to remain as chief trader while also being responsible for settling his trades, a job that is usually split. This made it easier for him to hide his losses in a secret account which he named after the Chinese lucky number, the '88888 account', where he hid his growing losses on the trading floor. In a later scene Leeson is shown as falsifying paperwork requested by auditors Coopers & Lybrand by setting up a fake electronic transaction to ensure the audit does not pick up on his deception. ☺ [**approximate running times: 9.40–14.20 mins; 59.25–1 hour 5.40 mins.**]

their use but what they signify. For Baudrillard, postmodernism entails the erosion of distinctions in society to such an extent that it even calls into question the distinction between the virtual and the real. This entails the unceasing reproduction of 'simulacra', copies or representations of objects or commodities that offer the impression that they are real but are simultaneously fictional. Simulacra persist in cultures where mass media and popular culture have altered the way that people encounter and interpret objects and events. The consumer is consequently reduced to relating to simulacra symbolically. This is what Baudrillard understands to be the basis of 'neoreality', or even 'hyperreality', a situation where our actions are dominated by the exchange of symbolic images which act as a substitute for real events or things, a theme which will be returned to in Chapter 8. Similarly, Denzin (1991, p. vii) suggests that film represents an important aspect of how meaning is constructed in hyperreal society, where individuals are 'voyeurs in a sea of symbols' who come to understand themselves by watching representations of the real. 'The postmodern person is a restless voyeur, a person who sits and gazes (often mesmerized and bored) at the movie or TV screen' (Denzin, 1991, p. 9). See Film Focus 5.10 for an example.

Postmodernism has implications for understanding self-identity that stem from managerial initiatives such as corporate culturism that have the potential to produce

FILM FOCUS 5.10: A political economy of signs in *Wall Street* (1987) and *Rogue Trader* (2000)

Denzin (1991) suggests that the film *Wall Street* (1987) illustrates many of the basic features of the postmodern world by contrasting Gekko who lives in a postmodern world where everything is commodified, including information, time, lifestyles, status and prestige, human feelings and art, with Bud Fox and his father Carl who represent a real, modern world, where hardworking individuals are rewarded. The people in this postmodern world seek to differentiate themselves from one another through the signifiers they attach to themselves. However, the signifiers in Gekko's world do not relate to signified things because in the world of commodity trading 'all that is purchased are the illusions of things and the money they cost' (Denzin, 1991, p. 88). Hence, Denzin argues, there is an unreality to Gekko's life because he creates nothing, instead he simply buys and sells illusions to which a financial value is attached. As a result, Gekko explains, 'the illusion becomes real, capitalism at its worst'. ☻ [approximate running times: 39–42.20; 1 hour 30.30–1 hour 34.20 mins.]

Continued

Denzin additionally observes that even Wall Street itself is not a real place but a computerized space where meaning is constructed through simulation. 'Go back to the floor of the Stock Exchange, and re-examine the green computer screens of the young brokers at Bud's firm. Numbers can be erased with the touch of a finger, or a loud voice. Numbers which point to imaginary properties or imaginary things. Companies with made-up names, whose productivity is measured by imaginary numbers concerning losses and gains. Money going in and out of hidden accounts. Money attached to nothing but imaginary numbers attached to made-up accounts, built on the transactions and imagined doings of imaginary companies. Careers built on who can best manipulate this imaginary political economy of signs' (Denzin, 1991, p. 91).

selective, calculative compliance from workers who seek to distance themselves from corporate values 'as a means of preserving and asserting self-identity' (Willmott, 1993, p. 537). However, this dramaturgical presentation of self (Goffman, 1959) is not without consequences, for while workers are able to engage in strategies of distancing from the demands of the organizational culture, in so doing they become engaged in a kind of cynicism which is also a part of the culture. Examples of the way that companies seek to build cultures that parody their own corporate culture as a means of a disarming critique are illustrated in Film Focus 2.9 and 2.10. The employee becomes locked into a vicious circle of cynicism and organizational dependence. Denzin (1991) also explores the effects of having to embody the multiple contradictions of postmodernism on employee self-identity. These include 'a nostalgic, conservative longing for the past, coupled with an erasure of the boundaries between the past and the present; an intense preoccupation with the real and its representations; a pornography of the visible; the commodification of sexuality and desire; a consumer culture which objectifies a set of masculine cultural ideals; intensive emotional experiences shaped by anxiety, alienation, resentment, and a detachment from others' (Denzin, 1991, p. vii) (see Film Focus 5.11).

particularly those relating to violence and aggression that the film suggests are essential to masculinity. The transition from identities based on production to those oriented towards consumption is represented through the film's narrator, who works as a recall coordinator for a major car company and aspires to acquire the perfect combination of Ikea furniture for his condo. The film can be read as a message about the futility of consumption as a basis for achieving selfhood and the construction of 'hyperreality' (Baudrillard, 1983), as indicated by the comment that 'everything is a copy of a copy of a copy'. It is also critical of the feminization of labour (see Film Focus 6.9) and represents men doing service work as essentially demeaning and degrading. ☉ [**approximate running time: 3.45–6 mins.**] These views are summarized by Tyler in his speech to the men at Fight Club. He states, 'man I see in Fight Club some of the smartest men who've ever lived. I see all this potential and I see it squandered. Goddamit! An entire generation pumping gas, waiting tables, slaves with white collars ... Working jobs we hate so we can buy shit we don't need. We're the middle children of history man, no purpose or place. We've got no Great War, no Great Depression. Our great war is a spiritual war. Our great depression is our lives. We've all been raised on television to believe that one day we'll all be millionaires and movie gods and rock stars, but we won't and we're slowly learning that fact. And we're very, very pissed off'. ☉ [**approximate running time: 1 hour 7–1 hour 8 mins.**]

Films such as *Fight Club* (1999) and *Office Space* (1998) can be read as exhibiting nostalgia for an authentic vision of human behaviour as a reflection of biological destiny. The characters in these films represent 'ressentiment', a form of emotionality involving 'the self-poisoning form of self-hatred which arises from the systematic repression of certain emotions, including envy, pride, anger, and the desire for revenge and self-conquest' (Denzin, 1991, p. 54) and reflects an underlying self-hatred and lack of self-worth. Denzin accounts for the ressentiment associated with the postmodern condition as caused by the inaccessibility of the American Dream (see Chapter 4) for large groups of people and their 'repeated inability to experience the pleasant emotions promoted by the popular culture' (Denzin, 1991, p. viii). They also reflect a nostalgia for masculine values of industrial labour which in films like *The Full Monty* (1997), *Brassed Off* (1996) and *Fight Club* (1999) are recommodified and revived in a process of circling back to create a new form of signification.

These films celebrate what was good about industrial labour through the construction of a mythical story in the present, regulating or 'mollifying' the negative aspects of masculine industrial labour within the narrative (Denzin, 1991) and inviting a return to the heroic industrial worker described earlier in this chapter. In so doing they appear to invoke a popularized version of evolutionary psychology which emphasizes biological compulsions as the basis for human actions in 'an attempt to rationalize what most of us would consider to be irrational and socially pathological behaviour' (Sewell, 2004, p. 925). These films can be read as implying that evolutionary determined drives developed by our ancient ancestors to ensure the continuation of the human species continue to exert a powerful influence on workplace behaviour and that these drives should be respected and encouraged rather than stifled. They suggest a potential mismatch between the natural instincts of the individual and the environment of the modern organization. This theme is illustrated in Film Focus 5.12.

FILM FOCUS 5.12: Masculinity and evolutionary psychology in *Office Space* (1998)

In *Office Space* (1998) masculinity can be read in the Gangsta Rap soundtrack which sets up a parallel between the angry impotence of white-collar male employees raging against the organization and the black male youth culture of the street, both groups portrayed as disaffected. One of the main messages in the film relates to the way that the modern organization denies white-collar male employees an aspect of their essential masculinity, thereby provoking frustration or even violence. This is exemplified in one scene where we see the three male co-workers taking the fax machine which has so frustrated them in the office to some waste ground where they smash it to pieces with a baseball bat and their bare hands to the rap sounds of *The Geto Boys* (see also Plate 5). Hassard and Holliday (1998, p. 121) discuss the way that objects in popular culture are used as metaphors. They cite as an example the relationship between men and guns in classic Westerns and note the emotion associated with their use. A similar dynamic is evident when the central character, Peter, takes possession of the maintenance man's drill and uses it to dismantle his office cubicle thereby liberating himself from the physical constraints of the organizational environment. In another scene we see him engaging in the stereotypically male pursuit of fishing then proceeding to gut the fish on his desk. These ideas are further reinforced in the conclusion to the film when Peter, who envies his neighbour's job as a construction worker, turns down the possibility of another white-collar job in favour of manual work on a construction site [http://wwwvdare.com/Sailer/060326_judge.htm – consulted 26.10.06]. ⊚ [**approximate running time: 53–54.40 mins.**]

The experience of the postmodern worker is suggested to be accompanied by different forms of malaise from those suffered by industrial workers. Rather than having to endure harsh, physically demanding working conditions like the industrial worker, or the competitive, aggressive mental pressures of the post-industrial worker, the postmodern worker is confronted by a lack of physical or mental pressure and a consequent emptiness and nothingness, a theme that will be explored further in Chapter 7. These films seek to depict the various forms of micro-resistance or 'micro-emancipation' that constitute workers' response to these conditions. Ackroyd and Thompson (1999) argue that the extent of misbehaviour varies in its intensity. One of the most serious and destructive involves sabotage, the mutilation or destruction of work environment including machinery or products, as represented for example in *Office Space* (1998) when co-workers destroy the fax machine (see Plate 5.1). Other examples include Tyler's acts of sabotage in *Fight Club* (1999), pissing in the soup while working as a waiter in an expensive restaurant and splicing pornographic images into reels of film when working as a cinema attendant.

Spicer (2001) describes this mode of resistance as predominantly one of 'passive cynicism', arguing that although the central characters in films such as *Fight Club* (1999) display ironic sensitivity, effectively parodying their predicament in a world dominated by corporations, they continue to act as if they accept it. Fleming and Spicer (2003) make a similar argument, pointing to research evidence which suggests employees may disidentify with the culture of an organization yet continue to act in a way which is supportive of it. They draw attention to the possibility of resistance to forms of cultural control that target their self-identities. Often this resistance takes the form of cynicism, as a means of distancing and protecting themselves from the corporate culture whilst continuing to enact the cultural rituals that are expected of them. Fleming and Spicer (2003) argue that this is a largely an ineffective form of resistance whilst employees continue to act as if they believe in the corporate culture. This is because the 'corporate culture does not necessarily need to colonize workers' "minds" ... only their discursive practices' (Fleming and Spicer, 2003, p. 164). What is more, cynicism can serve to support the corporate culture by providing workers with a sense of freedom in relation to it (see Film Focus 2.9 and 2.10).

Conclusion

The job of management is generally understood as being about controlling the behaviour of employees. Yet many of the representations of organized work in the films reviewed in this chapter depict workers as fundamentally uncontrollable and furthermore, as only limitedly engaged with management, instead going about their work with relatively little direct supervision and surveillance. These representations reinforce the social constructionist view that a work organization is the result of actions of all its members rather than simply, or even primarily, a small, if powerful, group of managers (Orr, 2006). They also challenge the view of the rational, modernist organization depicted in the previous chapter and call into question the role of the manager as the power behind the system.

By depicting workers as engaged in either trivial or significant acts of organizational misbehaviour they portray them as seeking to manage the tensions associated with their employment. The acts of resistance engaged in by the heroic industrial worker in films such as *Norma Rae* (1979) are purposive and clearly goal directed but this contrasts sharply with the resistance of the postmodern cynical worker which can be seen as a less directed form of organizational misbehaviour in texts such as *Fight Club* (1999). What is more, the focus of this resistance varies according to whether the text seeks to portray the industrial worker battling against the demands of mass production, the post-industrial worker fending off managerial attempts to colonize the self as an aspect of corporate culturalism, or the postmodern worker struggling against the meaninglessness of work as a means of consumption, a theme that will be returned to in Chapter 7. Some writers (Rhodes, 2001; Spicer, 2001) have been concerned to understand whether the acts of organizational misbehaviour represented in these texts constitute a significant form of resistance in the sense of challenging managerial discourses in a way which impacts on material practices in real organizations. However, the view taken here is that such questions tend to oversimplify the complex processes whereby people construct self-identity in relation to work as an economic and social as well as potentially politically motivated process.

To conclude this chapter we must consider the other to which these texts inevitably refer in their ongoing construction of meaning in relation to the organizational worker. The construction of the organizational worker within film relies upon establishing a contrast with manual or craft work associated with a pre-industrial era. Whether the hard working construction worker in *Office Space* (1998), the ethical organic baker in *Stranger than Fiction* (2006), or the entrepreneurial apple sauce maker in *Baby Boom* (1987), in their narrative conclusion these texts invoke a nostalgia for a remembered past in which the temporal and spatial boundaries between work and non-work are more fluid and permeable, thereby implying a return to meaningful work, a theme which constitutes the focus of Chapter 7.

Plate 6   JC Wiatt tries to juggle a high-flying career with motherhood in *Baby Boom* (1987)

Representing the other

Introduction

Representations of women in films about management and organization have remained relatively static in the decades since 1980, relying on a set of clearly defined signifiers of embodied identity which reinforce the subordinate status of women in the workplace and constitute them as the alien other. A relatively consistent range of characters can be read in the films described in this chapter, from the endearingly funny 'working girl' to the ruthlessly careerist 'devil woman', all of them defined in oppositional terms to organization man. Many of these films can be read as a commentary on the effects of gendered organizational cultures through their representation of norms, values and practices which have exclusionary effects on working women. However, it is the notion of the gaze which provides the basis for understanding some of the most frequently recurring representations of women in film through enabling analysis of the construction of subject-object relationships that draw attention to the female body which is constituted as a threat to the stability of the rational, modernist work organization.

The similarities that can be observed between the empirically based findings of organizational researchers such as Kanter (1977) and McDowell (1997) and the representations of working women contained within film might lead us to conclude that there is a close relationship between representations of gendered organizational practices in film and individual lived experience. If so, we might further speculate as to the direction of influence that is involved in this relationship. Is film, for example, a medium which simply confirms culturally constructed differences between working men and women in everyday life, making them seem natural and inevitable? This ideological approach tends to imply that the women who watch these films are socialised into false images of domestic femininity which prevent them from becoming full participants in the masculine world of work. Or does film contain contradictory meanings concerning gender relations in the workplace, so that successful working women who embody feminist principles can be represented alongside representations which contest these meanings?

Brundson (1997) takes the latter perspective, arguing that in the decades following Second Wave feminism of the 1970s, characters that are representative of 'the feminist' or 'the liberated woman' can be observed more frequently in film. Feminist discourses are articulated within these texts through characters who challenge gender discrimination in the workplace, while at the same time the strength of the dominant culture in suppressing feminism is often powerfully represented. This leads towards consideration of how readers respond to these representations and the final part of the chapter focuses on the role of the 'woman's film' about work as having gender specific appeal with certain audiences. Finally, it is important to note that analysis of the other in films that represent management and organization cannot be confined to female characters. In films like *Phildadelphia* (1993) and *The Associate* (1996) gay and black employees are also constituted as marginalized subjects in opposition to the superior sign of the heterosexual white male, the lesser frequency of these representations suggesting them to be even more of an absent presence than the working woman.

The male (and the female) gaze

Film theory has since the mid 1970s been dominated by psychoanalytic feminist theory (Taylor, 1995) informed by Lacan's model of sexual difference as the basis for understanding representations of women in film. Lacanian psychoanalysis explains the development of human subjectivity through child development, sexual difference and the child's relationship to the phallus. Driven by its fear of dependence upon the mother, the child's security is threatened by the realisation that the father possesses the phallus. In coming to see both the self and the mother as lacking, the child comes to equate sexual difference with the absence or presence of the phallus and to regard its possession as an indication of completeness. For the boy, this means he comes to identify with an idealised version of the father as in possession of the phallus. The girl on the other hand, has a more difficult task since her only hope of obtaining the phallus is to win the love of a male by identifying with the mother and learning to define herself as an object of male desire. Feminist psychoanalysis goes a step further in connecting specific social relations such as the patriarchal family to male and female psychosexual development in childhood and in particular to the child's changing relationship to the mother, proposing that these social conditions are the primary cause of unequal patterns of gender development in childhood, rather than innate psychosexual characteristics.

In an influential article, Mulvey (1985) suggests that film represents men as the active subjects of the narrative and women as objects of the film audience's gaze to be fought over by men. Women are thus the object of the narrative, rather than the subject, acted upon rather than active, desired rather than desiring. This structure of male looking and female to-be-looked-at-ness is suggested by Mulvey to underpin the visual pleasure that audiences derive from film. The female body is presented as a fetishized image. Signifiers of difference, including female body parts such as legs, breasts or lips are used to distract us from something that has the potential to threaten male power (e.g. the powerful business woman) by drawing attention to her essential difference (see Film Focus 6.1 for an example). The viewer is invited to identify with the male gaze at the passive, objectified female, thereby replicating the unequal power relations between men and women. However, the idea that women are never active subjects in film narrative is difficult to sustain in relation to all films, even those that have no female characters. Moreover, it tends to assume that audiences are comprised of heterosexual males who identify with the male gaze. If this analysis of film narrative were universally correct it would also imply that female audiences are universally willing to accept subordinate positions. Instead, the approach taken here suggests that film can be seen as a site of struggle where who is doing the 'gazing' and 'who is gazed at' is open to ongoing debate and contestation among audiences (Marshment and Gamman, 1988).

FILM FOCUS 6.1: The fetishized organizational woman in *Baby Face* (1933)

When Lily Powers, a beautiful blonde from Erie, Pennsylvania brought up by her father who runs a speakeasy and forces her into prostitution, arrives in Manhattan she is overwhelmed by the skyscrapers that are the home of New York's large corporations and becomes determined to achieve wealth, power and status by becoming a successful member of one of these organizations. However, unlike male heroes of this era such as John Sims in *The Crowd* (1928), her methods for getting to the top of the organization rely on sexual seduction and by putting her male bosses in compromising situations that enable her to move up another hierarchical level. The film follows Lily from the start of her career path as a secretary in the personnel department of a wealthy bank, to its conclusion when she marries the bank's president. Her journey entails a transition from secretary to wife, the two main role categories of organizational participation suggested by Kanter (1977) to have been available to women. However, organizational and material success does not bring her happiness. Lily is portrayed as a cold, heartless woman who cannot think of anything or anyone other than her own self-interest, claiming 'I'm not like other women, all the gentleness and kindness in me has been killed'. Eventually, Lily's husband is removed from his job at the bank and the couple give all their financial assets to the ailing bank to return to Pittsburgh where he becomes a labourer in the steel mills and a heroic industrial worker (see Chapter 5). ☯ [**approximate running time: 13.30–18.45 mins.**]

Either way, the notion of the gaze is important in understanding how film represents women in management and organization as the objects of male desire. While Lacan's ideas have been less widely applied within organization studies, Kerfoot (2000) argues that Lacanian theory is useful because it provides a means of studying the discursive category of woman as other in the context of organization and management, thereby 'allowing the separation of woman as signifier in language from real women' (Kerfoot, 2000, p. 238). This enables attention to be focused on the ways in which the symbolic order is established and maintained through the dualistic notions of 'woman' in relation to 'man'.

Working women's roles

Working women in film are positioned in a way which is supportive of the idea that they face the loneliness of a stranger intruding on an alien culture (Kanter, 1977) as 'travellers in a male world' (Marshall, 1984), where 'being female is something to compensate for' (Ehrenreich, 2006, p. 105). As demonstrated in Chapter 4, the very idea of the 'manager' is closely identified with signifiers of masculinity and man (Collinson and Hearn, 1996). It is therefore perhaps unsurprising that women in these contexts are represented as 'tokens', highly visible members of the organizational group whose actions are closely watched by other organization members. The characteristics of the dominant group are defined in contrast to the female token, this serving to further reinforce the boundaries of the dominant culture. In her study of a large bureaucratic organization in the 1970s, Kanter argues that working women are more easily stereotyped because of their difference from the dominant group, this having consequences for their assimilation. Furthermore, tokens are constantly reminded of their difference and are not trusted with information that is potentially damaging or embarrassing to dominants, thereby being excluded from important organizational decision-making situations.

McDowell (1998) argues that popular representations of work in the world of merchant banking 'affect the social practices and everyday interactions of "real" actors with specific class and gender, ethnic and personal attributes' (McDowell, 1998, p. 168). Based on a qualitative study of women and men working in the City of London she argues that the working 'woman' in the City is defined in relation to 'man' as the other (McDowell, 1997). One of the ways in which the exclusion of women is established and maintained in this context is through talk that involves the use of gendered metaphors such as those based on sport and war described in Chapter 4. A further category of sexualised vocabulary used by the bankers in McDowell's study to refer to their work, such as 'lift your skirts', (reveal your position); 'hard on', (rising market); 'on the scent of a deal', 'team players' and 'just bat it back to them' can also be identified in films about financial work such as *Boiler*

Room (2000) and *Rogue Trader* (2000). This is illustrative of how men can define the organizational culture in a way that excludes women by making their differences explicit. In *Boiler Room* this involves socializing new organization member Seth by introducing him to some sporting metaphors used to explain how the organization works. He is told to 'play the numbers, this is a contact sport'. He is also informed that they 'don't pitch the bitch' – sell stock to women – because 'they're a constant pain in the ass and you're never going to hear the end of it'. A further representation of sexualized language in a masculine organizational culture can be read in Film Focus 6.2.

FILM FOCUS 6.2: Masculine organizational culture in *Glengarry Glen Ross* (1992)

When a group of salesmen who sell real estate are called to a meeting at the office one wet evening in *Glengarry Glen Ross* (1992) they are visited by an anonymous man from the 'downtown' office of Mitch and Murray. His message to them, laced with a string of abuse, is 'if you can't play in the man's game, go home and tell your wife'. After asking them if they are 'man enough' to take people's money, he concludes 'you know what it takes to sell real estate? It takes brass balls to sell real estate'. ✆ [**approximate running time: 7–14.40 mins.**] The all male environment represented here should not distract from reading the absent other into this text, the message of the film clearly defining women as lacking what it takes to succeed in this masculine organizational culture.

As noted by McDowell (1997) the characteristics required for dealing, trading and selling are exactly the same as those associated with conventional masculinity. Hence, 'women are made to feel out of place on the trading floors and in the dealing rooms by the development of a particular type of heterosexual machismo culture in which crude bodily humour, pin-ups, practical jokes and various forms of verbal and non-verbal behaviour verging on sexual harassment are the norm' (McDowell, 1997, p. 178). Similar dynamics are represented in the film *In the Company of Men* (1997) where young aggressive male manager, Chad, continually trades in sexual jokes and insults with his colleagues in an effort to position himself as the superior in his relationships to women in general as well as with the junior male employees and other colleagues whom he dislikes. In one scene this entails demanding of a young black male 'intern' that he takes down his trousers to show him that he has 'got the balls' to succeed in business. Film Focus 6.3 provides further examples of representations which depict both manual industrial and elite business workplace cultures as excluding women.

FILM FOCUS 6.3: Exclusionary practices in *North Country* (2005) and *The Associate* (1996)

North Country (2005) is based on factual events relating to the first major successful sexual harassment case in the United States, 'Jenson vs. Eveleth Mines', where a female mineworker who was physically and verbally abused by her male co-workers won a landmark class action lawsuit in 1984. The film represents the sexual harassment of women mineworkers who were perceived by their male co-workers as having taken jobs which should have gone to men. In this scene, where a group of women are being inducted on their first day in the mine, Josey is made very aware of the visibility of her token status in this male-dominated environment where the women are referred to as 'ladies' and she is told to work in an industrial area referred to as 'the powder room'. The women are made aware that their presence is unwelcome through sexually abusive graffiti on their changing room door, a rubber penis placed in a lunchbox and the unwillingness of the management and unions to provide toilet facilities for the women. Once the portable toilets are installed, the men play another practical joke on one of the women and Josey decides to raise the issue of sexual harassment with the mine owner. In response, he invites her to resign. ☉ [**approximate running times: 16–20.40; 57–1 hour 2 mins.**]

Laurel Ayres is a highly capable financial analyst working for a major Wall Street company but being a black woman she finds herself passed over for promotion in favour of a less capable white male employee. When she decides to set up on her own, investors are reluctant to give her their business because she doesn't have the right 'image' so she creates a fictitious business partner, 'Robert S. Cutty', a cigar-smoking, golf-playing, Harvard-educated older white male who has all the right social connections to gain a foothold in this highly elitist community. When investors and the press become suspicious about the mysterious invisibility of Mr Cutty, Laurel with the help of her transvestite friend disguises herself as a white man and impersonates Mr Cutty. This gives her access into some exclusively male environments where 'old-boy networks' of structural power operate, including the men's toilets and a prestigious gentlemen's club where she receives an award for 'businessman of the year'. ☉ [**approximate running times: 1 hour 15–1 hour 16.30; 1 hour 36–1 hour 41 mins.**]

As a consequence of their marginal or 'token' status the everyday experience of working women in 'real' organizations is suggested by writers such as Pringle (1989), Marshall (1984) and McDowell (1997) to be shaped through the construction of particular stereotypical roles through which organizational gender relations are managed. These include nurturing, servicing and caring roles, such as the wife, mother and pet; or disciplinary roles, such as the schoolmarm, matron, governess and head-mistress. The inescapability of these roles is also highlighted by Jackall, who observes:

> If a female executive's public face presents a warm, engaging femininity that distinguishes her from the minions of female clerical workers adopting the "corporate clone" look and practicing the new techniques of self-assertiveness, she runs the risk of being seen by her male colleagues as a "cookie" or a "fluff-head" and dismissed as inconsequential. If she, on the other hand, assumes a public severity in her demeanour, especially if she seems ambitious, she may be labelled a "calculating bitch," a difficult label to shake. (Jackall, 1988, p. 52)

These identities thus serve to define women in ways that locate them within a broader patriarchal societal discourse about the status of women relative to men. Examples of these roles can be found in many films, the nurturing role is represented through the secretaries and wives discussed in Chapter 4 (see Film Focus 4.9), while disciplinary roles can be read, for example, in several of the minor female roles in *Erin Brockovich* (2000). One of the most obvious sources of signifiers through which the meaning of these gendered roles is encoded and communicated in film involves dress, signifiers such as the string of pearls, the brooch, conservative skirt-suit and handbag providing a means of communicating to the audience a particular working role for the female character. For example, the trend towards 'power dressing' amongst working women in the 1980s, an exaggerated masculine style of dress comprising dark suits with shoulder pads, high heels to add height and severe hairstyles, can be read in many films, including *Working Girl* (1988) and *Disclosure* (1994), as signifying the values of rationality and career ambition (Brewis, Hampton and Linstead, 1997). Conversely, in the film *Big Business* (1988), Rose Shilton's inability to keep her shoulder pads in place signifies her unsuitability for the demands of business (see Film Focus 6.4).

In addition to the nurturing or disciplinary roles, women can adopt the role of the 'careerist', 'embodying an unspoken neglect of familial responsibilities or, worse, a selfish rejection of motherhood' (McDowell, 1997, p. 152). Common stereotypes associated with the careerist are the bitch, dragon lady, witch, or iron maiden, a character who is tough, militant and dangerous. Examples of these representations can be found in *Erin Brockovich* (2000) and *Disclosure* (1994) (see Film Focus 6.4). In relation to the latter, Brewis (1998) suggests although the film was lauded for its portrayal of workplace sexual harassment as being 'about power, not sex', the female harasser is actually portrayed in a way that consolidates understandings of working women as overly competitive, aggressive and unnatural. Moreover, the highly eroticised portrayal of sexual harassment means that audiences may fail to accept that harassment is by definition unwanted and abusive and may see the victim as 'asking for it' or somehow 'enjoying it'. She suggests that men watching the film will not come to understand what it is like to be the victim of sexual harassment because the film portrays Johnson as an illegitimate occupant of her managerial role and suggests that sexual harassment is the fault of the victim. Hence it is significant that

Sanders and Johnson have been sexually involved before and that he is sexually attracted to Johnson. The film encodes Johnson as an object of desire by using camera angles and clothing to portray Johnson in a highly eroticised way. Brewis concludes that 'this representation of harassment could be seen to generate understandings that attribute at least some blame to the recipient of harassment' (Brewis, 1998, p. 95) and this may even contribute towards the reluctance of victims to speak out because they fear that they have somehow provoked, incited or welcomed this behaviour. Many of the careerist roles played by working women in films during the late 1980s and 1990s (see Film Focus 6.4), portray heroines as striving for success in a male-dominated organizational world and in the process becoming more ruthless and aggressive than their male colleagues (Brewis, 2004).

FILM FOCUS 6.4: The woman as ruthless careerist in *Big Business* (1988) and *Disclosure* (1994)

When the knuckle-cracking Sadie Shelton and her non-businesslike twin sister Rose decide to sell off and close down a subsidiary within their business empire Moramax, as part of deal involving open cast mining in *Big Business* (1988), they encounter more problems than they bargained for, The Hollowmade furniture factory in the sleepy town of Jupiter Hollow turns out to be run by twin sisters born in the same hospital on the same day who are also called Sadie and Rose. The identical twins were mismatched at birth, this providing the genetic explanation for Sadie Shelton and Sadie Ratliff's greed and ambition and the two Rose's lack of interest in material wealth. However, it is the highly successful, bullying Sadie Shelton who is portrayed as the only truly one-dimensional individual out of the foursome, having no interest in any relationship beyond those that are financially driven. 💿 [**approximate running time: 17.15–19.15 mins.**]

In *Disclosure* (1994) Meredith is represented as a ruthless, selfish careerist who has given up all vestiges of a private life in order to pursue a successful career. As Brewis (1998) notes, it is significant that we never see her anywhere except inside the DigiCom building where she even takes regular exercise on a running machine in the office. She is thereby positioned relationally in opposition to Tom who is signified as a well-adjusted family man through various signifiers that include his wife and children, his friends, his waterfront home, his well-used estate car, his casual clothes and stained tie. Tom's dismissal of Meredith as having nothing in her refrigerator except for 'two champagne bottles and an orange' is intended to make explicit that she has no life beyond the organization. However, Meredith is also represented as the 'pet' of her boss, Garvin, with whom she enjoys a benevolent, fatherly relationship since the death of his daughter. It is implied that Garvin's protectiveness of Meredith is the reason for her career success, since she is generally regarded as lacking the technical experience to have got the job on her own merit, or as one of Tom's team puts it 'she doesn't know the difference between software and a cashmere sweater'. These oppositions are established from the moment that Meredith and Tom first meet in Garvin's office. ☺ [approximate running time: 12.20–14 mins.]

Closely associated with these roles is the stereotypical role of the 'honorary man', a woman who dresses and behaves in a masculine way in the interests of being treated as an equal in a masculine culture. Women managers use body language to convey an impression of themselves as professional, everything from the way they sit to the way they shake hands being significant and carefully considered to present a more masculine, but not too threatening self-presentation (Sheppard, 1989; Tretheway, 1999). Although dressing and behaving in the role of the honorary man is a common strategy, it is suggested by McDowell (1997) that women who do this make their colleagues 'uneasy' and risk being seen as 'unfemale' and not sexually attractive, as the comments expressed by Jack Trainer in Film Focus 6.5 suggest. However, Pringle (1989) is more optimistic about the potential for dressing like a man as a means of empowering women. 'In wearing suits women are not transgressing gender, becoming 'men', but expressing a more masculine, instrumental relation to the body. To dress in this way is to *feel* like a man does, sexually empowered, an actor rather than an object to be looked at' (Pringle, 1989, p. 177, emphasis in original).

The analysis presented here suggests that over the course of many decades working women's organizational roles have been represented in film in clearly defined ways. However, the nature of these representations is far from entirely static. Brewis (2004) for example, observes that the roles played by working women in films of the 1980s and 1990s such as *Working Girl* (1988) and *Disclosure* (1994) were predominantly as work-obsessed 'career bitches', whereas more recent films such as *Bridget Jones's Diary* (2001) emphasise that being a woman is a full time job in itself and a woman's 'true job' is to love men (Basinger, 1993) (see also Film Focus 6.11). Kanter (1977) attributed this state of affairs to women's token status and consequent high visibility and predicted that these problems would be resolved once women were no longer minorities within organizations in a numerical sense. However, more recent studies have argued that these roles continue to be ascribed to working women because organizations are gendered in ways that inherently favour masculine identities (McDowell, 1997; Trethewey, 1999).

Female bodies

One of the consequences of the male gaze described earlier in this chapter is a focus on the female body in film and its role in signifying difference and constituting women as the object of male observation. McDowell (1997) suggests that women are marked out in the workplace because their bodies are defined as 'natural' and therefore out of place in the rational, cerebral world of work, especially in investment banking where the characteristics linked to success are closely associated with masculinity. She explains, 'my female interviewees openly discussed the ways they were reminded every day that they possessed a female body which classified them as inferior to men' (McDowell, 1997, p. 140). Because women continue to be marked out as exceptional in many organizational contexts, Trethewey (1999) argues that they learn to discipline their bodies in ways that can be traced back to well before the start of their professional lives, through diet and exercise, non-verbal behaviours, dress and makeup. Moreover, she argues, these gendered ordering practices render women's bodies in the workplace more 'docile', making them more focused on self-modification and more critical of each other in relation to the patriarchal gaze described earlier in this chapter. Such findings imply that women, especially those in professional-managerial positions, must prove that they are able to manage their own bodies through 'their ability to display the body in a manner that is culturally acceptable' (Kerfoot, 2000, p. 231).

The blurring of distinctions between work and leisure described in Chapter 5 is also suggested to have led to greater emphasis on how workers look, in terms of their style, or aesthetics, as well as their performance. The concept of aesthetic labour refers to the process whereby employees' bodies become part of the service provided to the consumer (Witz, Warhurst and Nickson, 2003). They argue that 'management intentionally mobilizes and develops aesthetic labour' pointing out that it is not only female labour 'that is subject to commodification via aestheticization' (Witz, Warhurst and Nickson, 2003, pp. 34–35). Aesthetic labourers are engaged in a staged performance in which they must deploy specific modes of embodiment in their interactions with customers or clients. In a case study of a rapidly expanding hotel chain, the authors suggest that hotel employees were carefully selected for their aesthetic qualities, including physical attractiveness, and then moulded into the desired aesthetic image through training on aspects of grooming and deportment. This echoes McDowell's (1997) finding that aesthetic labour is an aspect of women's experience of working in the city that is made manifest through the level of attention paid to the way a female worker dresses. 'If a woman's clothes are too bright, too tight, too revealing, this sends a message (albeit one that may be unintended) about her availability. However, wearing "frumpy", less sexy clothes also sends a message, even the conventional choice of a dark suit and plain blouse says something about their place in the workplace. They are therefore in an impossible position, since it is impossible for them to dress in a "neutral" fashion' (McDowell, 1997, p. 145) being caught in a series of 'complex, ambiguous, and precarious "in-betweens"' (Tretheway, 1999, p. 425) (see Film Focus 6.5).

FILM FOCUS 6.5: The impossibility of dressing neutrally in *Working Girl* (1988)

The transformation of the body of the female worker is represented in the film *Working Girl* (1988) where Tess, a hard working, ambitious New York secretary has just turned 30 and got a degree at night-school but continues to be passed over for any possibility of building a career in investment banking. In this scene, Tess who has just been reassigned to a new female boss of the same age, Catherine, is encouraged to modify her appearance. Catherine, wearing a simple grey suit with a skirt, plain blouse and a string of pearls, sets out her 'ground rules' which include some advice on what not to wear to work. 'We have a uniform, simple, elegant, impeccable. Dress shabbily they notice the dress, dress impeccably, they notice the woman'. Tess dutifully goes straight to the ladies room to remove her heavy gold jewellery and take off some of her eye makeup so as not to give her boss the wrong impression. Catherine is attempting to manage Tess in a way which communicates a specific style of organizational service. Yet it is Tess's inability to conform entirely to the stereotype of the 'honorary man' which makes investment banker, Jack Trainer, fall in love with her, as he indicates when he first meets her, 'You're the first woman I've seen at one of these damn things that dresses like a woman, and not like a woman thinks a man would dress if he was a woman'. ☻ [**approximate running times: 12.30–16.40; 35–44.40 mins.**]

Trethewey's (1999) study of how professional women see their own bodies suggests that physical fitness and not being overweight are important signifiers of self discipline and control, implying that the woman is more able to be trusted and to endure the requirements of work and hence more able to do their job effectively. However, 'the task of controlling and disciplining the female body', is 'made more difficult and complicated for women because the female body has a tendency to overflow' (Trethewey, 1999, p. 437). In competing with men, women in organizations may discover that their bodies are obstacles to full participation in contexts where few allowances are made for dealing with such body processes as menstruation, lactation, pregnancy or childbirth (Sheppard, 1989; Hassard, Holliday and Willmott, 2000) (see Film Focus 6.6 for an example). Several studies have indicated that women who have a family are likely to be stereotyped as less committed to work and hence devalued within the organization (Kanter, 1977; Hochschild, 1997). Interestingly, the interviewees in Tretheway's (1999) study actively perpetuated these stereotypes, suggesting that women can be disciplinarians of their own collective femaleness, actively participating in and perpetuating a masculine image of professionalism.

FILM FOCUS 6.6: Overflowing bodies in *Baby Boom* (1987)

In *Baby Boom* (1987) 'JC Wiatt', who graduated first in her class at Yale and got her MBA at Harvard, is a dedicated careerist who works as a management consultant. Nicknamed the 'Tiger Lady' she wears grey high-necked suits and cream cashmere sweaters, works 80 hours a week, earns six figures and has a firm handshake. Her big career break comes when her boss invites her to become a partner in the firm. He is eager to point out that, although he doesn't normally think of JC 'as a woman', he is concerned the promotion will entail certain sacrifices on her part, since she would not be able to 'marry and become a wife'. Unlike himself, he observes, she is unable to 'have it all'. Despite having no intentions to start a family, JC's life changes when her cousin dies and leaves his young daughter to her in his will. She intends to put the child up for adoption – 'I can't have a baby, because I have a 12.30 lunch meeting' but finds she cannot go through with it and so ends up keeping the child. It is not long before the tensions between the demands of JC's job and the pressures of looking after a young child begin to show. Even with her financial and organizational resources, the demands of motherhood literally spill into her life, disrupting the discipline and control that JC has carefully built into her working life to draw attention away from her female body. In this scene, JC has brought the child into the office, when her boss makes a surprise visit with his superior, as a prelude to making her partner in the firm. They are surprised to find a baby in her office. With her tousled hair, baby formula milk is spilt on the two men's suits and JC frantically tries to wipe it off. Later in an important presentation, JC is interrupted by a telephone call from her nanny in which she whispers furtively about where to find the 'nipples' or baby feeding teats. Even though she is not breastfeeding the child, these symbolic actions make the inappropriately sexual nature of her leaky female body in a working context explicit. The uncomfortable juxtaposition of signifiers of business (briefcase, power suit) and motherhood (baby feeding bottle) provide the basis for drama and humour within the film (see Plate 6). ☻ [**approximate running time: 3.30–6.20; 32.30–38.30 mins.**]

The dangers of revealing the body and making female sexuality explicit in an organizational context are highlighted by interviewees in Tretheway's (1999, p. 443) study who said that they avoided wearing short skirts, low cut blouses or any other kind of 'in your face attire' for fear that they would be treated as sexual rather than professional beings. These findings suggest that organizations are sexualised in asymmetrical ways, men being regarded as asexual and women as inherently sexual, for example by eliciting sexual overtures from men, therefore constantly having to desexualise themselves in order to fit into the modern workplace (Hearn et al., 1989). These findings support the notion that modernism leads to the repression or expulsion of sexuality from work organizations through a process of 'desexualization' (Burrell, 1984) in favour of rationalization and discipline. In this context, women in general and female sexuality in particular is represented as an uncontrollable, threatening and potentially disruptive or dangerous force that must be controlled or suppressed in order to ensure the smooth functioning of the modernist work organization. Such a view is summarized in the film *Working Girl* (1988) by Tess's seductive comment to her male drinking partner that she has a 'head for business and a bod[y] for sin'. This comment can be read as reflecting the Cartesian mind/body dualism, an organizing principle which separates emotions and passions from the rational mind so that the former can be controlled more effectively (Dale and Burrell, 2000). Consequently, 'rationality, reason and science become associated with masculinity whilst femininity is separated off and linked with nature and the body. Thus the Cartesian boundaries become gendered and the resulting structures take on a naturalistic gloss: the constructed dualism comes to seem inevitable' (Dale and Burrell, 2000, p. 17).

Rather than marginalizing or suppressing sexuality from work organizations, many of the films in this chapter are characterized by the 'over-inclusion' of sexuality within organizational life, representing it as 'an ordinary and frequent public process' that encompasses a wide range of practices from flirtation to sexual acts, 'rather than an extraordinary feature of private life' (Hearn et al., 1989, p. 13). Film represents sexual relations as a pervasive aspect of organizational life, particularly in relation to the heterosexual relationships through which organizational power relations are defined and exercised. Often this involves representing men using their sexuality at work in ways which exclude women from social settings and reinforce male power (Collinson and Collinson, 1989), for example by telling sexual jokes, using sexual terms to describe a particular work situation, making sexual comments to co-workers or displaying sexual posters or pictures, practices which can be read in films such as *In the Company of Men* (1997) and *North Country* (2005).

In addition, women's sexuality is represented in film as a means of pursuing strategic organizational goals and an integral aspect of the labour process. Workers are thus represented as using their 'tacit skills and assumed capacities as sexual subjects' to 'initiate sexual exchanges' (Hancock and Tyler, 2001, p. 159). An example of this can be read in *Erin Brockovich* (2000) where the female character uses her sexual characteristics to obtain information from the public records office (see Film Focus 6.7), a strategy which Gherardi, (1995) suggests is associated with 'boundary workers' who engage with environments or individuals outside the organization. However, as the film progresses Erin's physical appearance is gradually desexualized, her outfits becoming more understated and less revealing. This transition conveys the message that such displays of female sexuality are not appropriate in the workplace and confirms Erin as the successful career woman. This representation supports Brunsdon's (1997) analysis of the character of the post-feminist woman who is neither trapped by femininity nor rejecting of it. The post-feminist character instead uses her femininity to get what she wants, not being confined only to the pre-feminist goal of 'getting her man' but also reflecting the feminist idea of wanting control over her life. The popularity of the post-feminist working woman in film also supports Pringle's (1989) argument that women as well as men exercise sexual power in the workplace, sometimes actively seeking it out and taking pleasure in it. Hence, she argues, in addition to focusing on sexual harassment, there is a need for analyses that explore how female sexuality is used to disrupt male power in the workplace, thereby empowering women (see Film Focus 6.10 for examples).

FILM FOCUS 6.7: The sexualisation of work in *Erin Brockovich* (2000)

The female character in *Erin Brockovich* (2000) makes her sexuality explicit through the way that she dresses and behaves, her tight, low-cut tops, short skirts, high heels and long blonde hair positioning her in opposition to her female co-workers many of whom hardly speak in the film. Her overweight female supervisor is cast in the role of 'dragon lady' and the white female lawyers assume roles either of the pearl-wearing 'matron' or the suit and tie wearing 'honorary male'. In this context, Erin's sexuality is represented as a disruptive force in the workplace, threatening the organizational order through her lack of self-control. However, it is in her relationships with people who are external to the organization where she is best able to use her sexual characteristics. In her role as a boundary worker she is able to use her sexual skills to liaise with the working-class families who are the potential plaintiffs in the case against PG&E. In one scene she obtains copies of official documents relating to the water supply from the public records office by deploying her sexual skills to flatter and seduce the young male worker at the water records office into allowing her to photocopy documents. In the early part of the film it appears that her boss, Ed Masry, is unaware of the commercial value of this sexual exchange. However, as the narrative progresses he asks her, 'what makes you think you can just walk in there and find what we need?' to which she replies, 'they're called boobs Ed', thereby emphasising that she is not ashamed to use her sexuality to get the job done [http://www.usfca.edu/pj/brockovich-grant.htm – consulted 28.10.07] As the film progresses he consciously and deliberately deploys her sexual skills to get certain jobs done more effectively. ☻ [**approximate running times: 32–35 mins; 44–45.35 mins.**]

The working woman's film

The limitations of feminist psychoanalysis in arguing that film treats women as passive objects of male desire can be seen most clearly in relation to the category of the 'woman's film'. This comprises films which have gender-specific appeal, aimed at and enjoyed by a predominantly female audience, and often based on novels that are written by women and involving female-centred narratives where there is usually a central female character, the film's title often bearing the name of this woman (Jancovich, 1995) 'who is trying to deal with emotional, social and psychological problems that are specifically connected to the fact that she is a woman' (Basinger, 1993, p. 20). The appeal of these films, argues Basinger, stems from the fact that women are not marginalised in them; 'the woman's film is a genre that generously empowers a sex that society has relegated to secondary status' (Basinger, 1993, p. 15). Brunsdon (1997) argues that representations of women in contemporary film texts contain traces that reflect Western debates about appropriate feminine destinies that originate from the 1970s. She suggests that three interrelated ideas related to appropriate female roles circulate within these texts; the first emphasises the woman's right to fulfilment which may be located outside the domestic sphere of home and family. The second involves the notion of financial independence and earning more than 'pin-money'; and the third entails the separation of female sexuality from the consequences of maternity and domesticity. All three of these themes can be identified in the films discussed in this section.

FILM FOCUS 6.8: The woman's film about work: *Norma Rae* (1979) and *Baby Boom* (1987)

A key theme in the woman's film about work relates to the pressures associated with managing the competing demands of work and family. Norma Rae is a female-centered narrative about a young single mother in the Southern United States who works in a textile mill with her mother and father and most of the other members of her small town. Following the arrival of a labour union organizer and prompted by injustices suffered by her parents, Norma decides to join the union and fight to unionize the factory. However, her cause is also part of a broader project to become educated and to 'be somebody', in a way which extends her identity beyond being a factory worker and a mother. 💿 [**approximate running time: 1 hour 5.50–1 hour 8 mins.**]

Baby Boom (1987) centres on similar themes, the pressures of juggling work and family and the need for women to escape from them, through the story of

Continued

a highly successful New York career woman, whose escape comes when she resigns from her high-powered job in the city and moves to rural Vermont, where she uses her entrepreneurial skills to set up what becomes an extremely successful baby food company. The company is founded on a feminized model of work, run by an exclusively female workforce who make the products on the kitchen table and sell them to female storekeepers. She decides not to sell the company because she is not prepared to make the necessary sacrifices involved in giving up this new way of working. 💿 [**approximate running time: 1 hour 32–1 hour 39 mins.**]

The woman's film has historically concentrated on representing women's roles and lives in domestic and familial terms. Studies have therefore focused on defining films according to whether the suffering woman is a daughter, mother, wife or 'fallen woman' (Neale, 2000). However, another category of woman's film can be identified that focuses on representing the suffering of the working woman. The central dilemma for the heroine in these films is whether or not to have a career and how the demands associated with working in a demanding job can be managed without jeopardising love, marriage or her children. The woman is often represented as experiencing the repression of working in a patriarchal organization where she is subjugated and discriminated against. The films portray her resistance and refusal to submit to patri-archal ideology and its effects and sometimes her eventual triumph over them. Their appeal is thus based on recognition of the problems faced by women and the desire for things to be better (Basinger, 1993). For example, in *Erin Brockovich* (2000) the hero-ine is represented as having deserted her three children and supportive boyfriend, working long-hours and sacrificing her personal relationships in order to pursue her career. Consequently, she misses the moment that her daughter says her first word and must constantly appease her son by saying 'don't you want mommy to be good at her job?' The conflict between having a professional role and having a partner or children are made explicit in this and many other woman's films in which the central character is a woman. In *Silkwood* (1983) Karen works in a plutonium processing plant where management claims employees are exposed to 'acceptable levels' of contamination. When she gets involved with the union to try to improve conditions for the workers, her partner leaves her because he is unhappy with the person she has become.

As part of the desire for things to be better, films such as *Baby Boom* (1987) and *Nine to Five* (1980) represent and celebrate feminized workplaces where feminine subjectivities are encouraged. In *Baby Boom* (1987) this involves a return to the domestic space of the home as a site where female counterculture can be nurtured and where domestic skills, such as the making of gourmet baby apple sauce, 'can be revalued as a challenge to the male-dominated value system' (Hollows 2006, p. 102). In *Nine to Five* (1980) this entails the feminization of the workplace in a way that supports and seeks to ameliorate the practical and emotional tensions produced by women's domestic and working roles through, for example, job-sharing and the provision of on site childcare facilities (see Film Focus 6.9). The changes instigated by the women in their workplace promote values of emotional expressivity and aesthetics, for example through caring gestures towards sick employees and having flowers on employee's desks.

FILM FOCUS 6.9: Representing the feminization of labour in *Erin Brockovich* (2000) and *Nine to Five* (1980)

In the film *Erin Brockovich* (2000) the character of Erin is portrayed as having a feminine subjectivity, including relational skills, a capacity for empathy and interpersonal sensitivity which enables her to build relationships founded upon trust and understanding with the people whose case against PG&E, her legal firm is representing, and ensuring that a sufficient number of plaintiffs are willing to provide testimony. In contrast, female lawyer, Teresa, cast in the role of the honorary man, is represented as rational, uncaring and less able to engage appropriately with the plaintiffs. Consequently she is unable to get the testimonies needed in order to win the case. The film thereby represents some clearly defined class and gender stereotypes, including the jealous secretaries who victimise Erin and the asexual, masculinized female attorneys arguing that Brockovich is 'romanticised as an authentic member of the working class who can go in their and speak their lingo'. [http://www.usfca.edu/pj/brockovich-grant.htm – consulted 28.10.07] ☙ [**approximate running times: 59.20–1 hour; 1 hour 35.10–1 hour 36.10 mins.**]

After capturing their 'sexist, egotistical, lying, hypocritical bigot' of a boss Franklin Hart and holding him prisoner in his own home, the three female secretaries in *Nine to Five* (1980) develop a more feminized approach to the management of their department. This includes cultural changes, as indicated by the personalisation of employee's workspaces and warm colour schemes, and structural changes, in the form of the introduction of an equal opportunities policy, flexible working practices and a workplace day care centre. Rather than being disciplined by senior management for their activities, the women's efforts and the increases in productivity gained as a consequence of them are recognised and rewarded, although they are attributed to Hart. The organizationally hidden nature of their activities thereby re-establishes the dominance of the masculine hierarchy and shows the feminist workplace as unable to gain overt recognition. ☙ [**approximate running time: 1 hour 34.20–1 hour 41.20 mins.**]

Rather than simply concentrating on how women are dominated through film, Taylor (1995) suggests that we need to consider how women use fictional texts, including film, as a means of recognising and voicing their own interests and aspirations. For example, a number of women's films, such as *Baby Boom* (1987), *North Country* (2005), *Norma Rae* (1979) and *Erin Brockovich* (2000) represent the tensions between a woman having a career and a family through storylines that focus on the way that children and male partners feel neglected or deserted as a result of the heroine's career ambitions (see Film Focus 6.4). The resolution of these conflicts is often achieved by representing the woman as reconciled with her family once they realise that her commitment to her career was undertaken with them in mind. These films also sometimes contain an element of retribution or revenge which is visited by the woman on the man or men who are perceived to have caused her suffering (see Film Focus 6.10). These could be seen as examples of films that generously empower women in the way that Basinger (1993) suggests is a feature of the woman's film. However, they could also be interpreted as reinforcing stereotypes of women by representing them as unable to successfully balance the competing demands of work and family, highlighting the suffering of the family which results from this fundamental incompatibility and contributing towards the reproduction of patriarchal power relations.

As emphasized throughout this book, the relationship between audience and text is complex and readers are able to resist the dominant meaning of the text. Hence, women audiences may be critical of these representations while still using them as a means of expressing their aspirations and concerns about career and family. Yet their potential is limited by their textual form, the use of fantasy and comedy (see Film Focus 6.10) providing an 'alternative space' (Hermes, 2006) within which patriarchal workplace norms can be challenged but in a way that is unlikely to result in any kind of lasting transformation. On the other hand, as will be discussed in Chapter 7, possibilities for escaping and resisting the realities of work can take a variety of forms, including fantasies which provide the opportunity for some kind of temporary escape. By representing these 'escape attempts' (Cohen and Taylor, 1992) films like *Nine to Five* (1980) make explicit the women's fundamental discontent with the reality they inhabit in a way that audiences can potentially identify with.

FILM FOCUS 6.10: Reversing the gaze in *Nine to Five* (1980) and *What Women Want* (2000)

Since the 1980s there has been a trend towards more direct and contentious representations of the dilemmas faced by female corporate employees within film, especially in comedies (Boozer, 2002). These texts enable the incorporation of feminist discourses through female characters who seek to resist and challenge oppressive patriarchal workplace practices, often by reversing the subject-object relationship in a way which gives women control of the gaze. These scenarios often take the form of fantasies where socially impossible or unacceptable desires can be expressed in a way that is separate from the main film narrative. For example, in *Nine to Five* (1980) Dora Lee, a secretary who suffers constant sexual harassment from her male boss in her job at Consolidated Industries, gets high on drugs with her two female co-workers and fantasizes about being a cowgirl and subjecting him to oppressive practices similar to those she has had to endure from him. ✪ [**approximate running time: 37–40.30 mins.**]

Similarly, in *What Women Want* (2000), Nick Marshall is a successful advertising executive who sees women purely as objects of sexual desire and has no ability to empathize with them. Following a fall, he wakes up to find that he can hear the innermost thoughts of every woman he meets. This plot device enables women characters to express the things they would really like to say. For instance, when Nick comes into work he can hear the thoughts of his personal assistant who, after telling him about all the trivial details she has had to attend to for him, thinks aloud: 'do you realize that I have an Ivy League education and that running your stupid errands has put me into therapy? Why's don't you give me some real work to do? I know why, it's because I have a vagina!' ✪ [**approximate running time: 32–33.40 mins.**]

The woman's film represents women doing more influential jobs than in many other films, such as becoming a labour organizer, working as a legal assistant and helping to win an important case or acting as an assistant to the boss of one of the world's most prestigious fashion magazines. However, the appeal of the working woman's film to audiences is based upon a paradox that releases them into organizational contexts where they play active roles and are free to make choices and take action that changes the way that masculine organizations operate, while at the same time confirming to them that their own lives, constrained by marriage and motherhood are confirmed as the right path (Basinger, 1993). One of the key ways of doing this is through representing the liberated working woman falling in love, thereby communicating the message that although she can play important organizational roles she is still subject to her essential womanhood, hence, 'the woman's film suggests to women that until they figure out what to do about the fact that they are women, they can't expect anything else to work' (Basinger, 1993, p. 18) (see Film Focus 6.11 for an example). However, it may be that if feminist discourses enter popular film through showing women to be at the centre of narratives about management and organization, even if this is only the result of desires of producers to access a potentially lucrative market, they can be re-appropriated by audiences. Readers, especially experienced readers of these texts, may be able to explore commonsense notions about women in relation to management and organization and through this to come to a more complex and nuanced understanding of the representations and the reality they seek to represent.

FILM FOCUS 6.11: The return to essential womanhood in *Bridget Jones's Diary* (2001) and *Two Weeks Notice* (2002)

These films can be read as typical of a category of contemporary narrative in popular culture in which the heroine 'typically put[s] work a poor second to romantic entanglements, and long[s] for stable relationships with men' (Brewis, 2004, p. 1822). In *Bridget Jones's Diary* (2001) Bridget's friend Jude who is head of investment at Breitlings Bank 'spends most of her time locked in the ladies toilets crying over fuckwit boyfriend'. Meanwhile Bridget flirts with her new boss Daniel by email, deliberately wearing short skirts and revealing tops to attract his attention through his glass walled office and fantasizing about a white wedding. 💿 [**approximate running time: 11.20–15.30 mins.**] A further example of the return to essential womanhood can be read in *Two Weeks Notice* (2002). Lucy is a high-achieving Harvard educated attorney who campaigns on behalf of various community organizations and orders take away Chinese food to eat alone in her apartment until she meets George Wade, co-owner of a large construction company against which she has spent her career fighting. He offers her a job which she accepts despite her political and ethical principles on the condition that he will save a community centre that she has been fighting to save. George's demands, which extend to asking Lucy's advice on what to wear eventually cause her to hand in her notice, but her reluctance to accept any replacement for her post indicates that she has feelings for her boss that go beyond the professional. The final scene of the film, which shows Lucy and George together in her apartment ordering Chinese food for two, conveys the message that a woman's happiness depends more on hetero-sexual love and domestic companionship than a having a successful career or fighting for a cause. 💿 [**approximate running time: 47–50 mins.**]

Conclusion

This chapter has argued that through constructing the working woman as the alien other, film can be seen as reinforcing subject-object relations which constitute women as voyeuristic objects for the male gaze. It has also been argued that the high degree of consistency that can be observed between the many empirical studies of women's experience of organizations and management discussed in this chapter and the representation of these experiences in film texts would seem to imply that they are indicative of widely shared and collectively understood experience. In addition to reflecting the everyday experiences of women who work in real organizations these representations may also be partially responsible for constituting this reality (McDowell, 1998). It may therefore be that the narrowness of women's roles in organizations has been adversely affected by the representation of working women in film, an argument that is proposed by one of the women managers interviewed in Tretheway's (1999) study.

In evaluating the significance of representations of working women in film and in a manner consistent with the rest of this book, this chapter has argued that the meaning of these texts is the result of a complex dialectical interplay between text and reader which is influenced by the historical and cultural context in which the reading takes place. In taking this perspective it is argued that readers are not 'cultural dopes' (Garfinkel, 1967) socialized into accepting false images of working women through their consumption of these texts. Instead film constitutes one site among many within which the struggle for meaning in relation to these discursive categories is located. This helps to explain the incidence of competing discourses within the same text, for just as film has been used to construct and reinforce the dominant category of 'organization man', it has also been used to give voice to the subordinate category of 'working woman' through representing the marginalizing and exclusionary effects of gendered organizational practices as in films such as *The Associate* (1996) and *North Country* (2005). Film can therefore be seen as a complex medium which provides audiences with representations that challenge as well as endorse, through the communication of complex and sometimes contradictory messages.

Plate 7   Warren Schmidt celebrates his retirement after many years at Woodman insurance company in *About Schmidt* (2002)

Courtesy of Entertainment in Video

7

The search for meaning

Introduction

This chapter considers the preoccupation with the meaning of paid work and fears about the lack of meaning which run through representations of management and organization in film. Film commonly conveys a message about the triviality or futility of work, emphasizing its more mundane aspects and drawing attention to the boredom that employees experience in doing it. There is often a sense of time passing in these films combined with a message about the brevity of life, the need to ensure that it is not wasted through spending time in meaningless or unsatisfying work and several of these representations refer to the character's inevitable death as a means of emphasizing this. Film also represents the ways in which employees try to establish meaning in relation to their working lives, these often being quite different from the meaning that management seeks to impose upon them, drawing attention to the importance of social relationships over and above managerial objectives.

The pervasiveness of this theme invites the conclusion that the search for meaning and the place of work within this search is of fundamental concern. Many of the films discussed in this chapter were released in the mid to late 1990s. Explorations of the meaning of work in film may be connected with the spirit of the times or *Zeitgeist*, a *'fin-de-siècle'* uncertainty associated with the changing of centuries. The incidence of this theme can therefore be read as an indication of the changing meaning of work in the twenty-first century, confirmation of what writers like Sennett (1998) argue is the result of an increasing uncertainty in contemporary employment, organizations no longer providing a context for expression of the values discussed in Chapter 4 such as commitment, trust and loyalty due to an increasingly short-term orientation. Several of the films in this chapter represent these concerns through narratives which revolve around events such as corporate downsizing, redundancy and deskilling, particularly in relation to white-collar managerial and professional work.

However, while the search for meaning in relation to work is a frequently recurring theme within film it is rarely addressed directly within organizational behaviour and management studies. Instead the meaning of work is an issue which tends to be referred to indirectly, for example through studies of employee motivation or workplace spirituality. One potential explanation of this relates to the difficulty in studying beliefs rather than behaviour; the meaning of work is something that perhaps can only be alluded to rather than measured through empirical study, although some researchers have tried (see for example Wrzesniewski, Dutton and Debebe, 2003). This chapter will draw together the strands within this literature as it relates to the theme of meaning using these as a basis for making sense of these representations.

The meaning of work

Preoccupation with the meaning of work implies that having a job is not just about meeting basic material or even social and psychological needs by maintaining a source of income. Instead it is also related to the construction of individual self-identity through establishing a relationship between a person's sense of who they are and the paid work that they do for a living. The meaning of work is thus derived from its role in confirming self-worth. In addition, it provides a source of social relationships beyond the family or community, establishes a framework of activity that structures our time and imposes a rhythm on our lives, gives the opportunity to develop skills, acquire knowledge and practice creativity and fulfils a need for purpose through telling us what to do every day (Furnham, 1990; Ciulla, 2000). Meaningful work also provides the driving force behind the concept of career as a process of gradual progression throughout a person's life (see Chapter 4).

In Chapter 4 we discussed the concept of the Protestant ethic, based on Weber's (1930) thesis that the religious values associated with Protestantism, including the avoidance of idleness and the pursuit of industriousness, the virtues of thrift and frugality and the accumulation of wealth through work, provided the foundations for the expansion of contemporary capitalism. However, there is a further aspect of Weber's thesis which is relevant to exploring the meaning of work and that is the concept of work as a 'vocation' or calling. One of the implications of the Protestant ethic is that work provides a means through which an individual earns God's favour and ultimately achieves salvation. All work, however menial or badly paid, is therefore potentially defined as a calling. The medieval concept of religious vocation as a service to God that guided people for example towards joining monasteries was thereby 'transformed into the modern concept of secular work as a vocation', such that any type of work could be understood as 'requiring the individual's highest religious and ethical commitments' (Berger, 1964, p. 220). It is this concept of secularized vocation which Weber argues provides the basis for the success of modern capitalism since it encourages the belief that work should provide a fundamental source of fulfilment and meaning.

Meaningful work is often represented in film as involving making something that is useful or that has aesthetic value in contrast to work that creates nothing tangible or even leads to the destruction of useful or beautiful things. Some examples of the depiction of meaningful work include Bud Fox's father Carl, a skilled worker who makes aeroplanes in *Wall Street* (1987) and the vineyard manager in *A Good Year* (2006). In these films, work is conceived of as a vocation, a source of fulfilment and meaning for the characters who are engaged in it and a path to happiness (Ciulla, 2000). The dominant category of meaningful work is further defined in opposition to the subordinate category of work that lacks meaning, often represented as based on abstract calculations involving money, numbers and paperwork rather than face-to-face human interaction, through characters like 'Larry the liquidator' in *Other People's Money* (1991) (see Film Focus 3.1), Gordon Gekko in *Wall Street* (1987) (see Film Focus 5.10) and Harold Crick in *Stranger Than Fiction* (2006) (see Film Focus 7.3). What is more, the absence of meaningful work is depicted as a problem the effective resolution of which often involves the characters giving up their current jobs and going off to find work that is more meaningful.

The problem of meaning

The problem of meaning in relation to work is dealt with by many social thinkers including Karl Marx (1867 [1976]) who argued that, under capitalism, the meaning of human life decreases in direct proportion to the increased meaning attached to things which become 'fetishized' as commodities and invested with a significance based upon their marketable value. While Marx saw productive work as potentially meaningful, he regarded capitalism as having crushed the possibility of finding meaning through selling one's labour. The methods of the capitalist system 'mutilate the labourer into a fragment of a man, degrade him to the level of an appendage of a machine, destroy every remnant of charm in his work and turn it into a hated toil' (Marx 1876, quoted in McLellan, 2000, p. 520). In the absence of meaningful work, the individual relies on meaning attached to things. The construction of meaning based on commodity fetishism is a persistent theme within film wherein the value of an individual is signified by the financial value of his or her possessions. For example in *Glenglarry, Glen Ross* (1992) when the visitor from Mitch & Murray is asked his name by one of the salesmen he responds by saying 'I drove an $80,000 BMW [to get here tonight] that's my name!' A further example can be read in *American Beauty* (1999) when Carolyn chastises Lester for nearly spilling beer on the couch thereby putting an end to their rare moment of sexual intimacy. When Lester protests that it is 'just a couch' she retorts, 'this a $4,000 sofa upholstered in pure Italian silk!' Commodity fetishism is thereby presented in film as a source of alienation as well as meaning. This is related to a loss of control over work. As individuals become increasingly divorced from the creative and social rewards associated with their productive labour they are only able to make sense of who they are in the world through the things in their possession.

The intensive division of labour and principles of assembly-line production associated with large-scale, industrial capitalism are also suggested to be sources of alienation. Writers such as Braverman (1974) question whether it is possible for work to fulfil a meaningful role in such a context. Braverman's analysis of the impact of scientific management suggests that the purpose of management strategies is to reduce the power and knowledge held by workers through a gradual process of deskilling. He argues that scientific management will result in the deskilling of all jobs, not just manual ones, predicting that white-collar work as well as industrial labour will eventually become 'proletarianized', made repetitive, monotonous, and increasingly devoid of mental effort. Deskilling entails the increased specialisation of labour which means employees have fewer skills, earn lower wages and are subject to increased pressure over their productivity. In addition to enabling extension of managerial control over the worker, deskilling has consequences for the potential meaning that can be derived from work through removing the possibility of involvement in a task in its entirety. This is suggested to result in a situation where work becomes increasingly fragmented and is consequently less able to provide individuals with a clear source of self-identification. Some examples of films that represent the effects of deskilling on labour are given in Film Focus 7.1 (see also Film Focus 5.11).

FILM FOCUS 7.1: McJobs and nothingness in *Clerks* (1994) and *One Hour Photo* (2002)

The term 'McJob', popularized by novelist Douglas Coupland in his book *Generation X* (1991), refers to repetitive, monotonous jobs which require little mental effort and contain no opportunities for advancement that are often done by young people in service sector occupations such as the fast food industry. The jobs that Dante and Randall have in a convenience and video rental store in *Clerks* (1994) seem to satisfy all the criteria of a McJob. Even so, Dante seems to wish to deny this until his co-worker shatters his illusions by saying: 'You like to think the weight of the world rests on your shoulders. Like this place would fall apart if Dante wasn't here. Jesus, you overcompensate for having what is basically a monkey's job, you push fucking buttons! Anybody could waltz in here and do our jobs. You are so obsessed with making it seem so much more epic, so much more important than it really is. Christ you work in a convenience store Dante, and badly I might add. I work in a shitty video store, badly as well. You know that guy Jay has it right man. He has no delusions about what he does. Us, we like to make ourselves feel so much more important than the people that come in here to buy a paper, or God forbid cigarettes, we look down on them as if we're so fucking advanced. Well if we're so fucking advanced what are we doing working here?' ☺ [**approximate running time: 1 hour 23–24 mins.**]

In *One Hour Photo* (2002) Sy Parrish has been working in a one-hour photo lab for over twenty years. The lab is part of Savmart, which Ritzer (2007, p. 90) reads as a 'thinly disguised send-up of Wal-Mart'. Ritzer goes on to suggest that 'the Savmart store is clearly depicted as nothing', a '*non*place' lacking in distinctive character as signified by the 'white and icy blue colours' and populated by '*non*persons' as signified by the central character's nondescript clothes and his unassertive and affectless demeanor. The job requires that Sy behaves impersonally and efficiently, undertaking his tasks in a routine fashion and interacting with his customers in a scriptable manner without developing any personal attachment to either. This leads Ritzer to reflect that 'a sense of *loss* pervades Sy's life, the store, and the movie, but it is not made clear exactly what has been lost' (Ritzer, 2007, p. 195, emphasis in original); certainly it seems that the sense of personal fulfilment Sy formerly derived from his work has been threatened by organizational changes, this leading Ritzer to conclude that 'what has been lost in those contexts, and in the developed world more generally, are the locally conceived and controlled forms with distinctive substance associated with places, things, people and services' (Ritzer, 2007, p. 195). ☺ [**approximate running time: 6.50–8.20; 18.50–21.20 mins.**]

In addition, because as noted in earlier chapters, industrialization tends to result in the separation of the private from the public life-worlds, locating meaning in the former rather than the latter, work has tended to be constituted as a pseudo-reality where the individual plays a role in which they are not able to be authentic (Cohen and Taylor, 1992). The notion that corporate life requires the individual to behave in a way that is inauthentic is also picked up by more recent writers such as Jackall (1988) and Ehrenreich (2006) who talk about the mask that corporate managers must wear to conceal more complex and ambiguous emotions behind a bland, agreeable exterior. Berger (1964) concludes that the significance of work for an increasing number of people is neither as a source of fulfilment nor of oppression but instead as 'a sort of gray, neutral region in which one neither rejoices nor suffers, but with which one puts up with more or less grace for the sake of other things that are supposed to be more important – these other things typically being connected with one's private life' (Berger, 1964, p. 219). It is just this type of sentiment which is expressed by the character Lester in the film *American Beauty* (1999), when he describes how he feels permanently 'sedated' in his working and home life (see Film Focus 7.2). The representation of workplaces as lacking meaning is also conveyed metonymically by showing the scene to be colourless, such as in the pure white filing room in *Stranger than Fiction* (2006) or the vast empty white shelves of the store in *One Hour Photo* (2002) (see Film Focus 7.1).

A further dimension is introduced into this discussion through consideration of the meaning of managerial work, which several writers have suggested is particularly problematic. Gowler and Legge (1983) argue that management relies on the use of rhetoric, language that is rich in symbolic meaning, as a device through which it is legitimated as a moral order based on ideas such as having responsibility to others and the need for bureaucratic control. Through the use of rhetoric the manager is constructed as a morally superior guardian of scarce resources whose actions are governed by culturally specific principles of accountability and achievement. Watson (1994) argues that the meaning of managerial work is inherently ambiguous, to such an extent that even those who occupy such roles are unclear about what they are really about and whether they constitute 'real' jobs. He therefore characterizes management as an activity in search of itself. Within film, the meaning of management is frequently constructed as problematic and its reliance on rhetoric is depicted as a poor substitute for more classic vocations of 'butcher, baker or candlestick maker' or even 'scientist, pilot or accountant' (Watson, 1994, p. 30). See Film Focus 7.2 for two examples.

FILM FOCUS 7.2: The problem of meaning in managerial work in *About Schmidt* (2002) and *American Beauty* (1999)

In this opening scene we see Warren Schmidt sitting motionless in an empty office at Woodman, the insurance company where he has worked as an actuary for several decades, watching the clock until it reaches exactly 5pm before driving to a restaurant where his retirement party is being held. As Warren sits next to his wife at the head table (see Plate 7) his long-time colleague makes a speech in which he declares that none of the material rewards associated with employment or the ritual associated with retirement really matter, instead 'what really means something, is the knowledge that you devoted your life to something meaningful, to being productive and working for a fine company, hell, one of the top-rated insurance carriers in the nation! To raising a fine family, to building a fine home, to being respected by your community, to having wonderful, lasting friendships. At the end of his career if a man can look back and say I did it, I did my job, then he can retire in glory and enjoy riches far beyond the monetary kind, so all of you young people here take a good look at a very rich man!' After the speech has ended, the expressionless Warren gets up from the table leaving his dinner and colleagues to go to the bar for a drink.

☮ [approximate running time 0.30–7 mins.]

In *American Beauty* (1999) we meet Lester Burnham, a 42 year old advertising executive who works for a magazine publisher, whose wife and daughter

---

think he is a 'gigantic loser'. Lester, the film narrator, says 'They're right, I have lost something … I'm not exactly sure what it is, but I know I didn't always feel this sedated'. When he arrives at the office he is informed by his boss that staff must write their own job descriptions so that management can make a decision about who will lose their jobs. Lester's response to this challenge entails writing a statement which reads 'my job consists of basically masking my contempt for the assholes in charge'. Then he blackmails the organisation into giving him a large payoff, while his wife, Carolyn, continues to pursue the right image with the guidance of the 'King of Real Estate', Buddy Kane, whose career she has closely followed and admired. ☉ [**approximate running times 3.30–6; 49.18–52.10 mins.**]

Another threat to meaningful work comes in the form of emotional labour which involves being required to display a specific set of emotions as part of a job. Hochschild (1983) in *The Managed Heart* argues that organizations have turned emotions into commodities that individuals are required to convey as part of the service provided to the customer, particularly in service work. Emotional labour involves the expression of positive emotions such as happiness and friendliness even if they are not genuinely felt, combined with the suppression of inappropriate emotions such as anger or frustration. This places the employee in an extremely difficult situation; if they respond by 'surface acting', pretending to be friendly and cheerful while not really believing in what they are doing, they become cynical about their work and unable to see it as meaningful, like the 'cynical postmodern worker' described in Chapter 5. If, on the other hand, they engage in 'deep acting', identifying emotionally with the job in a way which endows what they are doing with meaning, they risk burnout and can become unable to express spontaneous emotion; in other words the heart becomes so well managed that it cannot express emotions honestly. The depiction of emotional labour as an aspect of meaningless work frequently arises in film particularly in relation to service work. For example Joanna, a waitress in a restaurant chain in *Office Space* (1998) finds the demands of her job to be intolerable following her supervisor's comments about her lack of 'flair', referring to the badges on her uniform, which can be read as a veiled comment about her unwillingness to express her identity and engage in 'deep acting'. In contrast, Lester in *American Beauty* (1999) is quite happy to engage in 'surface acting' in his job at the fast-food restaurant, Mr Smileys. Hochschild (1983) argues that the demand for emotional labour is primarily borne by women who are the traditional occupants of workplace roles where it is expected, such as the flight attendants in her study. However, *Fight Club* (1999) depicts male workers engaged in service work as bearing the brunt of these demands (see Film Focus 5.11), and as less willing to put up with them.

Yet despite these changes in the conditions of work which make it increasingly difficult to find meaning, the expectation that work will provide an opportunity for self-realization persists and if anything has grown stronger, through society's continuing expectation that individuals should find their work meaningful, this doing little to prepare them for the possibility of meaninglessness that awaits them in employment (Berger, 1964). This creates a paradox, as we are encouraged to be what we do and yet because of the precariousness of employment and incomprehensibly precise job roles there is a lack of inherent meaning contained within them. This is argued by Sievers (1986; 1994) to have generated a whole area of organizational behaviour research that is concerned with human motivation which, he argues, only became an issue for management when meaning was lost from work. Like Berger (1964) he suggests that the problem of meaning was caused by the increasing fragmentation of work which gave rise to a need to re-engineer meaning back into jobs through inventing theories of motivation, such as Maslow's (1943) hierarchy of needs and Herzberg's (1966) motivator-hygiene theory. Furthermore, Sievers argues, these theories are inadequate because they are limited to a micro-perspective that favours causal explanations and are used as a pragmatic instrument to influence human behaviour rather than to understand it. Such theories are based on a non-political, anti-historical and society-free bias that reduces the complexity of social reality into exclusive concerns of individual satisfaction and effectiveness.

Sievers (1994) further argues that one of the silences that exists within organizations surrounds the issue of what happens when work ends due to retirement (see Plate 7) or even death. The meaning of work is thus related to a broader question about the meaning of human existence. He argues that management seeks to deny the inescapable fact of mortality, both in relation to the organization itself which is constituted as immortal, and its members who are expected to privately face death as a fact of life. He suggests it is workers and managers who must carry the burden of this denial in a context where loss of employment and death is a metonym for isolation, loneliness and a confrontation with nothingness, all commonly represented in films that represent management and organization (see Film Focus 7.3). Meaningless death is also a common theme within film, for example through representation of the denial of deaths caused by defective vehicles in films such as *Fight Club* (1999) (see Film Focus 3.7), which can be read as an instance of an organization showing contempt and ignorance towards others such that 'living persons and their dead bodies are permanently reduced to mere market commodities' (Sievers, 1994, p. 147).

FILM FOCUS 7.3: Work and death in *Ikiru* (1952) and *Stranger than Fiction* (2006)

'This is an x-ray of our hero's stomach. He has stomach cancer but he is still unaware of it.' So the narrator begins in the film *Ikiru* (1952) which tells the story of a middle-aged Japanese local government bureaucrat who has done the same job for thirty years. Up until this point Watanabe has been 'just killing time', 'drifting through life'. The film narrator describes him as 'like a corpse, in fact he has been dead for 25 years', lacking 'all initiative and ambition' as a consequence of the 'meaningless intricacy' of his bureaucratic position. The narrator asks the audience 'is this how things should be?' When Watanabe finds out that he is dying of cancer this causes him to re-evaluate the role of work in his life. ☻ [**approximate running time: 2–6 mins.**]

The desire to escape from work before life runs out can also be seen in *Stranger than Fiction* (2006) where tax inspector Harold Crick discovers himself to be the central character in a story being planned by a novelist which must end in his death. Up until this point Harold's life is immensely tedious and repetitive, he never deviates from his daily routines, expresses any emotions or forms any meaningful relationships. The tax office is depicted as the perfect rational, bureaucratic organization for Harold, with its dull, colourless atmosphere where people who are suspected of not paying their taxes become 'files'. Yet once he becomes aware of the story being written about his life, Harold develops what his HR manager describes as 'cubicle fever', no longer observing the rules associated with his employment and breaking a taboo by developing a personal relationship with one of his clients whose tax record he is investigating. ☻ [**approximate running time: 6.20–9; 17.30–19.20 mins.**]

The crisis of meaning may also be related to the rise of a culture of the individual that is based on values of autonomy and self-realization. Rose (1999) argues that the human sciences, including psychology and psychiatry, became more important during the twentieth century because they offered new ways of thinking about self-identity and dealing with the burden of being 'obliged to be free'. The obligation of freedom is burdensome because 'however apparently external and implacable may be the constraints, obstacles and limitations that are encountered, each individual must render his or her life meaningful as if it were the outcome of individual choices made in furtherance of a biographical project of self-realization' (Rose, 1999, p. ix). What is more, work is accorded a central importance within this biographical project because it is suggested to provide a route to individual self-fulfilment and a means of producing, discovering and experiencing ourselves. Rose further argues that the Protestant work ethic no longer fits with the subjectivity of the modern worker whose identity is not shaped through hard work but by consumption.

We are obliged to make our lives meaningful by selecting our personal lifestyle from those offered to us in advertising, soap operas, and films, to make sense of our existence by exercising our freedom to choose in a market in which one simultaneously purchases products and services, and assembles, manages and markets oneself. (Rose, 1999, p. 103)

It is this obligation which is expressed by Jack, in the opening scenes of the film *Fight Club* (1999) when he describes how he, like so many others, 'had become a slave to the IKEA nesting instinct', believing that by owning a particular coffee table or sofa his life would become complete and meaningful. Rose (1999) makes specific reference to film as a source of material for constructing an appropriate self-identity. Through the development of what he refers to as 'technologies of subjectivity' in the form of psychological therapies communicated to us by 'experts', we learn to reshape our identities in a way which promotes the development of the autonomous self. Hence it is significant that Peter's repeated expression of disinterest in his work in *Office Space* (1998) is seen as a problem for which he seeks the help of an analyst (see Film Focus 7.8), while in *Stranger than Fiction* (2006) the counselling that Harold Crick receives from his HR manager is intended to address his apparent disinterest in self-actualization through work (Film Focus 7.3).

The role of consumption in the search for meaning is also taken up by Ritzer (2007) who sees consumer culture, Americanization and branding as evidence of a broader crisis related to the 'globalization of nothing', a social form that is 'generally centrally conceived, controlled, and comparatively devoid of distinctive substantive content' (Ritzer, 2007, p. 36) (see Film Focus 7.1 and 7.4 for examples). The characteristics of 'nothing' are knowable in relation to its opposite, the idea of 'something'. Whereas something is a unique product or service that is rich in distinctive substance often by virtue of its complexity, such as a gourmet meal, nothing is generic and interchangeable. Something is also tied to the local geographic area and is specific to the time period in which it is located, whereas nothing exists independently of time and space, its character being unaffected by this. Nothingness is also associated with impersonal, dehumanized relationships that are tightly controlled and scripted, in contrast to something 'which tends to be associated with deep, meaningful human relationships'. The final dimension through which something and nothing are differentiated draws the previous four dimensions together and concerns the magical. Ritzer argues that the predictability and rationality associated with nothing removes the possibility of enchantment (see Film Focus 7.11 for an example). Despite the 'monumental abundance' of our consumerist lives, he argues that we live in a world that is increasingly dominated by 'nothingness' which, although not inherently bad, threatens to overwhelm the possibility of something. This, argues Ritzer, gives rise to a form of deprivation or a sense of loss borne of the emptiness associated with nothing.

FILM FOCUS 7.4: The globalization of nothing in *Mondovino* (2004)

Mondovino (2004) is a documentary film which tells the story of small local wine producers in countries such as France and Italy being bought up by large conglomerates like Mondavi, a publicly-traded billion-dollar corporation based in the Californian Napa valley, or being forced to change their wines to fit with the preferences of influential wine critics, such as Robert Parker and magazines like the 'Wine Spectator', often hiring wine consultants, like Michel Rolland of Bordeaux, to tell them how to produce an American style. The central message of the film relates to the imposition of a kind of sameness in wine making and the way that globalization is 'changing many of the world's oldest and most established traditions' [IMDb user comment – http://imdb.com/title/tt0411674/#comment – consulted 08.08.07]. In this scene, wine makers from France and California discuss the role of branding and the relationship between traditional methods of manufacture and modern technology. One of the characteristics associated with French winemaking is the notion of *terroir*, which refers to the subtle aspects of the land on which vines are grown and the way that this influences a wine's character. However, globalization erodes the importance of place, hence contributing towards Ritzer's (2007) definition of 'nothingness'. This can be seen from the discussion relating to the French-Californian joint venture between winemakers Mouton Rothschild and Mondavi, in developing Opus One, where there is some debate as to whether this is a Franco-Californian or a Californian wine or a wine that can be geographically located in any way. This scene also illustrates the impact of Americanization and branding on wine production. The French winemakers use English terminology, such as 'winemaker', even when speaking in French, this illustrating the extent of Anglo-Saxon influence on the new managerial culture. ☉ [**approximate running time: 40–48 mins.**]

The threat of downsizing

Sennett (1988) argues that the meaning of work is changing in post-industrial society. In industrial society although work may have been routine or dull, it enabled pursuit of meaningful activities and contributed to the development of what he describes as 'character', principally through an individual's length of service and commitment to an organization. Most importantly, these principles were reciprocated by the organization. Work thus constituted an object of loyalty and commitment based on a social, long-term orientation. However, changes in the nature of work in post-industrial society have meant that such an orientation to work has been 'corroded' by short-term contracts, the expectation that one should take risks, lack of community at work, saying the 'right' thing and looking 'right', downsizing, individualism and the prioritization of personal responsibility. Film Focus 7.2 contains two examples, one of which seems to confirm Sennett's argument, the other to disconfirm it. In *American Beauty* (1999) it is suggested that Lester's character has become 'corroded' as a consequence of his experience of work in post-industrial society through having been exposed to the kinds of pressures that Sennett describes. Unlike his wife, Carolyn, who is still trying to survive in a high-pressure, short-term, results-focused career by taking personal responsibility for her own success and failure, Lester is no longer willing to withstand the pressures associated with his employment or to try to find meaning in his work as an advertising executive. However, in *About Schmidt* (2002) it is hard to see Warren's length of service and commitment to one organization throughout his working life as having produced the kind of meaning that Sennett suggests it should. Although it is clear that Warren's employment has been characterized by loyalty on both sides, the film's message involves Warren at the point of his retirement confronting the emptiness and lack of meaning in his life, his former employment being suggested as a principle reason for this (see Plate 7). However, *About Schmidt* (2002) is something of an exception as many other films, such as those discussed in Film Focus 7.5, contain narratives that are supportive of Sennett's thesis.

FILM FOCUS 7.5: The corrosion of character in *Jerry Maguire* (1996) and *In Good Company* (2004)

Jerry Maguire (1996) is a sports agent working for 'Sports Management International' who fears that he has become 'just another shark in a suit', negotiating ever larger financial deals for his clients in a way which is increasingly cynical and greedy. One night he wakes up and realizes that he hates who he has become. He therefore finds himself compelled to write a mission statement of how he would really like the business to be, the bottom line of which involves having fewer clients and less money. ☻ [**approximate running time: 5.30–9.50 mins.**] In discussing the film, director Cameron Crowe explains that one of the explicit aims was to start the narrative at the point where 1980s films traditionally ended, when the hero realizes that greed is not good after all, subsequently tracing how he deals with this realization (see Film Focus 3.1, 5.9 and 5.10).

In Good Company (2004) represents the fate that befalls employees working for the magazine 'Sports America' when the company they work for is acquired in a corporate takeover by 'Globecom', an empire-building conglomerate with a reputation for asset stripping. When the fabled CEO, Teddy K, makes a visit to the offices of the magazine, he is confronted by advertising-space salesman, Dan Foreman, who challenges his view of global capitalism, saying 'I'm not sure I understand how the way the world is changing is actually going to change how we do business, we're still selling a product, right, which hopefully someone needs. We're human beings with other human beings, for customers. Although I don't see how this company is like its own country, just because we sell different kinds of things, it doesn't mean we should operate by our own laws does it? Besides which countries, at least democratic ones, they have some obligation to their citizens don't they? So how do layoffs and bottom-line thinking fit into that?' ☻ [**approximate running time: 1 hour 23–1 hour 27.20 mins.**]

In films such as *Office Space* (1998), *American Beauty* (1999) and *In Good Company* (2004) increased insecurity surrounding managerial work is reflected by a discourse of corporate 'downsizing', 'restructuring' and 'de-layering'. This threat is often communicated to staff by the unexplained presence of outsiders in the workplace, such as management consultants, and signals impending job losses. These narratives can be read as depicting the phenomenon of business process re-engineering, as popularized by management writers such as Hammer and Champy (1993) who argue that a radical new approach to management is needed for the post-industrial age. The popularity of re-engineering is attributed to the fact that it provided an apparent solution to fears about declining American managerial effectiveness in the face of Japanese competition in the late 1980s and early 1990s, which Grint (1994) argues legitimated American culture, as can be read in the film *Gung Ho* (1986). The target of this new way of managing was the large organization which the re-engineering gurus argued had become inefficient, blaming the scientific management principle of breaking a task into its component parts for leading to excessive fragmentation and a blurring of accountability, where no one individual was able to see the whole of a task in its entirety. They were also critical of what they saw as excessive paperwork and bureaucracy, arguing that organizations instead needed to be guided by function, in the form of customer-oriented outputs, rather than process.

One might observe that the critique of scientific management and bureaucratic organization offered by the re-engineering gurus was not dissimilar to the way that industrial mass production and bureaucracy had been represented in films like *Modern Times* (1936), *Brazil* (1985), *Spotswood* (1991) and *The Hudsucker Proxy* (1994). However, the primary object of the re-engineering gurus' criticisms was middle-management the vast cost savings promised being achieved through the shedding of large numbers of employees (Grint, 1994) based on an ideology which proposed that the people 'doing the work' were more important than those supervising it (Hammer, 1990). Under this new regime, the value of managerial work could no longer be taken for granted. Middle-managers like Lester in *American Beauty* (1999) or Peter in *Office Space* (1998) could be called into the boss's office at any time and required to justify their value to the organization. In the meantime they were forced to live with the sense of constant apprehension and vulnerability that such a situation provoked. Such representations can be read as a reflection of what Scarbrough and Burrell (1996) suggest is an attempt to manage the middle layers of organization out of existence through breaking down traditional managerial career structures and removing their hierarchically-based privileges (see Chapter 4 for a summary). Downsizing tends to be portrayed critically within these films as a tool that offers a logic for making and justifying job cuts by placing responsibility for the loss of the job on the victim. As Sennett (1988) notes:

> The manager who declares that we are all victims of time and place is perhaps the most cunning figure to appear in the pages of this book. He has mastered the art of wielding power

without being held accountable; he has transcended that responsibility for himself, putting the ills of work back on the shoulders of those fellow "victims" who happen to work for him. (Sennett, 1988, pp. 115–116)

Survivor syndrome

Even for those who are fortunate enough to keep their jobs in a climate of downsizing the sense of insecurity that is provoked by such a situation leads to a form of survivor syndrome. Survivor syndrome is produced by the experience of witnessing the loss of colleagues and affects the behaviour of remaining employees in disturbing and potentially damaging ways. Job insecurity is suggested to have increased the extent to which white-collar workers feel obliged to demonstrate their commitment to the organization by working long hours and not having a life outside the organization (Ehrenreich, 2005). In one study employees adopted strategies for dealing with these pressures that included leaving their jackets on their office chairs or their keys on the desk in order to give their colleagues the impression that they were still at work even after they had left the office to go home (Collinson and Collinson, 1997). Hochschild's (1997) study of families at Fortune 500 company 'Amerco' also found that employees worked long hours. What is more, even though they expressed a desire to spend more time with their families and the organization had excellent family benefits, such as parental leave, the actual take-up of these initiatives was relatively low. However, rather being motivated to work long hours because of feelings of insecurity about their ongoing employment, Hochschild suggests that, for both women and men, the workplace had become a more attractive place to be than the home due to the greater possibilities for satisfaction in an orderly environment that the former provided, in contrast to the time pressures and stresses associated with the latter.

Films such as *Fun with Dick and Jane* (2005) (see Film Focus 3.11) and *The Devil Wears Prada* (2006) depict individuals as dealing with high pressure work environments characterized by a condition which Perlow (1999) describes as 'time famine', where they experience a scarcity of time, especially in specialist, high-skill occupations (see Film Focus 7.6). They are also depicted as experiencing temporal 'ever-availability' (Zerubavel, 1981) a condition enabled by technologies which increase the expectation to be available for work wherever they are and whatever they are doing. In addition, their work patterns are characterized by frequent interruptions to which they are expected to respond as heroic individuals, often dealing with a succession of crises for which they are rewarded by the organization. Perlow's (1999) study of high-tech engineers suggests that this creates a vicious cycle where the individual is never able to plan or manage their work effectively because they are constantly being interrupted to deal with urgent problems. For example, Dick does not question the decision of his bosses in *Fun with Dick and Jane* (2005) when they give him the task of appearing on a live TV news show only one day after he receives his promotion, having had no time to prepare for it. However, rather than celebrating and glorifying these organizational cultures, these films call into question such behaviours as a test of commitment to the organization through the introduction of narratives which end with the individual's departure from the organization (see also Film Focus 7.11).

FILM FOCUS 7.6: Time famine in *The Devil Wears Prada* (2006)

In *The Devil Wears Prada* (2006) Andy is expected to demonstrate her commitment to the organization and her boss, Miranda Priestly, through her heroic behaviours which constitute part of a vicious cycle of time famine. On one occasion she is asked by her boss to get her a flight home during a hurricane and in another to obtain a copy of the unpublished manuscript of a Harry Potter book. As she starts to achieve these heroic feats she is taken more seriously by her boss who starts to give her more status, responsibility and opportunity. Temporal 'ever-availability' is also a condition of Andy's employment. She can expect to be called on her mobile phone at all times of the day and night and asked to come into work whatever else she may be doing.
[**approximate running time: 26.10–30.30 mins.**]

The absence of work

Film represents the plight of the 'victims' of downsizing in the form of the unemployed white-collar workers who euphemistically describe themselves as 'in transition' in journalist Barbara Ehrenreich's (2006) depiction of contemporary corporate America. In the documentary film *Fired!* (2007), Annabelle Gurwitch, like Ehrenreich, visits career coaches and careers fairs, collecting people's tragicomic stories of losing their jobs. This illustrates an important point, for one of the clearest ways of representing the importance of work as a source of meaning is through illustrating the effects of its absence caused by unemployment. In Chapter 5, we analysed several examples of films that represent the absence of industrial work, such as *Brassed Off* (1996) and *The Full Monty* (1997). The meaning of white-collar work is also represented through its absence in films such as *Time Out* (2001) (see Film Focus 7.7).

FILM FOCUS 7.7: The absence of work in *Time Out* (2001) and *Fired* (2007)

Vincent appears to his family and friends to be a successful financial consultant in *Time Out* (2001). However, he lost his job weeks ago and since then has

Continued

constructed an elaborate fiction whereby he goes out driving around, eating in motorway service stations and calling his wife on his mobile phone to tell her about his many important meetings. This inversion of his domestic and work life entails getting changed into his suit and having a shave before he goes home, rather than before going to work. In one scene, he explains to a friend he meets on the road that driving was the thing he used to like best about his job, 'I felt so good in my car I had difficulty in leaving it', taking detours to extend the length of his business trips. Eventually, this led to him being told by his boss that he no longer 'fitted in' and his departure was negotiated. At the end of the film, Vincent is interviewed and offered another corporate job, which he is told, will be a 'human adventure' for which his 'personal investment' is required, but throughout the conversation he looks vacant as though he is somehow else-where. ☉ [**approximate running times: 4.35–10.38; 1 hour 23.50–1 hour 27; 2 hours 3.30–2 hours 6 mins.**]

In the documentary film *Fired!* (2007) Annabelle Gurwitch, an actress prompted by her experience of being fired from a play by Woody Allen to make a film about this subject, makes the point that almost everyone has a story to tell even if they are reluctant to tell it. She goes to a careers fair to encourage people to talk about their experiences of being fired and asks a former Human Resources manager to describe his technique for firing people. ☉ [**approximate running times: 19–21.20; 34.10–36 mins.**]

Meaning and the social group

The meaning of work in film is suggested to be derived not only from the job itself, the actual tasks and the significance that the individual undertaking them attributes to them, but also from the social and organizational settings in which work takes place, including the localised sense whereby meaning is established and maintained. One early research investigation that was highly influential in drawing attention to the importance of these sense making practices was the Hawthorne studies (1927–1932), which took place at the Western Electric Company and comprised a series of experiments designed to test the influence of various physical factors, including temperature, lighting and hours of sleep, on worker productivity (Roethlisberger and Dickson, 1939). The conclusions of these studies are well known, in that rather than being affected by changes in the physical conditions of work, of far more significant impact on worker productivity was the informal social group. Whether or not these interpretations were valid, some writers like Gilson (1940) having questioned the bias of the research in terms of its failure to consider issues of unionism and the assumptions that were made about women workers, the study became part of a received wisdom about management.

The importance of the informal social group in establishing and maintaining meaning at work was also considered by Roy (1958) on the basis of his participant observation study of social interaction in a small work group of factory operators. 'Since the operatives were engaged in work which involved the repetition of very simple operations over an extra-long workday, six days a week, they were faced with the problem of dealing with a formidable "beast of monotony"'. He goes on to observe: 'it was evident to me, before my first workday drew to a weary close, that my clicking career was going to be a grim process of fighting the clock' (Roy, 1958, pp. 158–160). The work group was left largely to its own devices and experienced very little interference from management. Roy described how the group used ritual acts of horseplay to punctuate working time thereby relieving the monotony and providing a solution to the problem of psychological survival. These revolved around designated 'times' for certain activities that entailed a break in the flow of production and often involved the consumption of food and drink, such as 'banana time' or 'coke time'. Also important were 'themes', topics of conversation which the group returned to repeatedly and they often involved an element of humour relating to a member of the group. It was thus the informal social activity of the work group rather than any external influence by management which provided a principle source of meaning in relation to work, this helping to alleviate the lack of meaning associated with fragmented work and the alienation of labour under capitalism. The importance of the informal work group in providing meaning can be read in several films that represent work, Film Focus 7.8 provides two examples.

FILM FOCUS 7.8: The informal work group as a source of meaning in *Clockwatchers* (1997) and *Office Space* (1998)

Clockwatchers (1997) follows the fortunes of four temporary secretaries who work for the Global Credit Association. The female secretaries constitute a distinct subculture which is separate from the 'permanents' who show so little interest in them that they fail even to learn their names, keeping the 'temps' working together and separating them from the 'permanents'. It gradually becomes clear that the 'temps' have very little work to do and their main task is to develop ways of 'looking busy' so as not to attract managerial attention. The members of this informal work group develop a variety of ingenious techniques for dealing with the boredom associated with their work including making a folder into a musical accordion, swivelling on an office stool while staring into space and sniffing coloured marker pens. Like the workers in Roy's (1958)

Continued

study, the meaning of work for the secretaries is based on social time, temporal rhythms, such as their regular Friday night socials, uniting them in their shared temporal perspective which can only ever be short-term because after all they are 'only temps'. ✆ [**approximate running times: 6.30–15.50; 29–31 mins.**]

The role of the informal work group in dealing with lack of meaning is also represented in the film *Office Space* (1998). In this opening scene, Peter arrives at work at Initech with a 'case of the Mondays', provoked by the female worker's irritating telephone voice in the next cubicle, his boss's petty reminders about coversheets and the fax machine that doesn't work. As a result, he appears to be experiencing signs of alienation including feelings of powerlessness, self-estrangement and meaninglessness, calling upon his two friends and co-workers to go for an early coffee break as a means of temporary escape, where he poses the question 'what if we are still doing this in our 50's?' When it becomes clear that the company is going to be downsized and the other members of his informal work group are going to lose their jobs, Peter once again invokes the theme of meaning as a basis for encouraging them to sabotage the company, saying 'We don't have a lot of time on this earth, we weren't meant to spend it this way. Human beings were not meant to sit in little cubicles staring at computer screens all day, filling out useless forms and listening to eight different bosses drone on about mission statements!' Although the problem of meaning is ultimately resolved through the pursuit of more 'authentic' work when Peter becomes a construction worker on a building site (see Film Focus 5.12), in the meantime it is the informal workgroup that provides him with a means of coping with his feelings of meaninglessness. ✆ [**approximate running times: 0–10.50; 44.50–48 mins.**]

Meaning is derived from the control of space as well as time within the informal work group. Baldry (1999) suggests that the working environment is a socially constructed space that comprises: the 'fixed environment' where conflict stems from struggles about the amount of control over the work space, the amount of space allocated being an indicator of status and power; the 'semi-fixed environment', wherein objects that may seem unremarkable outside the workplace take on significance as indicators of status and power; and the 'ambient environment' related to the degree of control employees have over privacy, heating and lighting, this being an indication of their hierarchical position within the organization. Baldry (1999) further argues that the work space is a 'contested terrain' within which struggles over space represent a struggle for power, for example when employees use the work space for activities other than those intended or move items around within their semi-fixed environment. These acts can also be seen as an attempt to manage the meaning of work as Film Focus 7.9 illustrates.

Film Focus 7.9: Control over space as a struggle for meaning in *Office Space* (1998) and *Clockwatchers* (1997)

In *Clockwatchers* (1997) the temps introduce meaning into their semi-fixed environment by personalizing their cubicles with items that are of symbolic importance to them. However, they fail to influence the ambient environment, management continuing to broadcast awful music through a loudspeaker system. When a series of items go missing from the office, management increases worker surveillance and suspicion focuses on the temps, security cameras are installed and their desks are moved into a central area where they can be more closely watched. This apparently confirms Baldry's (1999) assertion that poor conditions of working space are more common when workers' bargaining power is low, as for this group of temporary workers. 😊 [**approximate running time: 55.45–1 hour 3 mins.**]

In *Office Space* (1998) contestation over work space is most clearly represented through the character Milton adapted from a series of shorts by Mike Judge, who jealously guards his 'fixed environment' by trying to protect his office cubicle from size reduction, his 'semi-fixed environment' by guarding his stapler, and his 'ambient environment' by asserting his right to listen to the radio. However, Milton gradually loses all these battles and is eventually moved into the basement. In contrast, Peter, who is favoured by the management consultants in charge of the downsizing exercise, enjoys a steadily increasing amount of control over his work space and time. 😊 [**approximate running times: 31.30–32.40; 39.30–43.10 mins.**]

The possibility of escape

One of the most common visual conventions associated with representations of managerial work is the clerical open-plan office formerly known as the bullpen or, more recently, the office cubicle. Within this the individual is represented as trapped by the bleakness of office life and longing to escape from it (see Film Focus 7.10). Escape is a theme which runs through representations of industrial as well as post-industrial work; for example *Modern Times* (1936) ends with the factory worker escaping with his Gamine to live in the country. Many of these representations rely on a nostalgic view of pre-modern work as offering a solution to the problem of meaning and the fragmented self based on the reintegration of public and private spheres or life-worlds, as seen for example in *Baby Boom* (1987) (Film Focus 6.8). A potential explanation of the pervasiveness of this theme in film texts relates to the role of American cultural mythology in informing them, where escape is one of the foundational principles constituted through the history of a nation that has portrayed itself as a refuge for people fleeing from other countries (Sadar and Wyn Davies, 2004). Film offers a powerful medium through which the myth of 'escape as a reason for being' can be constructed.

Cohen and Taylor (1992) refer to escape attempts as the strategies, tactics and plans which we devise for escaping and resisting reality through identity work. They argue that the routinization of everyday life in consumer society so engulfs us, with its predictable scripts and standardised patterns of behaviour, that we are forced to search for an alternative reality from the one that we presently inhabit in order to escape from its oppressive nature. This, they argue, is a particular problem in contemporary society, where we have all the possibilities for our lives mapped out in front of us, hence 'the more predictable the life plan appears, the less we are able to sense ourselves as individuals possessing unique identities' (Cohen and Taylor, 1992, p. 48). So how do people escape from the workplace? One possibility is through fantasies, mind games that offer the promise of escape. However these are illusory and always involve a return to reality. Another possibility is through the creation of 'free areas', which enable a temporary absence from everyday life, perhaps by going on holiday or signing off sick with stress. For example, Vincent in the film *Time Out* (2001) creates a free area for himself by taking business trips when he can spend time alone in his car (see Film Focus 7.7). However, this temporary escape is not enough for him and eventually his escape becomes more permanent when he loses his job.

FILM FOCUS 7.10: Escaping from the workplace in *The Matrix* (1999)

In *The Matrix* (1999) work is represented as part of 'The System', from which people need to release themselves, in contrast to the 'real world' which Neo enters when he makes the decision to take the red pill that takes him into the world of the unknown rather than the blue one which would ensure his more mundane, conventional life is sustained. In this scene, Thomas 'Neo' Anderson, a program writer who works for a software company, is reprimanded for being late for work. He receives a package delivered to his office cubicle which turns out to be a message delivered on a telephone from Morpheus who remotely guides him through the maze of cubicles and away from the Agents who are looking for him. However, Neo cannot bring himself to jump from the building and so he gives himself up to the Agents. ☉ [**approximate running time: 11.30–16 mins.**]

Work and spirit

Further evidence of preoccupation with meaning can be discerned from the emergence of the workplace spirituality discourse as an attempt to overcome the perceived devaluation of work in contemporary organizations. The topic of spirituality in the workplace has become established as a focus of popular managerial interest and a field of academic study in the period since the mid 1990s. Interest is suggested to be a reaction against the attempted separation of the 'outer world' of production and consumption under modernism and the 'inner world' of spirituality and religion which is concerned with the meaning of being human (Neal and Biberman, 2003). One of the main assertions upon which this literature is based is that employees need to find work meaningful but that many organizational contexts fail to provide them with the opportunity to develop either meaning or fundamental purpose (Mitroff and Denton, 1999). The reasons for this relate to downsizing, careerism, consumerism, the fragmentation of self-identity and the separation of work from non-work life-worlds (see Bell and Taylor, 2003 for a summary). Several authors suggest that spirituality benefits both employees and management and some even seek to demonstrate a positive link between spirituality and organizational profitability (Ashmos and Duchon, 2000). This is an approach criticized by writers such as Bell and Taylor (2003), who argue that this paradoxically constructs spirituality as a reaction against modernist organization yet simultaneously seeks to shape it in ways that suggest it can be managed.

However, research indicates that the search for spirituality is driven by employees as well as management. Casey's (2002) study of highly skilled, well-paid, professional employees suggests that they seek out spirituality as a source of inner meaning that helps them to address the pressures associated with work. She contends that this is a type of 'revolt from within' in the form of a social movement based on diverse forms of spirituality driven by 'ordinary people' in an effort to transcend the 'emptiness' of the workplace. Referring to this 're-enchantment' of working life, Casey argues that one of the interesting things about these meaning-making explorations is that spirituality, which runs counter to the principles of scientific rationality associated with modernism, is being practiced within modernist organizations. This leads her to conclude that 'one-sided modernity now meets a counter-force it unintendedly helped generate' (Casey 2002, p. 165). What is more, she suggests, this exploration has the potential to become a precursor to more permanent disengagement from modernist organizations, as individuals with successful careers decide to opt out of organizational work. 'People from a wide range of working life backgrounds in Western societies are acting in ways which suggest that the modern societal privileging of work as ultimate *raison d'être* and of self and social value is being challenged and altered' (Casey, 2002, p. 167).

In this way spirituality is suggested to provide the basis for a more permanent escape from the post-industrial workplace based on challenging the notion of organizational work as a secularized vocation. Very often, this theme is pursued in film by constructing a binary opposition between fragmented work in rational, modernist organizations and craft work, involving creative self expression and enabling the reintegration of work and non-work life-worlds in harmony with the natural environment, the latter being portrayed as a more receptive environment in which the search for meaning can be pursued (see Film Focus 7.11).

FILM FOCUS 7.11: Spirituality and escape from modernist organization in *A Good Year* (2006) and *Stranger than Fiction* (2006)

Max Skinner is a highly successful London banker and bond trader who finds out that he has inherited a vineyard in Provence following the death of his uncle in *A Good Year* (2006). However, despite his commercial success, he is depicted as lacking a sense of vocation and therefore as unable to appreciate the meaning of the work involved in wine production. Hence when he finds out he has inherited the vineyard, his only concern is with the commodity value of the chateaux as a valuable piece of real estate. However, gradually his outlook changes, as his private and work lives merge in a way which implies that he comes to recognise the inauthentic nature of his working role as a banker, in contrast to making wine as a vocation which has the potential to provide a fundamental source of fulfilment and meaning. ☺ [**approximate running time: 3.50–6.50 mins.**]

Ana Pascal is the owner of a bakery in *Stranger than Fiction* (2006), a job which is depicted as a vocation, involving the creation of wonderful cakes, pastries and cookies that uplift the human spirit through the careful mixing of ingredients. The enchanted aspect of this work also stems from the human relationships involved in it. This contributes towards what Ritzer (2007) refers to as 'something' – locally conceived and controlled, distinctive work. The coffee shop also exhibits the characteristics of what Ritzer refers to as a 'great good place', an informal community meeting place that reflects the characteristics of its creator and its local environment. Ritzer argues that while some global restaurant chains like Starbucks try to present themselves as having these characteristics they depend on a highly centralized, controlled and standardized form of organization that has proliferated throughout the world. When she makes Harold Crick some cookies and gives them to him as a gift, there is a magical quality to the act which she manages to convey to him. However, when Harold offers to buy the cookies because he is not allowed to accept gifts from someone whose tax affairs he is investigating, the moment of meaning is lost through his attempt to turn them into a commodity. ☺ [**approximate running time: 37.10–46 mins.**]

Conclusion

This chapter has traced the search for meaningful work within film, drawing attention to representations of perceived threats and opportunities for constructing meaning and demonstrating their relationship to organizational analyses that provide commentary on and explanation of these conditions. Whereas representations of industrial work in film predominantly suggest it to be a source of suffering and a form of oppression (see Chapter 3), representations in the period leading up to and at the turn of the twentieth century articulate a different set of fears relating to dull, uninteresting and depersonalized work which leaves no lasting impression on either the employee, the customer, or other organization members whom they come into contact with. However, rather than simply depicting workers as trapped within meaningless work, film often presents the possibility of resistance and even escape from these stultifying conditions. Films such as *Fun with Dick and Jane* (2005), *Office Space* (1998) and *American Beauty* (1999) show the worker successfully dealing with the insecurities of the contemporary workplace by walking away from them or learning to cope without the organization, for example by blackmailing their boss into offering them a redundancy package in *American Beauty* (1999) (see Film Focus 7.2) or by presenting themselves as entirely unconcerned about employment in *Office Space* (1998). From an ideological perspective this could be interpreted as evidence of the 'safety-valve' function of film discussed in Chapter 1. By providing audiences with the opportunity of temporarily identifying with a character who escapes from meaningless work, their engagement with the text reduces the likelihood of any transformation in their everyday lives. Film can thus be seen as creating an illusion that is in itself a form of temporary escape, this constituting one of the potential 'gratifications' (Berger, 1991) that it offers to the audience.

However, as active readers of texts, audience engagement with film is more complex than this analysis suggests. As Cohen and Taylor (1992) argue, escape attempts can take multiple forms, including those which constitute a temporary escape by creating a fantasy of an alternative reality. Yet this does not necessarily make them valueless, since the identity work that is involved in such an activity may provide a precursor to more permanent forms of escape, as Casey's (2002) analysis of workplace spirituality suggests. Representations of modernist organization such as those depicted in earlier chapters may thereby be destabilized through these texts which question the assumption that modern work constitutes a source of meaning that provides the individual with a sense of purpose and fulfilment. What is more, as the boundaries between representation and reality are increasingly blurred (Baudrillard, 1995), the role of these texts as alternative realities becomes ever more complex, an issue that will be explored further in Chapter 8.

Plate 8 Chinese migrant workers in a duck processing factory which supplies a leading supermarket chain in *Ghosts* (2006)

8

Spectres of organization

Introduction

The concluding chapter of this book focuses on the use of film to give voice to those who tend to be silenced through contemporary managerial practices, such as the migratory workers who cross national borders in pursuit of low paid, often dangerous work, or those employed as call centre operators, construction workers, office temps, restaurant servers, cleaners, crop harvesting and food processing workers who provide the goods and services that consumers use every day. These texts represent various types of 'dirty work', physically or morally dirty, degrading or undignified work that 'runs counter to the more heroic of our moral conceptions' of labour (Hughes, 1958, p. 50, quoted in Dick, 2005, p. 1364). Dirty work also tends to be hidden from sight, both in terms of the lack of visibility of those who undertake it and the lack of research attention devoted to it. Film can therefore be understood as a means of making the invisible visible, giving form to the spectral bodies that remain unseen within organizations through the potential afforded by the medium to overcome these boundaries (see Film Focus 8.1). The role of film as a means of representing those who are marginalized also lends weight to the somewhat postmodern view that anything not represented in film seems not to happen completely, or even at all. By the same token, through representing the situation of these organization members film may make their situation more 'real' to audiences.

It is also significant that many of the films in this chapter are concerned with globalization, these texts often contrasting its optimistic promises with the less glamorous reality experienced by many people, such as sweatshop factory workers in developing countries whose exploitation enables the supply of cheap goods to consumers in the West. They thus seek to represent the negative human effects associated with global capital and the flow of investment across national borders focusing in particular on the role of multinationals, such as McDonalds and Wal-Mart, which have become the paradigmatic corporations of the twenty-first century (Zaniello, 2007) and the subject of several films (see Film Focus 8.5 and 8.7 for examples).

Many of the films in this chapter fall into the category of the documentary feature film. The popularity of feature-length documentary films can be gauged simply from the number of recent releases including *The Corporation* (2003), *The Take* (2004), *Super Size Me* (2004), *Mondovino* (2004), *Wal-Mart: The High Cost of Low Price* (2005), *McLibel* (2005), *Enron: The Smartest Guys in the Room* (2005), *Fast Food Nation* (2006), *Sicko* (2007) and *It's a Free World* (2007), all of which are highly critical of contemporary managerial practices. Although these films do not attract audiences as large as many of the other films discussed in this book, they are still popular in the sense that many people watch and derive meaning from them. It may even be suggested that we are in the midst of a 'documentary turn' which involves a reinvigoration of the documentary feature film as a means of resisting contemporary management ideas and practices.

However, there is a risk associated with reading documentary film that it is assumed to correspond to an objectively known and agreed upon reality. As has been argued throughout this book, the boundaries between fact and fiction in film are not as clear as this proposition suggests. This chapter therefore returns to consideration of the relationship between representation and reality, arguing that, even in documentary film, what we experience as the reality of organization is not the thing itself but a symbolic fiction through which reality is constituted and structured. This chapter explores the implications of this proposition for the way we read film and the significance we attribute to it, arguing that we come to understand the reality of organizations through encountering them on the screen as a mediated version of reality or as a spectre.

The final section of this chapter draws together the themes discussed previously and considers their implications. While the analysis developed has been broadly historical, drawing attention to the changing nature of representations of management and organization in film and exploring their relationship to changing socio-economic conditions and theories of management, it has also sought to emphasize the relative endurance of these representational themes. Rather than being superseded they are incorporated intertextually in a way which ensures that iconographic conventions established in an earlier era live on, thereby having the potential to continue to inform understandings of management and organization in everyday life.

FILM FOCUS 8.1: Spectral bodies in *Ghosts* (2006) and *It's a Free World* (2007)

Both of these films seek to represent migratory patterns of labour under globalization involving the movement of workers from economically deprived countries to the UK. *Ghosts* (2006) is a fictionalized representation based on real events in February 2004 when twenty-one Chinese migrant workers were drowned while cockle picking on Morecambe Bay in the northwest of England. The story follows the fate of Ai Qin, a young Chinese single mother, who cannot find work in her home country to support her son and who decides to become part of the global migration of labour by being smuggled into the UK in the back of a lorry. We follow Ai Qin as she becomes one of over one million undocumented workers currently employed in farms and factories across the UK, many working to provide food for restaurants and supermarkets. By the time the Chinese workers have paid inflated sums for their 'accommodation' (a mattress on the floor in a room shared with four other people) to their gangmaster and various 'taxes' to their employment agency they are left with very little money each week to send back to their families in China to pay back the heavy debts owed to the moneylenders who financed their travel to the UK. In one scene, we see Ai Qin working a shift in a duck processing factory that supplies to a leading supermarket chain [see Plate 8], in another she goes shopping with her co-worker in the supermarket only to find that they cannot afford most of the products, including the spring onions which only a few hours ago she was picking in a field. ☺ [**approximate running times: 28.50–33.50; 49.20–52.20 mins.**]

In *It's a Free World* (2007) two young women, Angie, who has had a series of jobs, with hollow promises of employment security and career prospects, and Rose, a university graduate who works in a call centre, set up an undeclared employment agency placing casual, hourly-paid, workers from Eastern Europe with London employers who are looking for a cheap source of labour. In this murky world, Angie discusses with one of her clients, the manager of a T-shirt factory, which of the people she has sent him he will accept back again, the client using racist, personalized judgements as the basis for his selection. It becomes clear, when Angie talks to her father about the social and employment conditions that have informed her decision to become the boss of the type of agency she was formerly employed by, that their values and life experiences are radically different and that responsibility for these employment conditions is borne by consumers as well as the gangmasters. ☺ [**approximate running time: 25.10–28; 55–57.30 mins.**]

Documentary film and reality

Before considering the impact of these spectres of organization, it is first necessary to review the status of the documentary film as a medium for their representation. Documentary feature film 'purports to present factual information about the world outside the film' (Bordwell and Thompson, 2004, p. 128) by recording events as they occur, using visual aids such as maps and artworks and staging events for the camera such as interviewing an expert or a witness to certain events with which the film is concerned. The documentary film provides evidence which is used to make a stand, develop an argument or advocate a solution to a problem. Hence, although the information presented in the film is suggested to be factually correct, a documentary may use it to present the subject in a particular light and in a way that is intended to appeal to beliefs that are dominant within a given culture at a particular historical moment. For example, the film *Super Size Me* (2004) echoes many of the arguments advanced by Schlosser in his bestselling book *Fast Food Nation* (2001) about the role of fast food as a commodity and a metaphor for American life; Schlosser's book was itself subsequently made into a film of the same name in 2007 (see Film Focus 8.11). These texts can therefore be read as part of a broader concern about large organizations and the global organization of the food industry at the turn of the century.

However, in seeking to differentiate documentary film from other types of films there is a risk that the former comes to be understood as corresponding more closely to the reality of management and organization as the very term 'documentary' implies that the purpose of such texts is to accurately document some phenomenon or event. One of the main points of this book has been to demonstrate that all film has the potential to either directly or indirectly present ideas about management and organization in the 'real' world. Furthermore, many non-documentary films such as *Erin Brockovich* (2000), *The Insider* (2000) or *Rogue Trader* (2000) are based on facts (see Film Focus 1.4), in the tradition of cinematic realism as a means of emphasizing the perceived authenticity of the text and ensuring the success of the film as a cultural product. Moreover, while the central purpose of many of the texts reviewed in this chapter is to provide an account of factual events in the real world, they often do so in a way which involves the development of a narrative which has a plot and contains characters. Therefore, the boundaries between documentary and fictional film are not as clear as they might initially seem.

One of the ways in which authenticity in documentary film is ensured is through the adoption of a 'guerrilla documentary' style (Barnouw, 1993), directors such as Michael Moore and Morgan Spurlock presenting themselves to audiences as slightly naïve but determined explorers who venture into the dangerous, hidden world of organizations in order to uncover their malevolent practices. This self-presentation partly explains why audiences are sometimes critical of documentary films that they perceive as being heavily biased, inaccurate or factually incorrect. For example, although the events shown in *Roger and Me* (1989) are accepted as having taken place, several commentators have suggested that the sequence in which they occur is misleading (see Film Focus 8.2 and 5.4). While the film represents events such as the visit by president Ronald Reagan or the opening of the indoor theme park AutoWorld as a response to the General Motors car plant closings shown earlier in the film, critics point out that this could not have been the case, since Reagan came to Flint in 1980, AutoWorld opened in 1985 and the plant closures did not start until 1986. However, Winston (2000) argues that the film never claimed to present a chronologically accurate account, instead suggesting that widespread criticism of the film's chronological accuracy was an expression of discomfort in the face of its political message about the uncaring nature of corporations in the late twentieth century.

FILM FOCUS 8.2: Presenting the facts in *Roger and Me* (1989)

Roger and Me (1989) is a semi-autobiographical story told by journalist and filmmaker Michael Moore about the history of the auto corporation General Motors in the town of Flint, Michigan, the birthplace of the company and where Moore grew up. The film begins by using historical film footage to represent General Motors in the 1950's with Moore narrating the story of a paternalistic company caring for its workers and describing how various members of his family had worked for the company over the years. This historical representation is immediately contrasted with a portrayal of General Motors in the 1980s following the announcement in November 1986 that the corporation intends to close eleven plants and cut 30,000 workers' jobs. Then Moore tells the audience how he returned to Flint, Michigan to try to find General Motors chairman Roger Smith, in an attempt to persuade him to spend a day in Flint to see what the town is really like. Moore thereby casts himself as an everyday kind of guy who is trying to make sense of the company's actions using his matter-of-fact storytelling style to challenge the corporate account of its own actions by telling his own story alongside those of other 'ordinary people' who are affected by them. Unusually for a critical documentary of this nature, the film achieved mainstream distribution and considerable commercial success.

⊙ [approximate running time: 0–10 mins.]

Narrative, categorical and rhetorical forms

Similar to non-documentary feature films many documentary films tend to be organized as narratives, having a beginning, middle and an ending which usually involves finding out what happened to the central characters, resolving conflicts and proposing a solution to the issues raised (see Film Focus 8.3). Others may be organised categorically, using a system through which the subject can be classified as a basis for developing understanding, an example is given in Film Focus 8.4. Documentary films also use rhetorical form (Film Focus 8.5), in which the filmmaker presents a persuasive argument; 'the goal in such a film is to persuade the audience to adopt an opinion about the subject matter and perhaps to act on that opinion' (Bordwell and Thompson, 2004, p. 140). Rhetorical form is recognisable by four basic attributes; first, it addresses the audience openly, trying to move them to a particular intellectual position, emotional attitude, and/or action. Second, it presents an opinion rather than a matter of broadly accepted scientific truth, and is thus explicitly ideological. Third, it appeals to our emotions, rather than just presenting factual evidence and fourth, it will seek to persuade the audience to make a choice that will affect their everyday life. However, while these categories provide a useful means of analysing the structure of documentary film, narrative, categorical and rhetorical forms should be seen as overlapping, any particular text potentially using aspects of them in combination.

FILM FOCUS 8.3: Narrative form in *Enron: The Smartest Guys in the Room* (2005) and *McLibel* (2005)

Just like other types of film, documentary films need human characters with whom the audience can identify. The film *Enron: The Smartest Guys in the Room* (2005) begins by introducing the character of Enron employee Cliff Baxter who in a scene based on these events being re-enacted is shown committing suicide by shooting himself in his car. In the final scene of the film we return once again to the subject of Cliff Baxter's suicide in an interview with a local chaplain who argues that what happened at Enron should not be seen as something exclusive to this particular organization, instead being a reflection of the corporate culture of America. The film ends by tying up the loose ends of the story by explaining what happened to the senior Enron executives following the collapse of the company. ☉ [**approximate running times: 0–5; 1 hour 37.10–1 hour 41.45 mins.**]

The film *McLibel* (2005) tells the story of two ordinary people, Helen Steel and Dave Morris, a gardener and a postman who were sued by the multinational corporation McDonalds for distributing a leaflet criticising the company's practices in relation to animal welfare, employment rights, advertising to children and health issues. McDonalds' legal action involved invoking strict UK libel laws to suppress criticism of its business practices. The main characters in the film are played by the people who were involved in the factual events. This involves them narrating their story to camera and re-enacting scenes directed by Ken Loach. Helen and Dave had to represent themselves because, unlike McDonalds who spent over £10 million in the action, they could not afford a legal team. Part way through the case they declined the terms of McDonalds' offer to settle out of court because they were not prepared to forfeit the right to comment on corporate malpractices in the future. Although they eventually lost the case against McDonalds, which turned into the longest court trial in UK history, taking up 314 days in court, the company was badly affected by the adverse publicity surrounding the case and did not pursue the campaigners for damages. Helen and Dave subsequently took their case to the European Court of Human Rights which ruled that the UK government had acted in breach of the Convention on Human Rights by denying them legal aid with which to fight the case. The film was made over a ten year period by film director Fanny Armstrong who describes her motivation for making the film as driven by the issues framed in terms of a David and Goliath styled human interest story. ☉ [**approximate running times: 29.20–33.45; 41.20–45.10 mins.**]

FILM FOCUS 8.4: Categorical form in *The Corporation* (2003)

Bordwell and Thompson (2004) suggest that categorical documentary films tend to be organized according to commonsensical groupings or classifications with which the audience can readily identify. The film begins by identifying its subject. For example, in *The Corporation* (2003) the subject is the organization which is characterized as a person, not only in a legal sense, but also as having a personality that is psychopathic (see Chapter 3). The anonymous female narrator then asks the audience, what kind of person the corporation is, this paving the way for the remainder of the film which is devoted to an analysis of it core characteristics in the form of a 'checklist', as a classificatory device. A series of 'talking head' interviews are provided in each of the film's separate segments in the form of experts who provide evidence in support of each personality characteristic. The first of these is a representation of the corporation as immoral, having no moral conscience being concerned only for its stockholders and the pursuit of profit, containing an interview with economist Milton Friedman who discusses the concept of externalities. Bordwell and Thompson (2004) suggest that one of the main challenges of using this device to structure a documentary film is that it can become repetitive and thus risks boring the audience. ☉ [**approximate running time: 10.55–19 mins.**]

FILM FOCUS 8.5: Rhetorical form in *Super Size Me* (2004)

In the film *Super Size Me* (2004) director and narrator Morgan Spurlock seeks to make his viewpoint seem the most plausible to the audience by presenting a series of arguments and evidence that support it. The film begins with 'The Con' and a group of kids singing a nursery song with fast-food lyrics. In the

Continued

opening scene Spurlock characterizes America as a nation of big, big businesses and big people, explaining that since 1980 the number of overweight people in the country has doubled. He refers to the 2002 law suit filed by two overweight girls in New York against the McDonalds Corporation for making them obese and uses cartoon graphics to represent the global spread of the fast food industry. Then he poses a question to the film audience, 'are the food companies solely to blame for this epidemic; where does personal responsibility stop and corporate responsibility begin?' The film narrates the 30 day story in which Spurlock is the human subject in an experiment to test whether fast food is really so bad for you by eating nothing but McDonalds meals. By making himself the subject of the experiment, the audience can follow his physical and emotional decline. The film thus appeals to our emotions in response to his suffering. The film ends on the thirtieth day when Spurlock holds a party at McDonalds to celebrate the end of his diet. We discover that the law suit against McDonalds was dismissed and discover the final analyses of Morgan's health; all three doctors are surprised at the ill effects on Spurlock's health and recommend that he come off the diet. Morgan challenges McDonalds to do away with their super-size option. His final statement is condemnatory of the organizations that he represents as responsible for the obesity epidemic: 'but why should these companies want to change? Their loyalty isn't to you, it's to the stockholders. The bottom line, they are a business, no matter what they say and by selling you unhealthy food, they make millions and no company wants to stop doing that.' ☉ [approximate running times: 0–4.25 mins; 1 hour 27–1 hour mins.]

The role of the author

Throughout this book there has been a concern to avoid becoming overly focused on the author of a particular film text as an intentional agent who has definitive authority over the production of meaning in relation to it (Derrida, 1974). Instead it has been argued that meaning is derived from a circuit of communication that involves reader and text as well as its author in a dynamic process that is open to ongoing revision. The notion of authorship in filmmaking is most strongly associated with the tradition of auteur theory in film studies which, in the 1950s and 1960s, focused on the expression of the author's intentions within the text. Certain film directors were seen as projecting their personality into their work in a way which led to the production of texts which displayed a series of consistent and recurring characteristics. However, at this point we shall attempt to bring the author back in to the analysis, in part because it is argued that critical representations of organization tend to be driven by certain filmmakers, like Michael Moore and Ken Loach, who have consistently sought to challenge dominant ideologies of management and organization through their film-making (see Film Focus 8.6).

FILM FOCUS 8.6: The author in *The Navigators* (2001)

The Navigators (2001), directed by Ken Loach, is a story about the deregulation and privatisation of the UK rail industry in the 1990s which can be read as a commentary on managerialism in UK public sector, and the potential costs associated with a rationalistic approach that balances economic considerations against human safety. Although the characters and events in the film are fictionalized, the script was written by an ex-rail worker, Rob Dawber, who worked on the railways for many years and died while the film was being made from cancer caused by exposure to asbestos while working on the tracks. A pivotal event in the film is provided by a scene involving the death of one of the rail workers working on the track. This incident raises issues about the responsibility of employers in ensuring the safety of employees and highlights the difficulties in bringing charges of corporate manslaughter in relation to work related incidents, despite the fact that Health and Safety Executive reports consistently demonstrate that most occupational deaths are avoidable, as they are due to lack of supervision, inadequate training and lack of attention to detail (Slapper, 1999). Filming of *The Navigators* began just days before the Hatfield rail crash in 2000 (Screenonline, 2006) [http://www.screenonline.org.uk/film/id/556980/index.html – consulted 27.11.06], which bore striking similarity to the film script and prompted a national inquiry into rail safety. The findings of the inquiry drew attention to the decline throughout the 1990s in the number of workers permanently employed to maintain and renew the infrastructure of the railways. As a result Network Rail was fined £3.5 million and their subcontractor Balfour Beatty £10 million; in summing up the judge noted that this was the 'worst example of sustained industrial negligence in a high-risk industry he had ever seen' (BBC News, 2005). Loach's critique of management and organization can also be read in his other films such as *Riff Raff* (1991), *Bread and Roses* (2000) and *It's a Free World* (2007) (see Film Focus 5.2 and 8.1). However, he does not see himself as an auteur in the traditional sense, instead emphasizing the collaborative aspect of his filmmaking in which the director is one producer of meaning among many [http://www.sensesofcinema.com/contents/directors/03/loach.html – consulted 27.11.06].

⚙ [**approximate running time: 1 hour 18.30–1 hour 27.40 mins.**]

Auteur theory has been criticised for its tendency to portray the filmmaker somewhat romantically as an artist engaged in acts of creative expression, similar to the role of the artist in literature or painting. This has led writers such as Barthes (1967) to suggest, in an essay provocatively entitled *The Death of the Author*, that the imperfect nature of the communication process entailed in the 'speech act' makes it impossible to identify a primary 'authorized' reading of the film text. Instead, for Barthes, the meaning of the text is the result of the relationship between the text and the reader which is constantly changing and is subject to ongoing intertextual influences. Similarly, Foucault (1984) argues that although the author cannot be understood as the principal originator of meaning in relation to the text, authorship is institutionalised in society as a mechanism whereby certain discourses are regulated. He describes this as the 'author function'. The author function is a process which indicates how a text should be received and the status it should be accorded within a given culture. It comprises three aspects. First, the author's name fulfils a classificatory function, grouping together groups of film texts and differentiating them from others. Second, the author's name serves a legal purpose, in holding the author responsible for the text and conferring certain rights of ownership upon them. Lastly, and most importantly, the author function is ideological, being used to regulate and shape discourses in certain ways that restrict the role of the author as 'regulator of the fictive'. The main point that can be taken from these debates about the role of the filmmaker as author is that while some caution needs to be exercised in seeking to interpret their actions and motives, we must not abandon all sense of the author as a key agent in shaping the meaning of the text.

Filmmakers as critics of management and organization

The notion of the auteur is helpful in making sense of the role of these filmmakers in attempting to hold management and organizations to account for their actions and practices. Some of them claim to be driven by their own experiences, such as Michael Moore who was brought up in the town of Flint, Michigan, the setting for *Roger and Me* (1989), and Annabelle Gurvitch who claims that her experience of being fired from an acting job in New York prompted her to make the film *Fired!* (2007) (see Film Focus 7.7). However, many of them also appear to be engaged in a political effort to ensure that companies and top managers are forced to bear responsibility 'for unemployment as well as employment, for pollution and ecological disasters, for psychic and social problems associated with the (often low) quality of work and for the exploitation of workers' (Alvesson and Willmott, 2003, p. 12) (see Film Focus 8.7 for an example). It would therefore seem that the sympathies of these filmmakers lie with those who are managed rather than managers, the relatively powerless rather than the relatively powerful. What is more, they seem to be using these texts as a vehicle for communicating basic messages about what is right and wrong, good and bad in relation to management and organization. In so doing they appear to be engaged in an exercise of 'de-naturalization' (Fournier and Grey, 2000; Grey, 2005), attempting to expose wrongful, exploitative organizational practices and encouraging a process of questioning whether they are necessary or right.

FILM FOCUS 8.7: The film author as a political agent in *Wal-Mart: The High Cost of Low Price* (2005)

Film director Robert Greenwald describes his rationale for *Wal-Mart: The High Cost of Low Price* (2005) as a desire to tell the personal stories of people affected by Wal-Mart's policies and tactics. The challenge was twofold, first in defining who to interview, as unlike in previous films Greenwald had directed such as *Outfoxed: Rupert Murdoch's War on Journalism* (2004) (see Film Focus 2.2), the number of potential interviewees was enormous. Greenwald explains that 'from this giant pool, we had to find people who were comfortable on camera, who would let us follow them around, and who were not afraid to go public'. However, the second problem, he explains, was due to the climate of fear that surrounds the corporation, which discouraged people from speaking out against it. 'We found heartbreaking stories from people who worked at Wal-Mart, but many of them were just too frightened to appear on camera. We found businesses run out of the country, with CEOs who were terrified of talking with us on or off camera because of retaliation by Wal-Mart. We had camera crews arrive at homes where folks had agreed to talk with us only to be turned away because they had since thought better of angering Wal-Mart. When we went public with the film, one of the first things I asked was a pledge from Wal-Mart not to fire anyone who cooperated with us on the film. They refused; the intimidation and fear continues'. [http://www.walmartmovie. com/intro.php – consulted 28.10.07] In addition to the personal stories that provide the basis for the characters in the film, Greenwald also wanted the corporation to have the opportunity to tell its side of the story. However, his efforts to get Wal-Mart CEO Lee Scott to be interviewed for the film were unsuccessful. He therefore came up with the idea of using existing film of Lee Scott, based on corporate film recordings and news footage, to construct an organizational narrative which runs through the film. For example, this scene begins with Lee Scott giving a speech promoting Wal-Mart as an equal opportunities employer. This is immediately contrasted with the personal stories of hourly paid workers who have been cheated of overtime pay, store lock-ins of illegal immigrants employed as cleaners and employees' experiences of gender and racial discrimination. Throughout the scene, the upbeat image promoted by the company through its advertising is juxtaposed against the experiences of its employees and former managers. ☻ [approximate running time: 33.30–44.30 mins.]

The efforts of film authors to force organizations to take responsibility for their unethical actions and exploitative practices are directed towards achieving practical as well as ideological outcomes. For example, the film *Ghosts* (2006) (see Film Focus 8.1) was used as a means of raising public awareness in the UK about the employment conditions involved in food production [http://www.ghosts.uk.com/ – consulted 11.05.07] and as a focus for charitable donations to help the families affected by the Morecombe Bay disaster. Similarly, *Black Gold* (2006) is a documentary film which aims to provide insight into the unbalanced struggle between poor coffee farmers in Ethiopia and greedy multinational coffee companies that promote 'fair trade' as a basis for changing consumer behaviour and their coffee buying habits. A further example relates to the film *Super Size Me* (2004) (Film Focus 8.5); at the time the film was being made a law suit was being brought in the United States against the company by two obese young women on the grounds that the food chain was responsible for their size. The case was dismissed but McDonalds subsequently removed super-size portions from its menus in the United States. This could be read as an example of how film can contribute towards public pressure which in turn encourages corporations to revise their business practices. The film also prompted a response by McDonalds in the form of a website www.supersizeme-thedebate.co.uk where counterarguments to those in the film are set out. Indeed it is not unusual for corporations to retaliate against negative representations of their activities in film. *Fast Food Nation* (2006) (see Film Focus 8.11) provoked a counter campaign of lobbyists and PR initiatives led by groups representing fast food, beef, dairy and potato companies such as the American Meat Institute and the Snack Food Association. However, this has the potential to generate more adverse publicity; this case also saw the launch and rapid dissolution (after only ten days) of a website called 'Fast Talk Nation' which sought to discredit Schlosser's (2001) book by (wrongly) suggesting that he favoured the legalisation of marijuana. The industry has now turned its efforts towards the website 'Best Food Nation' www.bestfoodnation.com which seeks to redress what it considers to be 'common myths' about the US food industry. Similarly the film *An Inconvenient Truth* (2006), in which Al Gore seeks to raise awareness of global climate change, prompted reactions from the Competitive Enterprise Institute, which received $2million from oil company Exxon between 1998 and 2005 in addition to contributions from Texaco and Amoco. The Institute released two advertisements promoting the view that climate change is exaggerated at the same time as the film's release (Patterson, 2007).

The role of film authors as political activists in seeking to challenge management and organizational practices can be read as a collective as well as an individualized project, as illustrated by the Anti-Corporate Film Festival, held in San Francisco, which aims to raise awareness and provoke discussion about 'how corporations actually operate, and what they *really* add to – and subtract from – humanity's "bottom line"'. The festival, organised by the pressure group CounterCorp, seeks to 'document, reduce, and ultimately prevent the corrosive political, economic, and social effects that large corporations have in the US and around the world' [http://www.countercorp.org/ – consulted 28.05.07]. The distribution of short films via the Internet further enables the use of this medium to challenge organizational practices as Film Focus 8.8 illustrates.

FILM FOCUS 8.8: The role of viral videos as a means of challenging organizational practice

Klein (2000) argues that the use of visual culture as a medium of protest against globalization has been enabled by 'newly accessible technologies that have made both the creation and circulation' (Klein, 2000, p. 285) of these texts much easier, including the growth of the Internet which allows them to be distributed to large audiences (see Film Focus 2.4). This is illustrated by the popularity of short, animated campaign-focused internet films, or 'viral videos' such as those made by creative media designers at Free Range Studios, including the award winning series *The Meatrix*, which is funded by a campaign group that lobbies to promote sustainable food production and is against factory farming. The series features 'Moopheus' who must defend pigs and chickens against the financially driven exploits of Agent Smith in the meat packing plant. http://meatrix.com/

Other examples of internet films which seek to challenge organizational practices can be seen at Participate.net [www.participate.net – consulted 20.08.07], a network organization which aims to produce films which 'deliver compelling entertainment that will raise awareness about important social issues, educate audiences and inspire them to take action'. This includes, amongst others, *Backwards Hamburger* and *The Fat Lane*, associated with the feature film, *Fast Food Nation* (2006), which campaigns against practices within the fast food industry. [http://www.backwardshamburger.com/; http://www.youtube.com/watch?v=5ey9M26W_pk – consulted 20.08.07]

The role of film authors in providing critical commentaries about management and organization is also linked to the anti-globalization movement. Some filmmakers, such as Naomi Klein (2000), are also leading anti-globalization protestors (see Film Focus 8.9). The use of film as a protest medium against globalization is informed by activists' use of various aspects of visual culture as a means of challenging dominant discourses and resisting the power of corporate branding. One of their main techniques is 'culture jamming' (Lasn, 1999), a symbolic form of resistance that involves sabotaging corporate images such as those found on advertising billboards in an attempt to disrupt their meaning through redefining the public environment and undermining the organizations that seek to control it. Through subverting the brands of large corporations anti-globalization activists seek to challenge the ideologies of capitalism and consumerism that they promote. Culture jamming has even found its way into film texts. For example the film *Super Size Me* (2004) uses images produced by the artist Ron English to portray the McDonald's marketing character Ronald McDonald in a variety of sinister ways.

FILM FOCUS 8.9: Film as an anti-globalization protest medium in *No Logo* (2003) and *The Take* (2004)

The Take (2004) is written and co-narrated by Naomi Klein, author of the book *No Logo* (2000), which was also made into a film in 2003. The film seeks to present an alternative to the capitalist methods of production which globalization is founded upon through telling the story of the Worker Controlled Factory Movement in Argentina, which began when female garment factory workers facing mass unemployment in the wake of the country's economic collapse, entered their factory and refused to leave until they had an official mandate to restart the machines, thereby becoming a self-managing cooperative. This scene tells the story of a worker occupied ceramic tile factory which has been controlled by its workers for two years and includes an interview with its owner, Mr Zanon, who intends to claim the factory back. ☻ [**approximate running time: 18–24 mins.**] A trailer for the film *No Logo* (2003) can be seen on You Tube. [http://www.youtube.com/watch?v=uI0itS3gQFU – consulted 08.08.07]

What is perhaps more interesting, however, is the extent to which anti-globalization films are popular with audiences and whether this is a reflection of a broader societal critique of the global power of large capitalistic organizations. If we accept the idea introduced in Chapter 2, that a cultural product like film relies on conveying a sense of authenticity to audiences, then certainly the number of films that focus on the downside of global capitalism would seem to imply that readers of these texts understand them to be a representation of a highly problematic and extremely destructive real-world phenomenon. Yet it could also be that the consumption of these films as a cultural product represents less of a backlash against globalization and more of a co-optation of its critics. Hence, as Klein (2000) herself acknowledges, many mainstream organizations have extremely effectively incorporated or co-opted the countercultural messages of culture jammers into their own brands, to such an extent that being critical of capitalism has become an integral part of their branding campaigns (see Film Focus 2.9 and 2.10 for examples that relate to the use of film). She argues, however, that 'by playing on sentiments that are already directed against them ... the process of co-optation runs the very real risk of amplifying the backlash, not disarming it' (Klein, 2000, p. 308).

Other commentators, however, are more sceptical about the potential for transformation enabled by countercultural critiques. Frank (1997) traces their emergence to the 1960s, when ideas about rebellion and liberation from the constraints of bureaucracy and conformity as represented by the character of 'organization man' described in Chapter 4 became popular, casting the former as 'a background of muted, uniform gray against which the counterculture went through its colourful chapters' (Frank, 1997, p. 6). The struggle for freedom from the constraints of stultifying organization can be read in many films since the 1960s, often in the form of fantasies, such as those described in Chapter 7 involving the overturning of conformity and deferred gratification by the character of the 'hipster' whose quest for authentic experience and escape involves resisting the ideology upon which the cultural system is founded. Heath and Potter's (2005) reading of *The Matrix* (1999) suggests this film to be particularly illustrative of these discourses (see Film Focus 8.10). However, rather than conceptualizing these cultural products as a 'fake counterculture', a commercial replica produced by corporations for the entertainment of audiences to subvert the threat posed by 'real' countercultural revolutionaries, Frank (1997) argues that the boundaries between authentic and inauthentic forms of protest are extremely blurred.

Film Focus 8.10: Countercultural revolution in *The Matrix* (1999) and *American Beauty* (1999)

Heath and Potter (2005) argue that the countercultural critique of management and organization casts the revolutionary as a hero who is seeking two things – consciousness of desire and the desire for consciousness, these texts conveying the message that both can be achieved through becoming independent from 'The System'. Morpheus sums up the countercultural analysis perfectly when describing The Matrix: 'the Matrix is a system, Neo. That system is our enemy. But when you're inside, you look around, what do you see? Businessmen, teachers, lawyers, carpenters. The very minds of the people we are trying to save. But until we do, these people are still a part of that system and that makes them our enemy. You have to understand, most of these people are not ready to be unplugged. And many of them are so inured, so hopelessly dependent on the system, that they will fight to protect it' (Heath and Potter, 2005, p. 9).

The countercultural critique can also be read in *American Beauty* (1999), which implies that 'it is simply not possible to be a well-adjusted adult in our society … one faces a stark choice. One can maintain one's adolescent rebelliousness … and remain free. The alternative is to "sell out", to play by the rules and thereby to become a neurotic, superficial conformist, incapable of experiencing true pleasure' (Heath and Potter, 2005, p. 57). They conclude that 'in a society that prizes individualism and despises conformity, being "a rebel" becomes the new aspirational category' (Heath and Potter, 2005, p. 130).

Counterculturalists further suggest that the system can be revolutionized through individual lifestyle and consumption choices, the choice of a particular T-shirt or a pair of running shoes having important political consequences. The rebel consumer is a theme pursued by Ritzer (2007) who argues that the solution to 'loss amidst monumental abundance' involves the construction of subjective meaning. Using the example of *Fight Club* (1999), Ritzer argues that this film represents an attempt to confront the globalization of 'nothing' (see Film Focus 7.1 and 7.4). Ritzer (2007, p. 203) suggests that 'dramatic change takes place when the movie's "hero" is introduced to the Fight Club, a place where he is able to find at least part of what has been lost in a modern consumerist society'. Ritzer goes on to comment that, 'the club devoted to fighting and depicted in this movie may be many things, but it is *not* empty', hence he views it favourably. Although he acknowledges that 'beating people senseless is obviously an extreme way of dealing with the loss' he suggests that 'it does highlight the idea that there are things that can be done to deal with this problem' (Ritzer, 2007, p. 203). While it is not entirely clear what things Ritzer advocates should be done, (presumably not participating in a fight club), he goes on to recommend 'craft consumerism', modifying products after their purchase as an act of creative expression.

However, this type of recommendation, argues Parker (2002), elevates the social actor to the status of a 'super-agent' who by engaging in minor acts of organizational resistance poses a significant challenge to the system. Moreover, Frank suggests that this cleverly supports capitalism through transforming 'all the complaints about conformity, oppression, bureaucracy, meaninglessness and the disappearance of individualism ... into rationales for consuming' (Frank, 1997, p. 31). This can be suggested to relate to the consumption of film just as much as other products, consumers being encouraged to believe that the consumption of certain texts which are critical of management and organization is a political act that helps to subvert the system. Through their consumption of film, audiences are constituted as engaged in a form of political action. These debates feed into the broader question of whether film provides a catalyst for transforming material practices in management and organization or acts as a safety valve that prevents audiences from initiating change in their everyday lives.

The hyper-real organization

In addition to the role of film as a medium for representing the spectres of organization whose voices are marginalized and silenced, the title of this chapter also refers to the spectre of the text itself. We come to understand the reality of organizations through encountering them on the screen as a mediated version of reality, a symbolic fiction or a spectre. This statement relates to Baudrillard's (1995) analysis of the first Gulf War in 1991 which he argues did not happen in the same way as wars previously.

For Baudrillard, the televised spectacle watched by mass audiences across the globe and involving military actions based on 'Star Wars' science fiction-like technology constituted a virtual 'non-war' of a particularly sinister nature, since it had already been 'won' in advance. What we encounter, he suggests, is therefore a 'simulacrum', a copy or symbolic representation of war as a one-sided, predetermined, deceptively-staged cultural campaign that blurs the distinction between real events and 'hyper-reality' based on the production and consumption of predetermined copies.

Baudrillard's ideas on the nature of reality and the growing indistinction between the real and the virtual have been used by filmmakers like the Wachowski brothers, directors of *The Matrix* (1999) trilogy (see Film Focus 5.1 and 7.10). The film pays tribute to the philosopher through, for example, the character Morpheus's line 'welcome to the desert of the real'. However, Baudrillard (2004) sought to distance himself from the film which he saw as an oversimplification of the relationship between reality and hyper-reality, suggesting that '*The Matrix* is surely the kind of film about the matrix that the matrix would have been able to produce' (Baudrillard, 2004) [http://www.ubishops.ca/BaudrillardStudies/vol1_2/genosko.htm – consulted 32.10.07]. Ideas about the construction of a pseudo-reality as an aspect of life within commodified capitalist culture are also taken up by Žižek (2005) who suggests that capitalism works on the public imagination in a way which produces a kind of 'false consciousness' – we feel free because we lack the language or cultural resources to express our non-freedom. Moreover, society promotes the illusion that we have a great deal of opportunity and choice in pursuing our desires yet simultaneously we are made to feel guilty if we do so. Hence, although capitalism provides us with a variety of ways of apparently fulfilling these desires, the very reason that we wished to consume them in the first place has been removed; in this way capitalism seeks to regulate the super-ego.

So what is the significance of these arguments about the nature of reality in relation to the current proliferation of documentary films as a critical commentary on management and organization? Instead of being a catalyst for change, by con-structing a pseudo-reality of organization on screen it may be argued that we are more, rather than less, inclined to accept these practices. We might further argue that rather than being a form of protest and resistance, the proliferation of documentary films that are critical of management and organization provides evidence to support the notion that protest and resistance is being 'increasingly absorbed and turned into fuel by the symbolic "system" of capitalism' (Baudrillard, 2004) through a variety of popular cultural forms including film. Hence, although we might be prompted to go and watch a documentary film that is critical of management and organization, then log on to the campaign website associated with the film afterwards, and perhaps even adjust our patterns of consumption slightly as a result by resolving to buy fair-trade coffee or not to eat at McDonalds, any potentially more significant protest is absorbed as a consequence of becoming part of the hyper-reality in which boundaries between fact and fiction, symbolic and material protest, become increasingly blurred.

FILM FOCUS 8.11: The hyper-real in *Fast Food Nation* (2006)

Based on the bestselling non-fiction book by Eric Schlosser (2001), *Fast Food Nation* (2006) is a fictionalised portrayal of a series of characters whose lives are in some way tied up with the American fast food economy. These include American High School girl Amber who works nights in the local branch of imaginary burger chain Mickey's to pay for her car and a group of Mexican illegal immigrants who risk industrial injury in the Colorado meatpacking plant that provides the fast food chain with its beef patties. When Mickey's marketing executive, Don Henderson visits the town to investigate claims that a high level of 'fecal matter' has been found in Mickey's burgers, he meets with a local meat supplier, Harry Rydell, who appraises him of his harsher view of American capitalism, concluding 'it is a sad fact of life, Don, but the truth is we all have to eat a little shit from time to time'. ☻ [**approximate running time: 48.35–56.30 mins.**] However, in blurring the boundaries between fiction and reality critics have argued that the film reduces serious and complex issues of corporate responsibility to a tale of a good-hearted manager who sets out to find out the truth about the company he works for. This leaves the 'real' story about corporations like McDonalds untold.

Conclusion

The central proposition of this book has been that film plays a role in producing systems of discourse which help to shape our collective perceptions of management that continue to inform our experience of organized work. It has sought to explore the role of film in shaping these discourses through demonstrating the coherence of certain themes, their recurrence across different film texts and their relative historical endurance despite significant socio-economic changes in the period since filmmaking began. Rather than being entirely superseded by a new management idea or a particular theoretical perspective, concepts like 'organization man' and the 'evil organization' are merely re-presented within texts in a way that makes them more acceptable within the societal context in which they are located. The reading of film presented here therefore suggests that management discourses about the way that complex organizations should be managed and how people should be treated within them never really disappear, instead they merely recede until societal conditions change in a way that permits their revival in a revised form (Eccles and Nohria, 1992; Barley and Kunda, 1992).

This book has further argued that the appeal of these texts is based on their ability to create resonance with the audience. The extent to which you, the reader, at any given moment, are able to identify with the characters, recognize the settings and empathize with the feelings that a film expresses is important in determining whether or not a particular text is successful and hence profitable. While the authors of these texts undoubtedly seek to convey certain ideological messages about management and organization, they are also influenced by collective perceptions of these phenomena in everyday life. Equally, since we are arguably all members of a postmodern society where the image is significant in defining what is considered to be real, these texts are important in articulating and reinforcing these discourses in ways that have a potential bearing on our everyday lives. To put this slightly differently, by turning people's experiences of management and work into film these texts provide a source of knowledge and understanding that individuals use to inform their own organizational experiences.

One of the central problems in developing such an argument arises from the difficulty in demonstrating this to be the case. As with other social phenomena, such as violent crime, the relationship between the phenomenon in everyday life and representations of it contained within popular culture are complex and interdependent. However, this is not a reason to disregard them, since by being aware of these discourses as a reader, you become better equipped to engage with them and also to question them. This book has therefore sought to provide the resources through which a questioning engagement with these discourses might be cultivated, an aim that can perhaps be best illustrated through telling a little story of my own. A couple of years ago I attended the graduation ceremony at the university where I worked to congratulate the business and management undergraduates who had successfully reached the end of their studies and to wish them well in whatever they were going on to do. At the social event that followed the formal ceremony I was approached by a student who had taken my course on reading management and organization in film. After the formal congratulations he told me that after completing the course he could no longer just watch a film as a pure form of entertainment; instead he found himself reading into the text various themes and messages related to management and organization. He seemed a little frustrated as well as amused by this, but for my own part I was quite pleased, since it seemed to confirm my reasons for designing the course and writing this book. When new films are released that revisit themes related to management and organization, perhaps reshaping and reinventing them in different and potentially significant ways, I like to imagine this student and how he might be reading these texts alongside older ones in the light of his knowledge, his everyday life and experience either as a manager or an employee in a contemporary work organization.

Filmography

A Good Year (2006) Dir. Ridley Scott. 118 mins.

About Schmidt (2002) Dir. Alexander Payne. 125 mins.

Aitraaz (2004) Dirs. Abbas Alibhai Burmawalla and Mastan Alibhai Burmawalla. 160 mins. India. Hindi with English subtitles.

Aliens (1986) Dir. James Cameron. 137 mins. UK/USA.

American Beauty (1999) Dir. Sam Mendes. 122 mins.

An Inconvenient Truth (2006) Dir. Davis Guggenheim. 100 mins.

Angry Silence, The (1960) Dir. Guy Green. 94 mins. UK. B&W.

Apartment, The (1960) Dir. Billy Wilder. 120 mins. B&W.

Associate, The (1996) Dir. Donald Petrie. 114 mins.

Baby Boom (1987) Dir. Charles Shyer. 110 mins.

Baby Face (1933) Dir. Alfred E. Green. 70 mins. B&W.

Bad and the Beautiful, The (1952) Dir. Vincente Minelli. 118 mins.

Big (1988) Dir. Penny Marshall. 104 mins.

Big Business (1988) Dir. Jim Abrahams. 97 mins.

Birth of the Robot, The (1936) Dir. Len Lye. 6 mins. (currently unavailable on DVD)

Black Gold (2006) Dirs. Mark Francis and Nick Francis. 78 mins. UK/USA.

Blade Runner (1982) Dir. Ridley Scott. 117 mins.

Blue Collar (1978) Dir. Paul Schrader. 114 mins.

Boiler Room (2000) Dir. Ben Younger. 120 mins.

Brassed Off (1996) Dir. Mark Herman. 107 mins. UK/USA.

Brazil (1985) Dir. Terry Gilliam. 132 mins.

Bread and Roses (2000) Dir. Ken Loach. 110 mins. UK.

Bridget Jones's Diary (2001) Dir. Sharon Maguire. 97 mins. UK/France.

Casino Royale (2006) Dir. Martin Campbell. 144 mins. USA/UK/Germany/Czech Republic.

Civil Action (A) (1998) Dir. Steven Zaillian. 115 mins.

Class Action (1991) Dir. Michael Apted. 110 mins.

Clerks (1994) Dir. Kevin Smith. 92 mins. B&W.

Clockwatchers (1997) Dir. Jill Sprecher. 96 mins.

Constant Gardener, The (2005) Dir. Fernando Meirelles. 129 mins.

Corporation, The (2003) Dirs. Mark Abbot and Jennifer Achbar. 145 mins. Canada.

Crowd, The (1928) Dir. King Vidor. 104 mins. B&W. Silent with intertitles. (currently unavailable on DVD)

Dealers (1989) Dir. Colin Bucksey. 87 mins. UK.

Desk Set (1957) Dir. Walter Lang. 103 mins.

Devil Wears Prada, The (2006) Dir. David Frankel. 109 mins.

Devil's Advocate, The (1997) Dir. Taylor Hackford. 144 mins.

Disclosure (1994) Dir. Barry Levinson. 128 mins.

Enron: The Smartest Guys in the Room (2005) Dir. Alex Gibney. 105 mins.

Erin Brockovich (2000) Dir. Steven Soderbergh. 130 mins.

Executive Suite (1954) Dir. Robert Wise. 104 mins. B&W.

Fast Food Nation (2006) Dir. Richard Linklater. 116 mins. UK/USA.

Fear and Trembling (Stupeur et Tremblements) (2003) Dir. Alain Corneau. 107 mins. France. French with English subtitles.

Fight Club (1999) Dir. David Fincher. 139 mins. USA/Germany.

Fired! (2007) Dirs. Chris Bradley and Kyle LaBrache. 71 mins.

Firm, The (1993) Dir. Sydney Pollack. 154 mins.

Full Metal Jacket (1987) Dir. Stanley Kubrick. 116 mins.

Full Monty, The (1997) Dir. Peter Cattaneo. 91 mins. UK.

Fun with Dick and Jane (2005) Dir. Dean Parisot. 90 mins.

Gattaca (1997) Dir. Andrew Niccol. 101 mins.

Ghosts (2006) Dir. Nick Broomfield. 96 mins. UK. Mandarin/English with English subtitles.

Glengarry, Glen Ross (1992) Dir. James Foley. 100 mins.

Godfather Trilogy (The): 1901–1980 (1992) Dir. Francis Ford Coppola. 583 mins.

Gung Ho (1986) Dir. Ron Howard. 112 mins.

Hoffa (1992) Dir. Danny DeVito. 140 mins.

How to Succeed in Business without Really Trying (1967) Dir. David Swift. 121 mins.

Hudsucker Proxy, The (1994) Dir. Joel Coen. 111 mins.

Human Resources (Ressources Humaines) (1999) Dir. Laurent Cantet. 100 mins. France. French with English subtitles.

I'm Alright Jack (1959) Dir. John Boulting. 104 mins. B&W. UK.

Ikiru (1952) Dir. Akira Kurosawa. 137 mins. B&W. Japan. Japanese with subtitles.

In Good Company (2004) Dir. Paul Weitz. 109 mins.

In the Company of Men (1997) Dir. Neil La Bute. 97 mins. Canada/USA.

Insider, The (2000) Dir. Michael Mann. 157 mins.

It's a Free World (2007) Dir. Ken Loach. 96 mins. UK/Italy/Germany/Spain.

Jerry Maguire (1996) Dir. Cameron Crowe. 139 mins.

Man in the Gray Flannel Suit, The (1956) Dir. Nunnally Johnson. 153 mins.

Matrix, The (1999) Dirs. Andy Wachowski and Larry Wachowski. 136 mins.

Matrix Revolutions, The (2003) Dirs. Andy Wachowski and Larry Wachowski. 129 mins.

McLibel (2005) Dirs. Franny Armstrong and Ken Loach. 85 mins. UK.

Men in Black (1997) Dir. Barry Sonnenfeld. 98 mins.

Metropolis (1927) Dir. Fritz Lang. B&W. Silent with intertitles. Germany.

Modern Times (1936) Dir. Charlie Chaplin. B&W. Silent with intertitles.

Mondays in the Sun (Los Lunes al Sol) (2002) Dir. Fernando León de Aranoa. 113 mins. Spain/France/Italy. Spanish with English subtitles.

Mondovino (2004) Dir. Jonathan Nossiter. 135 mins. Argentina, France, Italy, USA. English, French, Spanish, Italian, Portuguese with English subtitles.

Mr Deeds Goes to Town (1936) Dir. Frank Capra. 115 mins. B&W.

Navigators, The (2001) Dir. Ken Loach. 96 mins. UK.

Nine to Five (1980) Dir. Colin Higgins. 110 mins.

No Logo (2003) Dir. Suht Jhally. 42 mins.

Norma Rae (1979) Dir. Martin Ritt. 114 mins.

North Country (2005) Dir. Niki Caro. 126 mins.

Office Space (1998) Dir. Mike Judge. 90 mins.

One Flew Over the Cuckoo's Nest (1975) Dir. Milos Forman. 133 mins.

One Hour Photo (2002) Dir. Mark Romanek. 96 mins.

Other People's Money (1991) Dir. Norman Jewison. 103 mins.

Outfoxed: Rupert Murdoch's War on Journalism (2004) Dir. Robert Greenwald. 75 mins.

Patterns (1956) Dir. Fielder Cook. 83 mins. B&W.

Philadelphia (1993) Dir. Jonathan Demme. 125 mins.

Player, The (1992) Dir. Robert Altman. 124 mins.

Pursuit of Happyness, The (2006) Dir. Gabriele Muccino. 117 mins.

Riff Raff (1991) Dir. Ken Loach. 96 mins. UK.

Roger and Me (1989) Dir. Michael Moore. 91 mins.

Rogue Trader (2000) Dir. James Dearden. 101 mins. UK.

Saturday Night and Sunday Morning (1960) Dir. Karel Reisz. 89 mins. UK.

Secret of My Success, The (1987) Dir. Herbert Ross. 110 mins.

Severance (2006) Dir. Christopher Smith. 96 mins. Germany/UK.

Sicko (2007) Dir. Michael Moore. 113 mins.

Silkwood (1983) Dir. Mike Nichols. 131 mins.

Spotswood (1991) Dir. Mark Joffe. 85 mins. Australia.

Startup.Com (2001) Dirs. Chris Hegedus and Jehane Noujaim. 107 mins.

State and Main (2000) Dir. David Mamet. 105 mins. France/USA.

Stranger than Fiction (2006) Dir. Marc Forster. 113 mins.

Super Size Me (2004) Dir. Morgan Spurlock. 100 mins.

Symphony in F (1940) 9 mins.

Syriana (2005) Dir. Stephen Gaghan. 126 mins.

Take, The (2004) Dir. Avi Lewis. 87 mins. Canada. English and Spanish with subtitles.

Terminal, The (2004) Dir. Steven Spielberg. 128 mins.

Thank You for Smoking (2005) Dir. Jason Reitman. 92 mins.

Time Out (L'Emploi du Temp) (2001) Dir. Laurent Cantet. 134 mins. France. French with English subtitles.

Trading Places (1983) Dir. John Landis. 116 mins.

Tucker: The Man and His Dream (1988) Dir. Francis Ford Coppola. 115 mins.

Two Weeks Notice (2002) Dir. Marc Lawrence. 101 mins.

Wall Street (1987) Dir. Oliver Stone. 125 mins

Walmart: The High Cost of Low Price (2005) Dir. Robert Greenwald. 95 mins.

What Women Want (2000) Dir. Nancy Meyers. 127 mins.

Woman's World (1954) Dir. Jean Negulesco. 94 mins. (currently unavailable on DVD)

Workers Leaving the Lumière Factory (La Sortie des Usines Lumière) (1895) Dir. Louis Lumière. 1 min. France. Silent. (currently unavailable on DVD)

Working Girl (1988) Dir. Mike Nichols. 115 mins.

Your Studio and You (1995) Dir. Trey Parker. 17 mins.

Bibliography

Abrahamson, E. (1991) 'Managerial Fads and Fashions: The Diffusion and Rejection of Innovations', *Academy of Management Review*, 16(3): 586–612.

Ackroyd, S. and Thompson, P. (1999) *Organizational Misbehaviour*. London: Sage.

Adams, G.B. and Balfour, D.L. (2004) *Unmasking Administrative Evil*. Rev. Edition. Armonk, New York: ME. Sharpe.

Alloway (1963) 'Iconography and the Movies', *Movie*, 7: 4–6.

Alvesson, M. (2002) *Understanding Organizational Culture*. London: Sage.

Alvesson, M. and Willmott, H. (1996) *Making Sense of Management*. London: Sage.

Alvesson, M. and Willmott, H. (2003) *Studying Management Critically*. London: Sage.

Ang, I. (1991) *Desperately Seeking the Audience*. London: Routledge.

Ashmos, D.P. and Duchon, D. (2000) 'Spirituality at Work: A Conceptualization and Measure', *Journal of Management Inquiry*, 9(2): 134–145.

Bakan, J. (2004) *The Corporation: The Pathological Pursuit of Profit and Power*. London: Constable.

Baldry, C. (1999) 'Space – The Final Frontier', *Sociology*, 33(3): 535–553.

Barley, S.R. (1989) 'Careers, Identities, and Institutions: The Legacy of the Chicago School of Sociology', in M. Arthur, T. Hall and B. Lawrence (eds) *The Handbook of Career Theory*. Cambridge: Cambridge University Press.

Barley, S. (2006) 'When I Write My Masterpiece: Thought on What Makes a Paper Interesting', *Academy of Management Journal*, 49(1): 16–20.

Barley, S. and Kunda, G. (1992) 'Design and Devotion: Surges of Rational and Normative Ideologies of Control in Managerial Discourse', *Administrative Science Quarterly*, 37: 363–399.

Barnouw, E. (1993) *Documentary: A History of the Non-Fiction Film*. 2nd Edition. New York: Oxford University Press.

Barthes, R. (1967) *Image, Music, Text*. London: Fontana Press.

Barthes, R. (1972) *Mythologies*. London: Cape.

Barthes, R. (1975) *The Pleasure of the Text*. New York: Hill & Wang.

Barthes, R. (1988) *The Semiotic Challenge*. Oxford: Blackwell.

Basinger, J. (1993) *A Woman's View: How Hollywood Spoke to Women 1930–1960*. London: Chatto and Windus.

Baudrillard, J. (1983) *Simulations*. New York: Semiotext(e).

Baudrillard, J. (1995) *The Gulf War Did Not Take Place*. Bloomington: Indiana University Press.

Baudrillard, J. (1996) *The System of Objects*. London: Verso.

Baudrillard, J. (2004) 'The Matrix Decoded: Le Nouvel Observateur Interview with Jean Baudrillard', *International Journal of Baudrillard Studies*, 1(2).

Bauman, Z. (1989) *Modernity and the Holocaust*. Cambridge: Polity Press.

Bell, E. and Taylor, S. (2003) 'The Elevation of Work: Pastoral Power and the New Age Work Ethic', *Organization*, 10(2): 331–351.

Bellour, R. (1976) 'To Analyse, To Segment', *Quarterly Review of Film Studies*, 1(3): 331–354.

Belton, J. (1988) 'American Cinema and Film History', in J. Hill and P. Church Gibson (eds) *The Oxford Guide to Film Studies*. Oxford: Oxford University Press, 227–237.

Bendle, M.F. (2002) 'The Crisis of "Identity" in High Modernity', *British Journal of Sociology*, 53(1): 1–18.

Bennett, J.R. (1983) 'Corporate Sponsored Image Films', *Journal of Business Ethics*, 2: 35–41.

Berger, A.A. (1991) *Media Analysis Techniques*. London: Sage.

Berger, J. and Pratt, C.B. (1998) 'Teaching Business – Communication Ethics with Controversial Films', *Journal of Business Ethics*, 17: 1817–1823.

Berger, P. (1964) 'Some General Observations on the Problem of Work', in P. Berger (ed.) *The Human Shape of Work*. New York: Macmillan, 211–241.

Berger, P. (1972) *Ways of Seeing*. London: BBC and Penguin.

Bergman, A. (1971) *We're in the Money: Depression America and Its Films*. Chicago: Elephant Paperbacks.

Beynon, H. (1975) *Working for Ford*, 2nd Edition. Harmondsworth: Penguin.

Bittner, E. (1965) 'The Concept of Organization', *Social Research*, 32: 239–255.

Blair, H. (2001) '"You're Only as Good as Your Last Job": The Labour Process and Market in the Film Industry', *Work, Employment and Society*, 15(1): 149–169.

Bogliari, di F., Giorgi, S. Di, Lombardi, M. And Trupia, P. (2007) *Il Grande Libro del Cinema per Manager: 50 Film Letti in Chiave D'Impresa*. Collana: Management Files.

Boje, D. (2001) 'Spectacle and Inter-spectacle in *The Matrix* and Organization Theory', in M. Parker, W. Smith, G. Lightfoot and M. Higgins (eds) *Science Fiction and Organization*. London: Routledge, 101–122.

Boltanski, L. and Chiapello, E. (2005) 'The New Spirit of Capitalism', *International Journal of Political and Cultural Sociology*, 18: 161–188.

Boozer, J. (2002) *Career Movies: American Business and the Success Mystique*. Austin: University of Texas Press.

Bordwell, D. (2006) *The Way Hollywood Tells It*. Berkley: University of California Press.

Bordwell, D. and Thompson, K. (2004) *Film Art: An Introduction*. 7th Edition. Boston: McGraw Hill.

Bordwell, D., Staiger, J. and Thompson, K. (1985) *The Classical Hollywood Cinema: Film Style and Mode of Production to 1960*. London: Routledge and Kegan Paul.

Bourdieu, P. (1984) *Distinction: A Social Critique of the Judgement of Taste*. London: Routledge and Kegan Paul.

Bradley, H., Erickson, M., Stephenson, C. and Williams, S. (2000) *Myths at Work*. Cambridge: Polity.

Braverman, H. (1974) *Labour and Monopoly Capital: The Degradation of Work in the Twentieth Century*. London: Monthly Review Press.

Brenner, M. (1996) 'The Man Who Knew Too Much', *Vanity Fair*, May: 170–192.

Brewis, J. (1998) 'What is Wrong with this Picture? Sex and Gender Relations in Disclosure', in J. Hassard and R. Holliday (eds) *Organization Representation: Work and Organizations in Popular Culture*. London: Sage, 83–99.

Brewis, J. (2004) 'Sex and Not the City? The Aspirations of the Thirty-something Working Woman', *Urban Studies*, 41(9): 1821–1838.

Brewis, J., Hamption, M. and Linstead, S. (1997) 'Unpacking Priscilla: Subjectivity and Identity in the Organization of Gendered Appearance', *Human Relations*. 50(10): 1275–1304.

Brunsdon, C. (1997) *Screen Tastes: Soap Opera to Satellite Dishes*. London: Routledge.

Brunette, P. (2000) 'Post-structuralism and Deconstruction' in J. Hill and P. Church Gibson (eds.) *Film Studies: Critical Approaches*. Oxford: Oxford University Press, 89–93.

Brunette, P. and Wills, D. (1989) *Screen/Play: Derrida and Film Theory*. Princeton: Princeton University Press.

Bryman, A. (2004) *The Disneyisation of Society*. London: Sage.

Bryman, A. and Bell, E. (2007) *Business Research Methods*. 2nd Edition Oxford: Oxford University Press.

Buchanan, D. and Huczynski, A. (2004) 'Images of Influence: *12 Angry Men* and *Thirteen Days*', *Journal of Management Inquiry*, 13(4): 312–323.

Burrell, G. (1984) 'Sex and Organizational Analysis', *Organization Studies*, 5(2): 97–118.

Burrell, G. (1997) *Pandemonium: Towards a Retro-Organization Theory*. London: Sage.

Burrell, G. and Morgan, G. (1979) *Sociological Paradigms and Organisational Analysis*. Aldershot: Gower.

Butler, R. (1995) 'Time in Organizations: Its Experience, Explanations and Effects', *Organization Studies*, 16(6): 925–950.

Casey, C. (1995) *Work, Self and Society: After Industrialism*. London: Routledge.

Casey, C. (2002) *Critical Analysis of Organizations: Theory, Practice, Revitalization*. London: Sage.

Caves, R.E. (2000) *Creative Industries: Contracts Between Art and Commerce*. Cambridge, MA: Harvard University Press.

Champoux, J.E. (1999) 'Film as a Teaching Resource', *Journal of Management Inquiry*, 8(2): 206–217.

Champoux, J.E. (2001a) 'Animated Film as a Teaching Resource', *Journal of Management Education*, 25(1): 79–100.

Champoux, J.E. (2001b) *Organizational Behaviour: Using Film to Visualise Principles and Practices*. South Western Educational Publishing/Thompson Learning.

Champoux, J.E. (2004) *Our Feature Presentation: Management*. South Western College/Thompson Learning.

Champoux, J.E. (2005) *Our Feature Presentation: Organisational Behaviour*. South Western College/Thompson Learning.

Chandler, A.D. Jr. (1977) *The Visible Hand: The Managerial Revolution in American Business*. Cambridge, MA: Harvard University Press.

Christopherson, S. and Storper, M. (1989) 'The Effects of Flexible Specialization on Industrial Politics and the Labor Market: The Motion Picture Industry', *Industrial and Labor Relations Review*, 42(3): 331–347.

Ciulla, J.B. (2000) *The Working Life: The Promise and Potential of Modern Work*. New York: Three Rivers Press.

Clegg, S.R. (1990) *Modern Organizations: Organization Studies in the Postmodern World*. Newbury Park, CA: Sage.

Coffey, A. and Atkinson, P. (1996) *Making Sense of Qualitative Data*. London: Sage.

Cohen, C. (1998) 'Using Narrative Fiction within Management Education', *Management Learning*, 29(2): 165–181.

Cohen, L., Hancock, P. and Tyler, M. (2006) 'Beyond the Scope of the Possible: Art, Photography and Organizational Abjection', *Culture and Organization*. 12(2): 109–125.

Cohen, S. and Taylor, L. (1992) *Escape Attempts*. 2nd Edition. New York: Routledge.

Collinson, D. (1994) 'Strategies of Resistance: Power, Knowledge and Subjectivity in the Workplace', in J.M. Jermier, D. Knights and W.D. Nord. (eds) *Resistance and Power in Organisations*. London: Routledge, 25–68.

Collinson, D. and Collinson, M. (1989) 'Sexuality in the Workplace: The Domination of Men's Sexuality', in J. Hearn, D.L. Sheppard, P. Tancred-Sheriff and G. Burrell (eds) *The Sexuality of Organization*. London: Sage, 91–109.

Collinson and Collinson (1997) 'Delayering Managers, Time Space Surveillance and its Gendered Effects', *Organization*, 4(3): 373–405.

Collinson, D. and Hearn, J. (1996) (eds) *Men as Managers: Managers as Men*. London: Sage.

Collinson, D.L. (1992) *Managing the Shopfloor: Subjectivity, Masculinity and Workplace Culture*. Berlin: Walter de Gruyter.

Collinson, D.L. (2002) 'Managing Humour', *Journal of Management Studies*, 39(3): 269–288.

Comer, D.R. (2001) 'Not Just a Mickey Mouse Exercise: Using Disney's *The Lion King* to Teach Leadership', *Journal of Management Education*, 25(4): 430–436.

Comer, D.R. and Cooper, E.A. (1998) 'Gender Relations and Sexual Harassment in the Workplace: Michael Crichtons's *Disclosure* as a Teaching Tool', *Journal of Management Education*, 22(2): 227–241.

Cooper, R. and Burrell, G. (1988) 'Modernism, Postmodernism and Organizational Analysis: An Introduction', *Organization Studies*, 9(1): 91–112.

Corbett, M. (1995) 'Celluloid Projections: Images of Technology and Organizational Futures in Contemporary Science Fiction Film', *Organization*, 2(3/4): 467–488.

Costa-Gavras (1995) 'Resisting the Colonels of Disney', *New Perspectives Quarterly*, 12(4): 4–8.

Coupland, D. (1991) *Generation X: Tales for an Accelerated Culture*. New York: St Martin's Press.

Creadick, A. (2006) 'Postwar Sign, Symbol, and Symptom: "The Man in the Gray Flannel Suit" ', in E.H. Brown, C. Gudis and M. Moskowitz (eds) *Cultures of Commerce: Representation and American Business Culture 1877–1960*. Basingstoke: Palgrave Macmillan, 277–293.

Culler, J. (1982) *On Deconstruction*. Ithaca: Cornell University Press.

Czarniawska, B. (1999) *Writing Management: Organization Theory as a Literary Genre*. Oxford: Oxford University Press.

Czarniawska, B. and Rhodes, K. (2006) 'Strong Plots: Popular Culture in Management Practice and Theory', in P. Gagliardi and B. Czarniawska (eds) *Management Education and the Humanities*. London: Edward Elgar.

Czarniawska-Joerges, B. and Guillet de Monthoux, P. (eds) (1994) *Good Novels Better Management: Reading Organizational Realities in Fiction*. Chur: Harwood Academic Publishers.

Dale, K. and Burrell, G. (2000) 'What Shape Are We In? Organization Theory and the Organized Body', in J. Hassard, R. Holliday, H. Willmott (eds) *Body and Organization*. London: Sage, 15–30.

Davis, C. (2006) 'Girls in Gray Flannel Suits: White Career Women in Postwar American Culture', in E.H. Brown, C. Gudis and M. Moskowitz (eds) *Cultures of Commerce: Representation and American Business Culture 1877–1960*. Basingstoke: Palgrave Macmillan, 295–320.

Deacy, C. (2005) *Faith in Film*. Aldershot: Ashgate.

De Cock, C. and Land, C. (2006) 'Organization/Literature: Exploring the Seam', *Organization Studies*, 27(4): 517–535.

De George, R. (1981) 'Ethical Responsibilities of Engineers in Large Organisations: The Pinto Case', *Business and Professional Ethics Journal*, 1(1): 4.

Dekom, P.J. (2006) 'Movies, Money and Madness', in J.E. Squire (ed.) *The Movie Business Book*. 3rd International Edition. Maidenhead, Berkshire: Open University Press and McGraw Hill, 100–116.

Denzin, N.K. (1990) 'Reading Wall Street: Postmodern Contradictions in the American Social Structure', B.S. Turner (ed.) *Theories of Modernity and Postmodernity*. London: Sage.

Denzin, N.K (1991) *Images of Postmodern Society: Social Theory and Contemporary Cinema*. London: Sage.

Denzin, N.K. (1995) The Cinematic Society: The Voyeur's Gaze. London: Sage.

Derrida, J. (1974) *Of Grammatology*. Baltimore: Johns Hopkins University Press.

Derrida, J. (1980) 'The Law of Genre', translated by A. Ronell, *Critical Inquiry*, 7(1): 55–81.

Dick, P. (2005) 'Dirty Work Designations: How Police Officers Account for their Use of Coercive Force', *Human Relations*, 58(11): 1363–1390.

Doane, M.A. (2002) *The Emergence of Cinematic Time*. Cambridge, MA.: Harvard University Press.

Dorfman, A. and Mattelart, A. (1971) *How to Read Donald Duck: Imperialist Ideology in the Disney Comic*. New York: International General.

DuGay, P. (1996) *Consumption and Identity at Work*. London: Sage.

Dyer, R. (1979) *Stars*. London: British Film Institute.

Dyer, R. (2000) 'Introduction to Film Studies', in J. Hill and P. Church Gibson (eds) *Film Studies: Critical approaches*. Oxford: Oxford University Press, 1–8.

Eccles, R. and Nohria, N. (1992) *Beyond the Hype: Rediscovering the Essence of Management*. Harvard, MA.: Harvard University Press.

Eco, U. (1972) *Towards a Semiotic Inquiry into the Television Message*, Working Papers in Cultural Studies, 3: 103–121.

Eco, U. (1976) The Role of the Reader: Explorations in the Semiotics of Texts. London: Indiana University Press.

Eco, U. (1992) *Interpretation and Overinterpretation*. Cambridge: Cambridge University Press.

Ehrenreich, B. (2006) *Bait and Switch: The futile pursuit of the corporate dream*. London: Granta.

Epstein, E.J. (2005) *The Big Picture: The New Logic of Money and Power in Hollywood*. New York: Random House.

Etzioni, A. (1961) *A Comparative Analysis of Complex Organisations*. New York: Free Press.

Farrell, K. (2003) 'Naked Nation: *The Full Monty*, Working Class Masculinity, and the British Image', *Men and Masculinities*, 6(2): 119–135.

Faulkner, R.R. and Anderson, A.B. (1987) 'Short-Term Projects and Emergent Careers: Evidence from Hollywood', *American Journal of Sociology*, 92(4): 879–909.

Feingold, B.S. (2006) 'Home Video Business', in J.E. Squire (ed.) *The Movie Business Book*. 3rd International Edition. Maidenhead, Berkshire: Open University Press and McGraw Hill, 408–417.

Fleming, P. and Spicer, A. (2003) 'Working at a Cynical Distance: Implications for Power, Subjectivity and Resistance', *Organization*, 10(1): 157–179.

Foreman, J. and Thatchenkery, T.J. (1996) 'Filmic Representations for Organizational Analysis: The Characterization of a Transplant Organization in the Film *Rising Sun*', *Journal of Organizational Change Management*, 9(3): 44–61.

Foreman, J. and Thatchenkery, T.J. (2003) 'Representation of Organizational Change in Ron Howard's *Gung Ho*', in S. Linstead (ed.) *Text/Work: Representing Organization and Organizing Representation*. London: Routledge.

Foucault, M. (1977) *Discipline and Punish: The Birth of the Prison*. London: Penguin.

Foucault, M. (1984) 'The Author Function', in P. Rabinow (ed.) *The Foucault Reader*. Harmondsworth: Penguin, 101–120.

Fournier, V. and Grey, C. (2000) 'At the Critical Moment: Conditions and Prospects for Critical Management Studies', *Human Relations*, 53(7): 7–32.

Frank, T. (1997) *The Conquest of Cool: Business Culture, Counterculture, and the Rise of Hip Consumerism*. Chicago: University of Chicago Press.

Friedan, B. (1993) *The Feminine Mystique*. New York: W.W. Norton.

Frow, J. (2006) *Genre*. London: Routledge.

Furnham, A. (1990) *The Protestant Work Ethic: The Psychology of Work Related Beliefs and Behaviours*. London: Routledge.

Gabriel, Y. (2000) *Storytelling in Organizations: Facts, Fictions and Fantasies*. Oxford: Oxford University Press.

Gagliardi, P. (2006) 'A Role for Humanities in the Formation of Managers', in P. Gagliardi, and B. Czarniawska (eds) *Management Education and the Humanities*. London: Edward Elgar, 3–9.

Gamman, L. and Marshment, M. (1988) *The Female Gaze: Women as Viewers of Popular Culture*. London: Women's Press.

Gardels, N. (2007) 'Shock and Awe Versus Hearts and Minds', *New Perspectives Quarterly*, 24(2): 9–17.

Garfinkel, H. (1967) *Studies in Ethnomethodology*. Englewood Cliffs, NJ: Prentice Hall.

Garnham, N. (1990) *Capitalism and Communication: Global Culture and the Economics of Information*. London: Sage.

Gerse, S. (2006) 'Overseas Tax Incentives and Government Subsidies', in J.E. Squire (ed.) *The Movie Business Book*. 3rd International Edition. Maidenhead, Berkshire: Open University Press and McGraw Hill, 483–496.

Gerth, H. and Mills, C. (eds) (1948) *For Max Weber*. London: Routledge and Kegan Paul.

Gherardi, S. (1995) *Gender, Symbolism and Organizational Cultures*. London: Sage.

Gibson-Graham, J.K. (2001) 'Class Enchantment', *Theory & Event*, 5(3).

Giddens, A. (1990) *The Consequences of Modernity*. Cambridge: Polity.

Gilson, M.B. (1940) 'Review of Management and the Worker', *American Journal of Sociology*, 46: 98–101.

Glennie, P. and Thrift, N. (1996) 'Reworking E. P. Thompson's "Time, Work-discipline and Industrial Capitalism"', *Time & Society*, 5(3): 275–299.

Goetz, A. (2003) *Up Down Across: Elevators, Escalators and Moving Sidewalks*. London: Merrell.

Goffman, E. (1959) *The Presentation of Self in Everyday Life*. Harmondsworth: Penguin.

Goffman, E. (1968) *Asylums*. London: Penguin.

Gomery, D. (1998) 'Hollywood as Industry', in J. Hill and P. Church Gibson (eds) *The Oxford Guide to Film Studies*. Oxford: Oxford University Press, 245–254.

Gouldner, A.W. (1955) 'Metaphysical Pathos and the Theory of Bureaucracy', *The American Political Science Review*, 49(2): 496–507.

Gowler, D. and Legge, K. (1983) 'The Meaning of Management and the Management of Meaning: A View from Social Anthropology', in M.J. Earl (ed.) *Perspectives on Management*. Oxford: Oxford University Press, 197–234.

Grey, C. (1994) 'Career as a Project of the Self and Labour Process Discipline', *Sociology*, 28(2): 479–497.

Grey, C. (2005) *A Very Short, Fairly Interesting and Reasonably Cheap Book about Studying Organizations*. London: Sage.

Grey, C. and Sinclair, A. (2006) 'Writing Differently', *Organization*, 13(3): 443–453.

Grint, K. (1994) 'Reengineering History: Social Resonances and Business Process Reengineering', *Organization*, 1(1): 179–201.

Guest, D.E. (1990) 'Human Resource Management and the American Dream', *Journal of Management Studies*, 27(4): 377–397.

Hall, S. (1980) 'Encoding/Decoding', in S. Hall, D. Hobson, A. Lowe and P. Willis (eds) *Culture, Media, Language*. London: Hutchinson, 128–138.

Hall, S. (1981) 'Notes on Deconstructing "The Popular"', in R. Samuel (ed.) *People's History and Socialist Theory*, London: Routledge, 231–240.

Hammer, M. (1990) 'Re-engineering Work: Don't Automate, Obliterate', *Harvard Business Review*, July–August: 104–112.

Hammer, M.E. and Champy, J. (1993) *Re-engineering the Corporation*. London: Nicholas Brealey.

Hancock, P. and Tyler, M. (2001) *Work, Postmodernism and Organization: A Critical Introduction*. London: Sage.

Handy, C. (1994) *The Empty Raincoat*. London: Hutchinson.

Harrington, K.V. and Griffin, R.W. (1990) 'Ripley, Burke, Gorman and Friends: Using the Film "Aliens" to Teach Leadership and Power', *Journal of Management Education*, 14(3): 79–86.

Harrison, J. (2004) 'Film Review: Screening Classic Dilemmas in the Classroom', *Journal of Business Ethics*, 49: 105.

Harrison, J. Kline and Akinc, H. (2000) 'Lessons in Leadership form the Arts and Literature: A Liberal Arts Approach to Management Education through Fifth Discipline Learning', *Journal of Management Education*, 24(3): 391–413.

Harvey, D. (1990) *The Condition of Postmodernity*. Oxford: Blackwell.

Hassard, J. (1991) 'Aspects of Time in Organization', *Human Relations*, 44(2): 105–125.

Hassard, J. (1993) 'Postmodernism and Organizational Analysis: An Overview', in J. Hassard and M. Parker (eds) *Postmodernism and Organization*. London: Sage, 1–24.

Hassard, J. and Holliday, R. (1998) *Organization Representation: Work and Organizations in Popular Culture*. London: Sage.

Hassard, J., Holliday, R. and Willmott, H. (2000) *Body and Organization*. London: Sage.

Hatch, M.J. (1997) *Organization Theory: Modern, Symbolic and Postmodern Perspectives*. Oxford: Oxford University Press.

Hearn, J., Sheppard, D.L., Tancred-Sheriff, P. and Burrell, G. (1989) *The Sexuality of Organization*. London: Sage.

Heath, J. and Potter, A. (2005) *The Rebel Sell: How the Counterculture Became Consumer Culture*. Chichester: Capstone.

Hermes, J. (2006) ' "Ally McBeal", "Sex in the City" and the Tragic Success of Feminism', in J. Hollows and R. Moseley (eds) *Feminism in Popular Culture*. Oxford: Berg, 79–95.

Herzberg, F. (1966) *Work and the Nature of Man*. Cleveland, OH: World Publishing Company.

Hill, J. (2000) 'General Introduction', in J. Hill and P. Church Gibson (eds) *Film Studies: Critical approaches*. Oxford: Oxford University Press, xiii–xv.

Hochschild, A. (1983) *The Managed Heart: Commercialization of Human Feeling*. Berkeley, CA: University of California Press.

Hochschild, A. (1997) *The Time Bind*. New York: Metropolitan Books.

Hoffman, M. (1984) 'The Ford Pinto', in M. Hoffman, R.E. Frederick and M.S. Schwartz (eds) *Business Ethics: Readings and Cases in Corporate Morality*. Boston: McGraw Hill, 552–559.

Hollows, J. and Jancovich, M. (1995) 'Popular Film and Cultural Distinctions', in J. Hollows and M. Jancovich (eds) *Approaches to Popular Film*. Manchester: Manchester University Press, 1–14.

Hollows, J. (1995) 'Mass Culture Theory and Political Economy', in J. Hollows and M. Jancovich (eds) *Approaches to Popular Film*. Manchester: Manchester University Press, 15–36.

Hollows, J. (2002) 'Vocation to Profession: Changing Images of Nursing in Britain', *Journal of Organizational Change Management*, 15(1): 35–47.

Hollows, J. (2006) 'Can I Go Home Yet? Feminism, Post-feminism and Domesticity', in J. Hollows and R. Moseley (eds) *Feminism in Popular Culture*. Oxford: Berg, 97–118.

Holmes, R.A. (2005) 'Finding OB in Disney's Finding Nemo', *Organization Management Journal*, 2(2): 70–79.

Höpfl, H. with Maddrell, J. (1996) 'Can You Resist a Dream? Evangelical Metaphors and the Appropriation of Emotion', in D. Grant and C. Oswick (eds) *Metaphors and Organizations*. London: Sage, 200–212.

Horkheimer, M. and Adorno, T. (1944 [2002]) *Dialectic of Enlightenment: Philosophical Fragments*. Stanford, CA: Stanford University Press.

Hoskin, K.W. and Macve, R.H. (1998) 'The Genesis of Accountability: the West Point Connections', *Accounting, Organization and Society*, 13(1): 37–73.

Huczynski, A. and Buchanan, D. (2004) 'Theory from Fiction: A Narrative Process Perspective on the Pedagogical Use of Feature Film', *Journal of Management Education*, 28(6): 707–724.

Hughes, E. (1951) *Men & Their Work*. Glencoe, IL: Free Press.

Hutchings, P. (1995) 'Genre Theory and Criticism', in J. Hollows and M. Jancovich (eds) *Approaches to Popular Film*. Manchester: Manchester University Press, 59–77.

Huxtable, A.L. (1984) *The Tall Building Artistically Reconsidered: The Search for a Skyscraper Style*. New York: Pantheon.

Jackall, R. (1988) *Moral Mazes: The World of Corporate Managers*. New York: Oxford University Press.

Jacques, R. (1996) *Manufacturing the Employee*. London: Sage.

Jaffee, D. (2001) *Organization Theory: Tension and Change*. Singapore: McGraw Hill.

Jameson, F. (1992) *Signatures of the Visible*. London: Routledge.

Jancovich, M. (1995) 'Screen Theory', in J. Hollows and M. Jancovich (eds) *Approaches to Popular Film*. Manchester: Manchester University Press, 123–150.

Jeffcutt, P. (2000) 'Culture and Industry, Exploring the Debate', *Studies in Cultures, Organizations and Societies*, 6(2): 129–143.

Jeffcutt, P. and Pratt, A.C. (2002) 'Managing Creativity in the Cultural Industries', *Creativity and Innovation Management*, 11(4): 225–233.

Jones, C. (2001) 'Co-evolution of Entrepreneurial Careers, Institutional Rules and Competitive Dynamics in American Film, 1895–1920', *Organization Studies*, 22(6): 911–944.

Kanter, R.M. (1977) *Men and Women of the Corporation*. New York: Basic Books.

Kerfoot, D. (2000) 'Body Work: Estrangement, Disembodiment and the Organizational "Other"', in J. Hassard, R. Holliday, H. Willmott (eds) *Body and Organization*. London: Sage, 230–246.

Kets de Vries, M.F.R. and Miller, D. (1984) *The Neurotic Organization*. San Francisco: Jossey Bass.

Klein, N. (2000) *No Logo*. London: Flamingo.

Kress, G. and van Leeuwen, T. (1996) *Reading Images: The Grammar of Visual Design*. London: Routledge.

Kunda, G. (1992) *Engineering Culture: Control and Commitment in a High-tech Corporation*. Philadelphia: Temple University Press.

Lasn, K. (1999) *Culture Jam: The Uncooling of America*. New York: Eagle Brook/William Morrow.

Lederer, R. (2006) 'Management: New Rules of the Game', in J.E. Squire (ed.) *The Movie Business Book*. 3rd International Edition. Maidenhead, Berkshire: Open University Press and McGraw Hill, 160–166.

Legge, K. (2005) *Human Resource Management: Rhetorics and Realities*. Basingstoke: Palgrave Macmillan.

Lewis, J. (1998) 'Money Matters: Hollywood in the Corporate Era', in J. Lewis (ed.) *The New American Cinema*. Durham: Duke University Press, 87–121.

Linstead, S. (1993) 'From Postmodern Anthropology to Deconstructive Ethnography', *Human Relations*, 46(1): 97–120.

Linstead, S. (2003) (ed.) *Text/Work: Representing Organization and Organizing Representation*. London: Routledge.

Livingstone, S.M. (1993) 'The Rise and Fall of Audience Research: An Old Story with a New Ending', *Journal of Communication*, 43(4): 5–12.

Locke, R.R. (1996) *The Collapse of the American Management Mystique*. Oxford: Oxford University Press.

Lopate, P. (2001) 'Hollywood Looks at the Business Office', *New Labour Forum*, Fall/Winter.

Mangham, I. (1979) *The Politics of Organisational Change*. London: Associated Business Press.

Marshall, J. (1984) *Women Managers: Travellers in a Male World*. Chichester: John Wiley.

Marshment, M. and Gamman, L. (1988) 'Introduction', in M. Marshment and L. Gamman (eds) *The Female Gaze: Women As Viewers of Popular Culture*. London: Women's Press, 1–7.

Marx, K. (1867 [1976]) *Capital: Volume 1*. London: Penguin.

Marx, R.D. and Frost, P.J. (1998) 'Towards Optimal Use of Video in Management Education: Examining the Evidence', *Journal of Management Development*, 17(4): 243–250.

Marx, R.D., Jick, T.J. and Frost, P.J. (1991) *Management Live! The Video Book*. Englewood Cliffs, NJ: Prentice Hall.

Maslow (1943) 'A Theory of Human Motivation', *Psychological Review*, 50: 370–396.

McDowell, L. (1997) *Capital Culture: Gender at Work in the City*. Oxford: Blackwell.

McDowell, L. (1998) 'Fictional Money (or, Greed Isn't so Good in the 1990s)', in J. Hassard and R. Holliday (eds) *Organization Representation: Work and Organizations in Popular Culture*. London: Sage, 167–183.

McGregor, D. (1960) *The Human Side of Enterprise*. New York: McGraw Hill.

McLellan, D. (2000) *Karl Marx: Selected Writings*. 2nd Edition. Oxford: Oxford University Press.

McNeill, D. (2005) 'Skyscraper Geography', *Progress in Human Geography*, 29(1): 41–55.

Merton, R.K. (1940) 'Bureaucratic Structure and Personality', *Social Forces*, 18(4): 560–568.

Mezias, J.M. and Mezias, S.J. (2000) 'Resource Partitioning, the Founding of Specialist Firms, and Innovation: The American Feature Film Industry, 1912–1929', *Organization Science*, 11(3): 306–322.

Milgram, S. (1963) 'A Behavioral Study of Obedience', *Journal of Abnormal and Social Psychology*, 67: 371–378.

Milgram, S. (1974) 'The Perils of Obedience', *Harper's Magazine*, December, 62–77.

Miller, T. (1998) 'Hollywood and the World', in J. Hill and P. Church Gibson (eds) *The Oxford Guide to Film Studies*. Oxford: Oxford University Press, 371–381.

Miller, T., Govil, N., McMurria, J., Maxwell, R. and Wang, T. (2005) *Global Hollywood 2*. London: BFI Publishing.

Mills, C.W. (1951) *White Collar: The American Middle Classes*. Oxford: Oxford University Press.

Mintzberg, H. (2004) *Managers Not MBAs: A Hard Look at the Soft Practice of Managing and Management Development.* New York: Barrett-Koehler.

Mishna, V. (2002) *Bollywood Cinema: Temples of Desire.* New York: Routledge.

Mitroff, I. and Denton, E. (1999) *A Spiritual Audit of Corporate America.* San Francisco: Jossey Bass.

Monaco, J. (2000) *How to Read a Film: Movies, Media, Multimedia.* New York: Oxford University Press.

Morgan, G. (1997) *Images of Organization.* Thousand Oaks, CA: Sage.

Moudry, R. (2006) 'The Metropolitan Life Tower: Architecture and Ideology in the Life Insurance Enterprise', in E.H. Brown, C. Gudis and M. Moskowitz (eds) *Cultures of Commerce: Representation and American Business Culture 1877–1960.* Basingstoke: Palgrave Macmillan, 199–228.

Mulvey, L. (1985) 'Visual Pleasure and Narrative Cinema', in B. Nichols (ed.) *Movies and Methods, Vol. II.* Berkeley: University of California Press.

Neal, J. and Biberman, J. (2003) 'Introduction: The Leading Edge in Research on Spirituality and Organizations', *Journal of Organizational Change Management*, 16(4): 363–366.

Neale, S. (2000) *Genre and Hollywood.* London: Routledge.

Newitz, A. (2006) *Pretend We're Dead: Capitalist Monsters in American Pop Culture.* Stanford, CA: Duke University Press.

Nichols and Beynon, H. (1977) *Living with Capitalism: Class Relations and the Modern Factory.* London: Routledge and Kegan Paul.

O'Sullivan, J. and Sherridan, A. (2005) 'The King is Dead, Long Live the King', *Gender, Work and Organization*, 12(4): 299–318.

Orr, J. (2006) 'Ten Years of Talking About Machines', *Organization Studies*, 27(12): 1805–1820.

Orwell, G. (1949) *Nineteen Eighty-Four.* London: Secker and Warburg.

Pahl, R. (1984) *Divisions of Labour.* Oxford: Blackwell.

Pahl, R. (1995) *After Success: Fin-de-Siècle Anxiety and Identity.* Cambridge: Polity.

Parker, M. (2001) ' "Repent Harlequin!" Said the Ticktockman', in W. Smith, M. Higgins, M. Parker and G. Lightfoot (eds) *Science Fiction and Organization.* London: Routledge, 193–214.

Parker, M. (2002) *Against Management.* Cambridge: Polity.

Patterson, J. (2007) 'Down with This Sort of Thing', *The Guardian.* 21–27 April, 9–10.

Perlow, L.A. (1999) 'The Time Famine: Towards a Sociology of Work Time', *Administrative Science Quarterly*, 44(1): 57–81.

Perrow, C. (1991) 'A Society of Organizations', *Theory and Society*, 20(6): 725–762.

Peterson, R.A. (1997) *Creating Country Music: Fabricating Authenticity.* Chicago, IL: Chicago University Press.

Phillips, N. (1995) 'Telling Organizational Tales: On the Role of Narrative Fiction in the Study of Organizations', *Organization Studies*, 16(4): 625–649.

Pillai, P. (1992) 'Rereading Stuart Hall's Encoding/Decoding Model', *Communication Theory*, 2(3): 221–233.

Prasad, P. (2005) *Crafting Qualitative Research: Working in the Postpositivist Traditions.* Armonk, NY: M.E. Sharpe.

Pringle, R. (1988) *Secretaries Talk: Sexuality, Power and Work.* London: Verso.

Pringle, R. (1989) 'Bureaucracy, Rationality and Sexuality: The Case of Secretaries', in J. Hearn, D.L. Sheppard, P. Tancred-Sheriff, and G. Burrell (eds) *The Sexuality of Organization.* London: Sage, 158–177.

Rhodes, C. (2001) 'D'Oh: *The Simpsons*, Popular Culture, and the Organizational Carnival', *Journal of Management Inquiry*, 10(4): 374–383.

Rhodes, C. and Brown, A. (2005) 'Writing Responsibly: Narrative Fiction and Organization Studies', *Organization*, 12(4): 467–491.

Rhodes, C. and Westwood, R. (2007) *Critical Representations of Work and Organization in Popular Culture.* London: Routledge.

Ribstein, L. E. (2005) *Wall Street and Vine: Hollywood's View of Business.* University of Illinois Law and Economics Research Paper No. LE05-010.

Ritzer, G. (1993) *The McDonaldization of Society: An Investigation into the Changing Character of Contemporary Social Life.* Thousand Oaks, CA: Pine Forge Press.

Ritzer, G. (2007) *The Globalization of Nothing 2.* Thousand Oaks: Pine Forge Press.

Roethlisberger, F.J., and Dickson, W.J. (1939) *Management and the Worker: An Account of a Research Programme Conducted by the Western Electric Company, Hawthorne Works, Chicago.* Cambridge, MA: Harvard University Press.

Roper, M. (1994) *Masculinity and the British Organisation Man Since 1945.* Oxford: Oxford University Press.

Rorty, R. (1979) *Philosophy and the Mirror of Nature.* Princeton, NJ: Princeton University Press.

Rose, N. (1999) *Governing the Soul: The Shaping of Private Self.* 2nd Edition. London: Free Association Books

Rothman, T. (2006) 'A Chairman's View', in J.E. Squire (ed.) *The Movie Business Book.* 3rd International Edition. Maidenhead, Berkshire: Open University Press and McGraw Hill, 148–159.

Roy, D. (1958) 'Banana Time: Job Satisfaction and Informal Interaction', *Human Organization*, 18: 156–68.

Roy, W.G. (1997) *Socializing Capital: The Rise of the Large, Industrial Corporation in America.* Princeton, NJ: Princeton University Press.

Sadar, Z. and Wyn Davies, M. (2004) *American Dream: Global Nightmare.* Cambridge: Icon Books.

Sampson, A. (1995) *Company Man: The Rise and Fall of Corporate Life.* London: Harper Collins.

Saunders, J. (2001) *Celluloid Skyline: New York and the Movies.* London: Bloomsbury.

Saussure, F. de (1966) *Course in General Linguistics.* New York: McGraw Hill.

Scarbrough, H. and Burrell, G. (1996) 'The Axeman Cometh', in S. Clegg and G. Palmer (eds) *The Politics of Management Knowledge.* London: Sage. 173–189.

Schatz, T. (1989) *The Genius of the System.* London: Faber and Faber.

Schlosser, E. (2001) *Fast Food Nation.* London: Allen Lane.

Sennett, R. (1998) *The Corrosion of Character: The Personal Consequences of Work in the New Capitalism.* New York: W.W. Norton and Company.

Sewell, G. (2004) 'Yabba-dabba-doo! Evolutionary Psychology and the Rise of Flintstone Psychological Thinking in Organization and Management Studies', *Human Relations*, 57(8): 923–955.

Shapiro, B. (1990) 'Collaring the Crime, Not the Criminal: Reconsidering the Concept of White-Collar Crime', *American Sociological Review*, 55: 346–65.

Shaw, B. (2004) 'Hollywood Ethics: Developing Ethical Issues … Hollywood Style', *Journal of Business Ethics*, 49: 167–177.

Shenhav, Y. (1999) *Manufacturing Rationality: The Engineering Foundations of the Managerial Revolution.* Oxford: Oxford University Press.

Sheppard, D.L. (1989) 'Organizations, Power and Sexuality: The Image and Self Image of Women Managers', in J. Hearn, D.L. Sheppard, P. Tancred-Sheriff, and G. Burrell (eds) *The Sexuality of Organization.* London: Sage, 139–157.

Sievers, B. (1986) 'Beyond the Surrogate of Motivation', *Organization Studies*, 7(4): 335–351.

Sievers, B. (1994) *Work, Death and Life Itself.* Berlin: DeGruyter.

Sklar, R. (1975) *Movie-Made America: A Cultural History of American Movies.* New York: Random House.

Slapper, G. (1999) *Blood in the Bank: Social and Legal Aspects of Death at Work.* Aldershot: Ashgate.

Smith, W. (2001) *Science Fiction and Organization.* London: Routledge.

Spicer, A. (2001) 'Out of the Cynical Bind? A Reflection on Resistance in *Fight Club*', *Ephemera*, 1(1): 92–102.

Spradley, J. and McCurdy, D. (1973) *The Cultural Experience.* Chicago: Science Research Associates.

Squire, J.E. (2006) 'Introduction', in J.E. Squire (ed.) *The Movie Business Book.* 3rd International Edition. Maidenhead, Berkshire: Open University Press and McGraw Hill, 1–12.

Stein, M. (2000) 'The Risk Taker as Shadow: A Psychoanalytic View of the Collapse of Barings Bank', *Journal of Management Studies*, 37(8): 1215–1229.

Storey, J. (1992) *Developments in Human Resource Management.* Oxford: Blackwell.

Tashiro, C.S. (2002) 'The *Twilight Zone* of Contemporary Hollywood Production', *Cinema Journal*, 41(3): 27–37.

Taylor, (1995) 'Psychoanalytic Theory in Film', in J. Hollows and M. Jancovich (eds) *Approaches to Popular Film.* Manchester: Manchester University Press, 151–171.

Taylor, F.W. (1911) *Principles of Scientific Management.* New York: Harper.

Thompson, E.P. (1967) 'Time, Work-Discipline and Industrial Capitalism', *Past and Present*, 38: 56–97.

Thompson, K. (1999) *Storytelling in the New Hollywood*. Cambridge, MA: Harvard University Press.

Tolliver, J.M. and Coleman, D.F. (2001) 'Metropolis, Maslow and the Axis Mundi', in W. Smith, M. Higgins, M. Parker and G. Lightfoot (eds) *Science Fiction and Organization*. London: Routledge, 43–60.

Trethewey, A. (1999) 'Disciplined Bodies: Women's Embodied Identities at Work', *Organization Studies*, 20(3): 423–450.

Umansky, E. (2003) 'Erin Brockovich's Weird Science', *New Republic*, 229(21): 18–23.

UNESCO (2000) *A Survey on National Cinematography*. Paris: UNESCO.

Van Es, R. (2003) 'Inside and Outside *The Insider*: A Film Workshop in Practical Ethics', *Journal of Business Ethics*, 48: 89–97.

Van Gelderen, M. and Verduyn, K. 'Entrepreneurship in the Cinema: Feature Films as Case Material in Entrepreneurship Education', *International Journal of Entrepreneurship Education*, 1(4): 539–566.

Waterman, D. (2005) *Hollywood's Road to Riches*. Cambridge, MA: Harvard University Press.

Watson, T. (1994) *In Search of Management: Culture, Chaos and Control in Managerial Work*. London: Routledge.

Watson, T. (2000) 'Ethnographic Fiction Science: Making Sense of Managerial Work and Organizational Research Processes with Caroline and Terry', *Organization*, 7(3): 489–510.

Weber, M. (1930) *The Protestant Ethic and the Spirit of Capitalism*. London: Allen & Unwin.

Weber, M. (1947) *The Theory of Social and Economic Organization*. New York: Free Press.

Westwood, A. (2003) *Is New Work Good Work?* London: The Work Foundation.

White, P. (2000) 'Feminism and Film', in J. Hill and P. Church Gibson (eds) *Film Studies: Critical approaches*. Oxford: Oxford University Press, 115–129.

Whyte, W.H. (1956 [2002]) *Organization Man*. Philadelphia: University of Philadelphia Press.

Williamson, J. (1991) ' "Up Where You Belong": Hollywood Images of Big Business in the 1980s', in J. Corner and S. Harvey (eds) *Enterprise and Heritage: Crosscurrents of National Culture*. London: Routledge, 151–161.

Willmott, H. (1993) 'Strength is Ignorance; Slavery is Freedom: Managing Culture in Modern Organizations', *Journal of Management Studies*, 30(4): 515–552.

Winston, B. (2000) *Lies, Damn Lies and Documentaries*. London: British Film Institute.

Witz, A., Warhurst, C. and Nickson, D. (2003) 'The Labour of Aesthetics and the Aesthetics of Organization', *Organization*, 10(1): 33–54.

Wright Mills, C. (1951) *White Collar: The American Middle Classes*. New York: Galaxy Books.

Wright, D. (2005) 'Mediating Production and Consumption: Cultural Capital and "Cultural Workers" ', *British Journal of Sociology*, 56(1): 105–121.

Wright, W. (1975) *Sixguns and Society: A Structural Study of the Western*. Berkeley: University of California Press.

Wrzesniewski, A.C., Dutton, J.E. and Debebe, G. (2003) 'Interpersonal Sensemaking and the Meaning of Work', *Research in Organizational Behavior*, 25: 93–135.

Zaniello, T. (2007) *The Cinema of Globalization*. Ithaca: Cornell University Press.

Zaniello, T. (1996) *Working Stiffs, Union Maids, Reds, and Riffraff: An Expanded Guide to Films about Labor*. Ithaca: Cornell University Press.

Zerubavel, E. (1981) *Hidden Rhythms: Schedules and Calendars in Social Life*. Chicago: University of Chicago Press.

Zimbardo, P.G., Haney, C., Banks, W.C. and Jaffe, D. (1973) 'The Mind is a Formidable Jailer: A Pirandellian Prison', *The New York Times Magazine*, April 8, 38–60.

Žižek, S. (2002) 'Are We in a War? Do We Have an Enemy?', *London Review of Books*, 10, 23 May: 3–6.

Žižek, S. (2005) *Interrogating the Real*. London: Continuum.

Index

225